HERE COMES TROUBLE

HERE COMES TROUBLE

STORIES FROM MY LIFE

MICHAEL MOORE

ALLEN LANE
an imprint of
PENGUIN BOOKS

ALLEN LANE

Published by the Penguin Group
Penguin Books Ltd, 80 Strand, London WC2R 0RL, England
Penguin Group (USA) Inc., 375 Hudson Street, New York, New York 10014, USA
Penguin Group (Canada), 90 Eglinton Avenue East, Suite 700, Toronto, Ontario, Canada M4P 2Y3
(a division of Pearson Penguin Canada Inc.)
Penguin Ireland, 25 St Stephen's Green, Dublin 2, Ireland (a division of Penguin Books Ltd)
Penguin Group (Australia), 250 Camberwell Road, Camberwell,
Victoria 3124, Australia (a division of Pearson Australia Group Pty Ltd)
Penguin Books India Pvt Ltd, 11 Community Centre, Panchsheel Park, New Delhi – 110 017, India
Penguin Group (NZ), 67 Apollo Drive, Rosedale, Auckland 0632, New Zealand
(a division of Pearson New Zealand Ltd)
Penguin Books (South Africa) (Pty) Ltd, 24 Sturdee Avenue,
Rosebank, Johannesburg 2196, South Africa

Penguin Books Ltd, Registered Offices: 80 Strand, London WC2R 0RL, England

www.penguin.com

First published in the United States of America by Grand Central Publishing, a division of Hachette
Book Group, Inc. 2011
First published in Great Britain by Allen Lane 2011
1

Printed in Great Britain by Clays Ltd, St Ives plc

A CIP catalogue record for this book is available from the British Library

HARDBACK ISBN: 978–0–713–99701–9
TRADE PAPERBACK ISBN: 978–0–713–99866–5

www.greenpenguin.co.uk

MIX
Paper from
responsible sources
FSC
www.fsc.org   FSC™ C018179

Penguin Books is committed to a sustainable
future for our business, our readers and our
planet. This book is made from paper certified
by the Forest Stewardship Council.

For
my mother
who taught me to read
and write
when I was four

Growing up it all seems so one-sided
Opinions all provided
The future pre-decided
Detached and subdivided
In the mass production zone
Nowhere is the dreamer
Or the misfit
So alone...
                    — *"Subdivisions"*
                    Neil Peart/Rush

A Note from
the Author

This is a book of short stories based on events that took place in the early years of my life. Many of the names and circumstances have been changed to protect the innocent, and sometimes the guilty. They say that memory can be a strange and twisted amusement park, full of roller coaster rides and funhouse mirrors, frightening freak shows and gentle contortionists. This is my first volume of such stories. I wanted to commit them to paper while paper (and bookstores and libraries) still existed.

Stories

SANDY BATES [WOODY ALLEN]: Shouldn't I stop making movies and do something that counts, like helping blind people or becoming a missionary or something?

THE ALIEN: Let me tell you, you're not the missionary type. You'd never last. And incidentally, you're also not Superman; you're a comedian. You want to do mankind a real service? Tell funnier jokes.
> —from *Stardust Memories*/
> Woody Allen

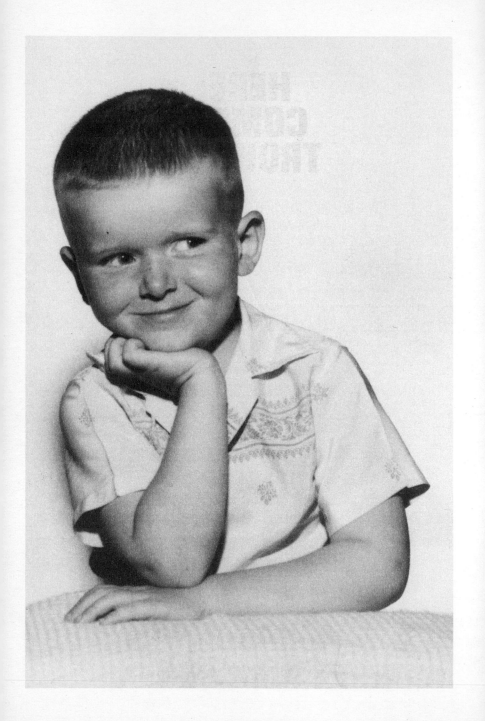

HERE COMES TROUBLE

The Execution of Michael Moore

I'm thinking about killing Michael Moore, and I'm wondering if I could kill him myself, or if I would need to hire somebody to do it . . . No, I think I could. I think he could be looking me in the eye, you know, and I could just be choking the life out [of him]. Is this wrong? I stopped wearing my "What Would Jesus Do?" band, and I've lost all sense of right and wrong now. I used to be able to say, "Yeah, I'd kill Michael Moore," and then I'd see the little band: What Would Jesus Do? And then I'd realize, "Oh, you wouldn't kill Michael Moore. Or at least you wouldn't choke him to death." And you know, well, I'm not sure.

Glenn Beck,
live on the Glenn Beck *program,*
May 17, 2005

Wishes for my early demise seemed to be everywhere. They were certainly on the mind of CNN's Bill Hemmer one sunny July morning in 2004. He had heard something he wanted to run by me. And so, holding a microphone in front of my face on the floor of the 2004 Democratic National Convention, live on CNN, he asked me what I thought about how the American people were feeling about Michael Moore:

"I've heard people say they wish Michael Moore were dead."

I tried to recall if I'd ever heard a journalist ask anyone that question before on live television. Dan Rather did not ask Saddam Hussein that question. I'm pretty sure Stone Phillips didn't ask serial killer and cannibal Jeffrey Dahmer, either. Perhaps, maybe, Larry King asked Liza once — but I don't think so.

For some reason, though, it was perfectly OK to pose that possibility to *me,* a guy whose main offense was to make documentaries. Hemmer said it like he was simply stating the obvious, like, "of course they want to kill you!" He just assumed his audience already understood this truism, as surely as they accept that the sun rises in the east and corn comes on a cob.

I didn't know how to respond. I tried to make light of it. But as I stood there I couldn't get over what he had just said live on a network that goes out to 120 countries and Utah. This "journalist" had possibly planted a sick idea into some deranged mind, some angry dittohead sitting at home microwaving his doughnut-and-bacon cheeseburger while his kitchen TV (one of five in the house) is accidentally on CNN: *"Well, more chilly weather today across the Ohio Valley, a cat in Philadelphia rolls its own sushi, and coming up, there are people who want Michael Moore dead!"*

Hemmer wasn't finished with his dose of derision. He wanted to know who gave me these credentials to be here.

"The DNC [Democratic National Committee] did not invite you here, is that right?" Hemmer asked, as if he were some cop checking ID, something I'm sure he would ask no one else attending the convention that week.

"No," I said, "the Congressional Black Caucus invited me here." My anger was building, so I added, for effect, "Those *black* congressmen, you know." The interview ended.

Over the next few minutes, off air, I just stood there and glared at him as other reporters asked me questions. Hemmer went over to be interviewed by some blogger. Finally, I couldn't take it anymore. I walked back up to him and said, with Dirty Harry calm, *"That is absolutely the most despicable thing ever said to me on live television."*

He told me not to interrupt him and to wait until he was done talking to the blogger. *Sure, punk, I can wait.*

And then, when I wasn't looking, he slipped away. *But there would be nowhere for him to hide!* He took refuge inside the Arkansas delegation — *the refuge of all scoundrels!* — but I found him, and I got right up in his face.

"You made my death seem *acceptable*," I said. "You just told someone it was OK to kill me."

He tried to back away, but I blocked him in. "I want you to think about your actions if anything ever happens to me. Don't think my family won't come after you, because they will." He mumbled something about his right to ask me anything he wanted, and I decided it wasn't worth breaking my lifelong record of never striking another human, certainly not some weasel from cable news (*Save it for* Meet the Press, *Mike!*). Hemmer broke loose and got away. Within the year he would leave CNN and move to Fox News, where he should have been in the first place.

To be fair to Mr. Hemmer, I was not unaware that my movies had made a lot of people mad. It was not unusual for fans to randomly come up and hug me and say, "I'm so happy you're still *here!*" They didn't mean in the building.

Why *was* I still alive? For over a year there had been threats, intimidation, harassment, and even assaults in broad daylight. It was the first year of the Iraq War, and I was told by a top security expert (who is often used by the federal government for assassination prevention) that "there is no one in America other than President Bush who is in more danger than you."

How on earth did this happen? Had I brought this on myself? Of course I did. And I remember the moment it all began.

It was the night of March 23, 2003. Four nights earlier, George W. Bush had invaded Iraq, a sovereign country that not only had *not* attacked us, but was, in fact, the past re-cipient of military aid from the United States. This was an illegal, immoral, stupid invasion — but that was not how Americans saw it. Over 70 percent of the public backed the war, including liberals like Al Franken and the twenty-nine Democratic senators who voted for the war authorization act (among them Senators Chuck Schumer, Dianne Feinstein, and John Kerry). Other liberal war cheerleaders included *New York Times* columnist and editor Bill Keller and the editor of the liberal magazine the *New Yorker,* David Remnick. Even liberals like Nicholas Kristof of the *Times* hopped on the bandwagon pushing the lie that Iraq had weapons of mass de-struction. Kristof praised Bush and Secretary of State Colin Powell for "adroitly" proving that Iraq had WMDs. He wrote this after Powell presented phony evidence to the United Nations. The *Times* ran many bogus front-page stories about how Saddam Hussein had these weapons of mass destruction. They later apologized for their drumbeating this war into existence. But the damage had been done. The *New York Times* had given Bush the cover he needed *and* the ability to claim, heck, if a liberal paper like the *Times* says so, it must be true!

And now, here it was, the fourth night of a very popular war, and my film, *Bowling for Columbine,* was up for the Academy Award. I went to the ceremony but was not allowed, along with any of the nominees, to talk to the press while walking down the red carpet into Hollywood's Kodak Theatre. There was the fear that someone might say *something*—and in wartime we need everyone behind the war effort and on the same page.

The actress Diane Lane came on to the Oscar stage and read the list of nominees for Best Documentary. The envelope was opened, and she announced with unbridled glee that I had won the Oscar. The main floor, filled with the Oscar–nominated actors, directors, and writers, leapt to its feet and gave me a very long standing ovation. I had asked the nominees from the other documentary films to join me on the stage in case I won, and they did. The ovation finally ended, and then I spoke:

I've invited my fellow documentary nominees on the stage with us. They are here in solidarity with me because we like nonfiction. We like nonfiction, yet we live in fictitious times. We live in a time where we have

fictitious election results that elect a fictitious president. We live in a time where we have a man sending
us to war for fictitious reasons. Whether it's the fiction of duct tape or the fiction of orange alerts: we are
against this war, Mr. Bush. Shame on you, Mr. Bush.
Shame on you! And anytime you've got the Pope and
the Dixie Chicks against you, your time is up! Thank
you very much.

About halfway through these remarks, all hell broke
loose. There were boos, very loud boos, from the upper
floors and from backstage. (A few—Martin Scorsese, Meryl
Streep—tried to cheer me on from their seats, but they were
no match.) The producer of the show, Gil Cates, ordered
the orchestra to start playing to drown me out. The microphone started to descend into the floor. A giant screen with
huge red letters began flashing in front me: "YOUR TIME
IS UP!" It was pandemonium, to say the least, and I was
whisked off the stage.

A little known fact: the first two words every Oscar winner hears right after you win the Oscar and leave the stage
come from two attractive young people in evening wear hired
by the Academy to immediately greet you behind the curtain.

So while calamity and chaos raged on in the Kodak, this
young woman in her designer gown stood there, unaware of
the danger she was in, and said the following word to me:
"Champagne?"

And she held out a flute of champagne.

The young man in his smart tuxedo standing next to her
then immediately followed up with this: "Breathmint?"

And he held out a breathmint.

Champagne and *breathmint* are the first two words all Oscar winners hear.

But, lucky me, I got to hear a *third*.

An angry stagehand came right up to the side of my head, screaming as loud as he could in my ear:

"ASSHOLE!"

Other burly, pissed-off stagehands started toward me. I clutched my Oscar like a weapon, holding it like a sheriff trying to keep back an angry mob, or a lone man trapped and surrounded in the woods, his only hope being the torch he is swinging madly at the approaching vampires.

The ever-alert security backstage saw the rumble that was about to break out, so they quickly took me by the arm and moved me to a safer place. I was shaken, rattled, and, due to the overwhelming negative reaction to my speech, instead of enjoying the moment of a lifetime, I suddenly sunk into a pit of despair. I was convinced I had blown it and let everyone down: my fans, my dad out in the audience, those sitting at home, the Oscar organization, my crew, my wife, Kathleen—anyone who meant anything to me. It felt like at that moment I had ruined their night, that I had tried to make a simple point but had blundered. What I didn't understand then—what I couldn't have known, even with a thousand crystal balls—was that it had to start somewhere, someone had to say it, and while I didn't plan on it being me (*I just wanted to meet Diane Lane and Halle Berry!*), this night would later be seen as the first small salvo of what would become, over time, a cacophony of anger over the actions of George W. Bush. The boos, in five years' time, would go the other way, and the nation would set aside its past and elect a man who looked absolutely like no one who was booing me that night.

I understood none of this, though, on March 23, 2003. All I knew was that I had said something that was not supposed to be said. Not at the Oscars, not *anywhere*. You know what I speak of, fellow Americans. You remember what it was like during that week, that month, that year, when no one dared speak a word of dissent against the war effort—and if you did, you were a traitor and a troop hater! All of this elevated Orwell's warnings to a new height of dark perfection, because the real truth was that the only people who hated the troops were those who would put them into this unnecessary war in the first place.

But none of this mattered to me as I was hidden away backstage at the Oscars. All I felt at that moment was alone, that I was nothing more than a profound and total disappointment.

An hour later, when we walked into the Governors Ball, the place grew immediately silent, and people stepped away for fear their picture would be taken with me. *Variety* would later write that "Michael Moore might have had the briefest gap between career high and career low in show business history." The Oscar-winning producer Saul Zaentz (*One Flew Over the Cuckoo's Nest, Amadeus*) was quoted as saying, "He made a fool of himself."

So there I stood, at the entrance of the Governors Ball, alone with my wife, shunned by the Hollywood establishment. It was then that I saw the head of Paramount Pictures, Sherry Lansing, walking determinedly up the center aisle toward me. Ah, yes—so *this* was how it would all end. I was about to be dressed down by the most powerful person in town. For over two decades, Ms. Lansing ran Fox, and then Paramount. I prepared myself for the public humiliation of being asked to leave by the dean of studio heads. I stood there, my shoulders hunched, my head bowed, ready for my execution.

And that was when Sherry Lansing walked right up to me, and gave me a big, generous kiss on my cheek.

"Thank you," she said. "It hurts now. Someday you'll be proved right. I'm so proud of you." And then she hugged me, in full view of Hollywood's elite. Statement made. Robert Friedman, Lansing's number two at Paramount (and a man who years ago had helped convince Warner Bros. to buy my first film, *Roger & Me*) hugged my wife and then grabbed my hand and shook it hard.

And that was pretty much it for the rest of the night. Sherry Lansing's public display of unexpected solidarity kept the haters at bay, but few others wanted to risk association. After all, everyone knew the war would be over in a few weeks—and no one wanted to be remembered for being on the wrong side! We sat quietly at our table and ate our roast beef. We decided to skip the parties and went back to the hotel where our friends and family were waiting. And as it turned out, they were anything but disappointed. We sat in the living room of our suite and everyone took turns holding the Oscar and making *their* Oscar speeches. It was sweet and touching, and I wished *they* had been up there on that stage instead of me.

My wife went to bed, but I couldn't sleep, so I got up and turned on the TV. For the next hour I watched the local TV stations do their Oscar night wrap-up shows—and as I flipped between the channels, I listened to one pundit after another question my sanity, criticize my speech, and say, over and over, in essence: "I don't know what got into him!" "He sure won't have an easy time in this town after that stunt!" "Who does he think will make another movie with him now?" "Talk about career suicide!" After an hour of this, I turned off the TV and went online — where there was *more* of the same, only *worse* — from all over America. I began to get sick. I could see the writing on the wall — it was curtains for me as a filmmaker. I bought everything that was being said about me. I turned off the computer and I turned off the lights and I sat there in the chair in the dark, going over and over what I had done. Good job, Mike. And good riddance.

Over the next twenty-four hours I got to listen to more boos: Walking through the hotel lobby, where Robert Duvall complained to management that my presence was causing a commotion ("He did not like the smell of Michael Moore in the morning," one of my crew would later crack to me), and going through the airport (where, in addition to the jeers, Homeland Security officials purposefully keyed my Oscar, scratching long lines into its gold plate). On the plane ride to Detroit, hate took up at least a dozen rows.

When we got back to our home in northern Michigan, the local beautification committee had dumped three truck-loads of horse manure waist-high in our driveway so that we wouldn't be able to enter our property — a property which, by the way, was freshly decorated with a dozen or so signs nailed to our trees: GET OUT! MOVE TO CUBA! COMMIE SCUM! TRAITOR! LEAVE NOW OR ELSE!

I had no intention of leaving.

Two years before the Oscars and before the war, in a calmer, more innocent time — March 2001 — I received an envelope one day in the mail. It was addressed to "Michael Moore."

And the return address? "From: Michael Moore."

After pausing a moment to consider the Escher-esque nature of what was in my hand, I opened the letter. It read:

Dear Mr. Moore,

I'm hoping when you saw that this letter was from you — not really! — that you might open it. My name is also Michael Moore. I have never heard of you until last night. I am on Death Row in Texas and am scheduled for execution later this month. They showed us your movie last night, Canadian Bacon, and I saw your name and I saw that we had the same name! I never saw my name in a movie before! You probably never saw your name in a headline, "MICHAEL MOORE TO BE EXECUTED." I am hoping you can help me. I do not want to die. I did something terrible which I regret but killing me will not solve anything or undo what I did. I did not receive a best defense. My court-appointed lawyer fell asleep during the trial. I am appealing one last time to the Texas Prison Board. Can you use your influence

```
to help me? I believe I should pay for my
crime. But not by killing me. Below are
the names of my new attorneys and the
people who are helping me. Please do what
you can. And I like your movie! Funny!
   Yours,
   Michael Moore
   #999126
```

I sat and stared at this letter for the longest time. That
night I had a bad dream. I was at the execution of Michael
Moore — and, needless to say, I didn't want to be there. I
tried to get out of the room but they had locked the door.
Michael Moore started laughing. "Hey! You're next, good
buddy!" I froze in place, and as they administered the lethal
injection, he would not take his dying eyes off me as his life
expired.

The following day I called the anti–death penalty advo-
cates who were helping him. I offered to do whatever I could.
They told me that things seemed pretty hopeless — after all,
this *was* Texas, and *no one* gets a stay or a pardon from the
governor here — but they were filing one last appeal nonetheless. They said I could write a letter to the governor or
the Court of Criminal Appeals.

I did more than that. I began a letter-writing drive on
my website and appealed to the half-million people on my
e-mail list to help me. I spoke out publicly against Michael
Moore's execution. I told people the story of a young man,
a Navy veteran of nine years, who was severely abused as a
child and never mentally recovered from the abuse. Now at
the age of thirty, he kept a notebook of the high school girls

in town he liked to stalk. One night he thought he would sneak into one of the girls' homes and steal what he could. She wasn't home. Her mother was. He was drunk and he freaked out and killed her. Pulled over an hour later for a traffic violation, he volunteered to the police (who were unaware a murder had been committed) that he had just done something bad. And that was that. He got a lousy lawyer (who, to his credit, filed a statement on behalf of his appeal, admitting he didn't do a good job for Michael) and a quick trial. Michael Moore was found guilty and given the maximum sentence: death.

Thousands responded to my appeal to stop the execution of Michael Moore. The Texas governor and prison board were deluged with letters and calls from people protesting his killing.

And then something unusual happened: on the day before he was to be put to death, the Texas Criminal Court of Appeals granted a stay of execution for Michael Moore. Michael Moore to live! In *Texas*! Unbelievable. No, really, *unbelievable*.

I can't describe the relief I felt. Michael Moore wrote me another letter, thanking me. But now the hard work of the real appeal would begin.

And then 9/11 happened. You know the cliché "9/11 changed everything"? This was one of those things. Compassion for killers went *way* out the window. It was killing time in America, and if an innocent man could be killed while eating a danish during a business meeting 106 floors above Manhattan, then a murderer in Texas certainly could not expect to be kept alive. Kill or be killed was all that mattered to us; we were now a people ready to go to war, anywhere, one war after another, if need be. You would soon be able to sum us up the way D. H. Lawrence once did: "The essential American soul is hard, isolate, stoic, and a killer."

Plans for the execution of Michael Moore were placed on the fast track. All appeals were rejected. Michael put me on the list to attend his execution—if I so chose to come. I could not. I could not go to Texas and watch Michael Moore die. I wanted to be there for him, but I simply couldn't do it.

At 6:34 p.m. on January 17, 2002, Michael Moore became the first execution of the year in the state of Texas.

And yes, the headline read: MICHAEL MOORE EXECUTED.

———

The hate mail after the Oscar speech was so voluminous, it almost seemed as if Hallmark had opened a new division where greeting card writers were assigned the task of penning odes to my passing. (*"For a Special Motherfucker..."* *"Get Well Soon from Your Mysterious Car Accident!"* *"Here's to a Happy Stroke!"*)

The phone calls to my house were actually creepier. It's a whole different fright machine when a human voice is attached to the madness and you think, *This person literally risked arrest to say this over a phone line!* You had to admire the balls—or insanity—of that.

But the worst moments were when people came on to our property. At that time we had no fence, no infrared cameras, no dogs with titanium teeth, no electrocution devices. So these individuals would just walk down the driveway, always looking like rejects from the cast of *Night of the Living Dead,* never moving very fast, but always advancing with single-minded purposefulness. Few were actual haters; most were just crazy. We kept the sheriff's deputies busy until they finally suggested we might want to get our own security, or perhaps our own police force. Which we did.

We met with the head of the top security agency in the country, an elite, no-fucking-around outfit that did not hire ex-cops ("Why are they *ex*-cops? Exactly."), nor any "tough guys" or bouncer-types. They preferred to use only Navy SEALs and other ex–Special Forces, like Army Rangers. Guys who had a cool head and who could take you out with a piece of dental floss in a matter of nanoseconds. They had to go through an additional nine-week boot camp with the agency to work for them. They already knew how to kill quietly and quickly with perfection; now they would also learn how to save a life.

I started by having the agency send me one of their ex-SEALs. By the end of the year, due to the alarming increase of threats and attempts on me, I had *nine* of them surrounding me, round-the-clock. They were mostly black and Hispanic (you had to volunteer to be on *my* detail, thus the lopsided but much-appreciated demographic). I got to know them well and, suffice it to say, when you live with nine hardcore SEALs who also happen to like you and what you do, you learn a lot about how to "floss."

After the Oscar riot and the resulting persona-non-grata status I held as the most hated man in America, I decided to do what anyone in my position would do: make a movie suggesting the president of the United States is a war criminal. I mean, why take the easy road? It was already over for me, anyway. The studio that had promised to fund my next film had called up after the Oscar speech and said that they were backing out of their signed contract with me — and if I didn't like it, I could go fuck myself. Fortunately, another studio picked up the deal but cautioned that perhaps I should be careful not to piss off the ticket-buying public. The owner of the studio had backed the invasion of Iraq. I told him I had already pissed off the ticket-buying public, so why don't we just make the best movie possible, straight from the heart—and, well, if nobody liked that, there was always straight-to-video.

In the midst of all this turmoil I began shooting *Fahrenheit 9/11*. My crew found Bush White House footage that the networks wouldn't run. I lifted it from their news departments because I thought the people had a right to see the truth.* I told everyone on my crew to operate as if this was going to be the last job we were ever going to have in the movie business. This wasn't meant to be an inspirational speech—I really believed that this was going to be it, that we were lucky to even be making *Fahrenheit* considering all that had rained down on me. So let's just make the movie we want to make and not worry about our "careers." Careers are overrated anyway! And so we spent the next eleven months putting together our cinematic indictment of an administration and a country gone mad.

The release of the film in 2004, just a little over a year after the start of the war, came at a time when the vast majority of Americans still backed the war. We premiered it at the Cannes Film Festival after the Walt Disney Company had done everything it could to stop the film's release (our

---

* I am still banned from one of these networks for liberating their footage of Deputy Defense Secretary Paul Wolfowitz licking his comb, and George W. Bush making faces and clowning around just seconds before he went live on national TV to announce the bombing and invasion of Iraq.

distributor, Miramax Films, was owned by Disney). We went to the *New York Times* with the story of how they were silencing the movie, and the *Times,* still smarting from the revelation that their pre–Iraq invasion stories were false, put the whole sordid affair on the front page. That saved us and the film, and we got to Cannes—where the movie received the longest standing ovation in the festival's history. We were awarded the top prize, the Palme d'Or, by an international jury headed by Quentin Tarantino. It was the first time in nearly fifty years a documentary had won the prize.*

This initial overwhelming response to *Fahrenheit 9/11* spooked the Bush White House, convincing those in charge of his reelection campaign that *a movie* could be the tipping point that might bring them down. They hired a pollster to find out the effect the film would have on voters. After screening the movie with three different audiences in three separate cities, the news Karl Rove received was not good.

The movie was not only giving a much-needed boost to the Democratic base (who were wild about the film), it was, oddly, having a distinct effect also on female Republican voters.

The studio's own polling had already confirmed that an amazing one-third of Republican voters—*after watching the movie*—said they would *recommend* the film to other people. The film had tiptoed across the partisan line. But the White House pollster reported something even more dangerous: 10 percent of Republican females said that after watching *Fahrenheit 9/11,* they had decided to either vote for John Kerry or to just stay home.

---

* It went on to become the largest-grossing documentary in the history of cinema, and the largest-grossing Palme d'Or winner ever (a list of winners that included films like *Apocalypse Now* and *Pulp Fiction*).

In an election that could be decided by only a few percentage points, this was devastating news.

The Bush campaign was strongly advised to get out
ahead of the movie and make sure their base never even
thought about checking it out. "You must *stop* them from entering the theater. *Republicans and independents must not see
this movie.*" Because if they did, a certain, small percentage
of them would not be able to overcome their "emotional"
reaction to the death and destruction the movie attributed
to George W. Bush. Although they knew most Republicans
would dismiss the movie sight unseen, nothing could be left
to chance. The pollster himself sat in the back at the screenings and saw firsthand what he called "the fatal blows" the
film delivered, especially when it went to a scene with the
mother of a deceased American soldier. It was too devastating for a small but significant part of the audience. "If we
lose the November election," he told me shortly after the
film's release, "this movie will be one of the top three reasons why."

I had crossed the Rubicon into mainstream America with
Fahrenheit 9/11. But now that I had crossed it, I didn't realize there would be no return to the semiquiet life of quasi-
anonymity. (I had had a strong, but respectfully small, cult
following that had made my life pleasant and functional up
to that point.) I had now entered dangerous territory, and
while it meant that I would never have to worry about a roof
over my head again, it also meant that my family and I would
pay a high price for this "success."

This was now no longer just some little documentary we

had made—and I was no longer seen as some "gadfly" that could be ignored like a nettlesome pest. This was now cover of *Time* magazine territory. This was now me being seated in the presidential box next to President Jimmy Carter at the Democratic National Convention. There would be a record four appearances in six months on *The Tonight Show.* The movie would open at #1 all across North America (the first time ever for a documentary). And, to make matters worse for the White House, it opened at #1 in *all fifty states,* even in the Deep South. Even Wyoming. Yes, even Idaho. It opened at #1 in military towns like Fort Bragg. Soldiers and their families were going to see it and, by many accounts, it became the top bootleg among the troops in Iraq. It broke the box office record long held by the *Star Wars* film *Return of the Jedi* for the largest opening weekend *ever* for a film that opened on a thousand screens or less. It was, in the verbiage of *Variety,* major boffo, a juggernaut.

And in doing all of that, it had made me a target. Not just a target of the Right or of the press. This movie was now affecting a sitting president of the United States and his chances for a second term.

So, the film—and especially its director—had to be portrayed as so repulsively anti-American that to buy a ticket to this movie would be akin to an act of treason.

The attacks on me were like mad works of fiction, crazy, made-up stuff that I refused to respond to because I didn't want to dignify the noise. On TV, on the radio, in op-eds, on the Internet—everywhere—it was suggested that Michael Moore hates America, he's a liar, a conspiracy nut, and a croissant-eater. The campaign against me was meant to stop too many Republicans from seeing the film.

And it worked. Of course, it also didn't help that Kerry was a lousy candidate. Bush won the election by one state, Ohio.

There was a residual damage from all the hate speech generated toward me by the Republican pundits. It had the sad and tragic side effect of unhinging the already slightly unglued. And so my life went from receiving scribbly little hate notes (think of them as *anti-Valentines*) to full-out attempted physical assaults — and worse.

The ex–Navy SEALs moved in with us. When I walked down a public sidewalk they would literally have to form a circle around me. At night they wore night-vision goggles and other special equipment that I'm convinced few people outside Langley have ever seen.

The agency protecting me had a Threat Assessment Division. Their job was to investigate anyone who had made a credible threat against me. One day, I asked to see the file. The man in charge began reading me the list of names and the threats they'd made and the level of threat that the agency believed each one posed. After he went through the first dozen, he stopped and asked, "Do you really want to keep going? There are four hundred and twenty-nine more."

Four hundred and twenty-nine *more?* Four hundred and twenty-nine files of people who wanted to harm me, even kill me? Each file contained minute details of these people's lives and what they might be capable of. I really didn't want to hear any more. My sister was surprised at the number.

"I thought it would be around fifty," she said, as if "fifty" was a doable number we could handle.

I could no longer go out in public without an incident happening. It started with small stuff, like people in a restaurant asking to be moved to a different table when I was seated next to them, or a cab driver who would stop his cab in mid-traffic to scream at me. There were often people who would just start yelling at me, no matter where the location: on a highway, in a theater, in an elevator. I was often asked by bystanders, "Does this happen to you a lot?" as they would be shocked at the intensity and randomness of it. One hater decided to let me have it at Mass on Christmas Day. "Really?" I said to her. "On Christmas? You can't even give it a rest on *this* day?"

The verbal abuse soon turned physical, and the SEALs were now on high alert. For security reasons, I will not go into too much detail here, partly on the advice of the agency and partly because I don't want to give these criminals any more of the attention they were seeking:

- In Nashville, a man with a knife leapt up on the stage and started coming toward me. The SEAL grabbed him from behind by his belt loop and collar and slung him off the front of the stage to the cement floor below. Someone had to mop up the blood after the SEALs took him away.

- In Portland, a guy got on the outdoor stage and started coming at me with a blunt object that he apparently was going to use over my head. My assistant blocked him momentarily, and that gave the SEALs the jump they needed to grab him and take him away.

- In Fort Lauderdale, a man in a nice suit saw me on the sidewalk and went crazy. He took the lid off his hot, scalding coffee and threw it at my face. The SEAL saw this happening but did not have the extra half-second needed to grab the guy, so he put his own face in front of mine and took the hit. The coffee burned his face so badly, we had to take him to

the hospital (he had second-degree burns)—but not before
the SEAL took the man face down to the pavement, placing
his knee painfully in the man's back, and putting him in cuffs.

• In New York City, while I was holding a press conference outside one of the theaters showing *Fahrenheit,* a man
walking by saw me, became inflamed, and pulled the only
weapon he had on him out of his pocket—a very sharp and
pointed #2 graphite pencil. As he lunged to stab me with it,
the SEAL saw him and, in the last split second, put his hand
up between me and the oncoming pencil. The pencil went
right into the SEAL's hand. You ever see a Navy SEAL get
stabbed? The look on their face is the one we have when we
discover we're out of shampoo. The pencil stabber probably
became a convert to the paperless society that day, once the
SEAL was done with him and his sixteenth-century writing
device.

• In Denver, I appeared at a screening of my movie. Security found a man carrying a gun and had him removed.
There were often guns found on people—always legal, of
course, thanks to the new laws that let people carry hand-
guns into public events.

• More than once, some white guy just wanted to punch
me. One time it was a group of skinheads. Another time it
was a realtor. Each time, the SEALs stepped in and put their
bodies between mine and the assailant's. Most times we did
not involve the police as we didn't want it to become public,
thinking that would only encourage copycats.

And then there was Lee James Headley. Sitting alone at
his home in Ohio, Lee had big plans. The world, according to
his diary, was a place dominated and being ruined by liber-

als. His comments read like the talking points of any given day's episode of *The Rush Limbaugh Show.*

And so Lee made a list. It was a short list, but a list nonetheless of the people who had to go. The names on it were former attorney general Janet Reno, Senator Tom Harkin, Senator Tom Daschle, Rosie O'Donnell, and Sarah Brady. But at the top of the list was his number one target: "Michael Moore." Beside my name he wrote, "MARKED" (as in "marked for death," he would later explain).

Throughout the spring of 2004, Lee accumulated a huge amount of assault weapons, a cache of thousands of rounds of ammunition, and various bomb-making materials. He bought *The Anarchist's Cookbook* and the race-war novel *The Turner Diaries.* His notebooks contained diagrams of rocket launchers and bombs, and he would write over and over: "Fight, fight, fight, kill, kill, kill!" He also had drawings of various federal buildings in Ohio.

But one night in 2004, he accidentally fired off a round inside his home from one of his AK-47s. A neighbor heard the shot and called the police. The cops arrived and found the treasure trove of weapons, ammo, and bomb-making materials. And his hit list. And off to jail he went.

I got the call some days later from the security agency.

"We need to tell you that the police have in custody a man who was planning to blow up your house. You're in no danger now."

I got very quiet. I tried to process what I just heard: I'm... in...no...danger...now.

For me, it was the final straw. I broke down. I just couldn't take it anymore. My wife was already in her own state of despair over the loss of the life we used to have. I asked myself again, What had I done to deserve this? Made a *movie?* A *movie* led someone to want to blow up my home? What happened to writing a letter to the editor?

It seemed that my crime was bringing questions and ideas to a mass audience (the kind of thing you do from time to time in a democracy). It wasn't that my ideas were dangerous; it was the fact that millions suddenly were eager to be exposed to them. And not just in the theater, and not just at lefty gatherings. I was invited to talk about these ideas on… *The View!* On *The Martha Stewart Show.* On *Oprah*—four times! Then there's Vanna White, turning the letters of my name on *Wheel of Fortune.* I was allowed to spread the ideas of Noam Chomsky and Howard Zinn, of I. F. Stone and the Berrigan brothers, everywhere. This drove the Right totally batshit crazy. I didn't mean for that to happen. It just did.

And so the constant drumbeat against me grew louder, with conservative talk radio and TV describing me as something that was subhuman, a "thing" that hated the troops and the flag and everything about America. These vile epithets were being spoon fed to a poorly-educated public that thrived on a diet of hate and ignorance and had no idea what the word *epithet* meant. Here's Bill O'Reilly making a crack to Mayor Rudolph Giuliani, live on his Fox News TV show, in February of 2004:

"Well, I want to kill Michael Moore. Is that all right? All right. And I don't believe in capital punishment—that's just a joke on Moore." *Ha ha.*

As the months wore on, even after Bush's reelection, the campaign to stop me only intensified. When Glenn Beck said over the airwaves that he was thinking of killing me, he was neither fined by the FCC nor arrested by the NYPD. He was, essentially, making a call to have me killed, and no one in the media at that time reported it. No FCC commissioner condemned it. It was simply OK to speak of me in this manner over the public airwaves.

And then a man trespassed on our property and left something outside our bedroom window when I wasn't home. It terrorized my wife. He even videotaped himself doing this. When the police investigated, he said he was making a "documentary." He called it *Shooting Michael Moore*. And when you went to his website, and the words *Shooting Michael Moore* came on the screen, the sound of a gunshot went off. The media ate it up, and he was asked to be on many TV shows (like Sean Hannity's). *"Coming up next—He's giving Michael Moore a taste of his own medicine! Moore now has somebody after him!" (Cue sfx: KA-BOOM!)* He then provided video and maps of how to not only get to our house, but how to illegally get onto the property. He failed to mention, though, what the ex-SEALs would do to you when they caught you.*

And now a man from Ohio had drawn up plans and gathered the necessary materials to do to our house what Timothy McVeigh did in Oklahoma City.

"He'll be going away to prison for a long time, Mike," the

---

* Right-wing groups and talk-show hosts weren't the only ones behind the attacks. Corporate interests began to spend large sums of money to stop me. When I announced that my next film would be about health care in this country, a consortium of health insurance companies and drug manufacturers formed a group to try and stop the film, mainly by spending hundreds of thousands of dollars on a disinformation campaign intended to discredit me and the film. And if that plan didn't work, then they would do what they had to do to "push Michael Moore off the cliff." Wendell Potter, the vice president of CIGNA Insurance, blew the whistle on this to the journalist Bill Moyers and in his own book, *Deadly Spin*.

security chief reassured me. "The reason that he and others always fail is because of the systems you have in place."

"And because he had a nosy neighbor who called the cops," I added.

"Yes, that too."

I will not share with you the impact this had, at that time, on my personal life, but suffice it to say I would not wish this on anyone. More than once I have asked myself if all this work was *really* worth it. And, if I had it to do over again, *would I?* If I could take back that Oscar speech and just walk up on the stage and thank my agent and tuxedo designer and get off without another word, *would I?* If it meant that my family would not have to worry about their safety and that I would not be living in constant danger—well, I ask you, what would *you* do? You know what you would do.

For the next two and a half years, I didn't leave the house much. From January 2005 to May 2007, I did not appear on a single television show. I stopped going on college tours. I just took myself off the map. I wrote the occasional blog on my website, but that was pretty much it. The previous year I had spoken on over fifty campuses. For the two years following that, I spoke at only one. I stayed close to home and worked on some local town projects in Michigan where I lived, like renovating and reopening a closed-down historic movie palace, starting a film festival, and trying to sleep at night.

And then to my rescue rode President Bush. He said something that helped snap me out of it. I had heard him say it before, but this time when I heard him, I felt like he was speaking directly to me. He said, "If we give in to the terrorists, the terrorists win." And he was right. *His* terrorists were winning! Against me! *What was I doing sitting inside the house? Fuck it!* I opened up the blinds, folded up my pity party, and went back to work. I made three films in three years, threw myself into getting Barack Obama elected, and helped toss two Republican congressmen from Michigan out of office. I set up a popular website, and I was elected to the board of governors of the same Academy Awards that had booed me off the stage.

And then Kurt Vonnegut invited me over to his house one night for dinner. It would be one of four dinners I would have with him and his wife in the final year of his life. The conversations were intense, funny, provocative—and they *resuscitated me,* literally breathed life right back into me, and brought me back to a place in the world.

He told me he had been observing for some time "the crucifixion" (as he called it) that I was experiencing—and he had a few things he wanted to tell me.

"The extremes to which the Bush people have gone to get you, they directly correlate to just how effective you've been," he told me over his third after-supper cigarette one night. "You have done more to put the brakes on them than you realize. It may be too late for all of us, but I have to say you have given me a bit of hope for this sad country."

One night I went to his house and he was sitting out on the stoop by himself waiting for me. He told me that he had stopped contemplating the "meaning of life" because his son, Mark, had finally figured it out for him: "We're here to help each other get through this thing, whatever it is." And that's what he was doing for me.

Vonnegut had, in his final years, turned to writing nonfiction.

"This has been my greatest challenge," he told me, "because the current reality now seems so unreal, it's hard to make nonfiction seem believable. But you, my friend, are able to do that."

We went for a walk to meet his wife and some friends for dinner. I asked him if any of this—the writing, the movies, the politics—was worth it.

"No, not really," he replied in typical Vonnegut style. "So you might as well quit complaining and get back to work. You have nothing to worry about. No harm will come to you." And then, realizing I might not be buying it, he added with the voice of God: "SO SAYETH I!" I stood there on East Forty-eighth Street looking at this mad son of Mark Twain and broke down into laughter. That was all I really needed to hear. If not the voice of God, then at least a gentle plea from Billy Pilgrim. And so it goes.

That night he gave me one of his drawings with the inscription, "Dear Iraq: Do like us. After 100 years let your slaves go. After 150 let your women vote. Love, Uncle Sam." He signed it, "For Michael Moore, my hero—KV."

I came back alive. I chose not to give up. I wanted to give up, badly. Instead I got fit. If you take a punch at me now, I can assure you three things will happen: (1) You will break your hand. That's the beauty of spending just a half hour a day on your muscular-skeletal structure—it turns into kryptonite; (2) I will fall on you. I'm still working on my core and balance issues, so after you slug me I *will* tip over and crush you. It won't be on purpose, and while you are attempting to breathe, please know I'll be doing my best to get off you; (3) My SEALs will spray mace or their own homemade concoction of jalapeño spider spray directly into your eye sockets while you are on the ground. I hear this is excruciatingly painful. As a pacifist, please accept my apologies in advance — and never, ever use violence against me or anyone else again. (SERMON ALERT)

> Only cowards use violence. They are afraid that their ideas will not win out in the public arena. They are weak and they are worried that the people will see their weakness. They are threatened by women, gays, and minorities — *minorities,* for chrissakes! You know why they're called "minorities"? Because they don't have the power — YOU do! That's why you're called the "majority"! And yet you're afraid. Afraid of fetuses not coming to term, or of men kissing men (or worse!). Afraid someone will take your gun away — a gun that you have in the first place because you're...*afraid!* Please, please, for the sake of all of us — RELAX! We like you! Heck, you're an American!

One night in Aventura, Florida, I took my new buff self, along with a friend, to the mall alongside the William Lehman Causeway to see a movie. A young guy in his thirties passed by me, and as he did, he had this to say: "Shithead."

He continued on his walk. I stopped and turned back toward him.

"Hey! You! Come back here!"

The guy kept walking.

"Hey, don't run away from me!" I shouted louder. "Don't be a chicken. Come back here and face me!"

"Chicken" is a dish not well served to the gender with testosterone for their fluid. He abruptly halted, turned and headed back toward me. As he got five feet from me, I said the following in a gentle voice:

"Hey, man — why would you say such a thing to me?"

He sneered and steeled himself for a fight. "Because I know who you are, and you're a shithead."

"Now, there you go again, using that word. You haven't the foggiest idea who I am or what I'm really about. You haven't even seen *one* of my movies."

"I don't need to!" he replied, confirming what I already suspected. "I already know the anti-American stuff you put out there."

"OK, dude, that's not fair. You can't judge me based on what someone else has told you about me. You look way smarter than that. You look like a guy who makes up his own mind. Please watch one of my movies. I swear to God, you may not agree with all the politics, but I can guarantee you that (1) you will instantly know that I deeply love this country; (2) you will see that I have a heart; and (3) I promise you'll laugh quite a few times during the film. And if you still wanna call me a shithead after that, then fine. But I don't think you will."

He calmed down, and we talked for at least another five minutes. I listened to his complaints about the world, and I told him that we probably have more that we agree on than disagree on. He relaxed even more, and eventually I got a smile out of him. Finally, I said I had to go or we were going to miss our movie.

"Hey man," he said, holding out his hand to shake mine. "I'm sorry I called you that name. You're right, I don't really know anything about you. But the fact that you just stopped and talked to me after I called you that—well, that's got me thinking—I really didn't know you. Please accept my apology."

I did, and we shook hands. There would be no more disrespecting me or threatening me—and it was *that* attitude that made me safe, or as safe as one can be in this world. From now on, if you messed with me, there would be consequences: I may make you watch one of my movies.

A few weeks later I was back on *The Tonight Show* for the first time in a while. When it was over and I was leaving the stage, the guy who was operating the boom microphone approached me.

"You probably don't remember me," he said nervously. "I never thought I would ever see you again or get the chance to talk to you. I can't believe I get to do this."

Do what? I thought. I braced myself for the man's soon-to-be-broken hand.

"I never thought I'd get to apologize to you," he said, as a few tears started to come into his eyes. "And now, here you are, and I get to say this: I'm the guy who ruined your Oscar night. I'm the guy who yelled 'ASSHOLE' into your ear right after you came off the stage. I…I…[he tried to compose himself]. I thought you were attacking the president—but

you were right. He *did* lie to us. And I've had to carry this
with me now all these years, that I did that to you on your
big night, and I'm so sorry…"

By now he was starting to fall apart, and all I could think
to do was to reach out and give him a huge hug.

"It's OK, man," I said, a big smile on my face. "I accept
your apology. But you do *not* need to apologize to me. You
did nothing wrong. What did you do? You believed your
president! You're supposed to believe your president! If we
can't expect that as just the *minimum* from whoever's in office, then, shit, we're doomed."

"Thank you," he said, relieved. "Thank you for
understanding."

"Understanding?" I said. "This isn't about understanding.
I've told this funny story for years now, about the first two
words you hear when you're an Oscar winner—and how I
got to hear a bonus word! Man, don't take that story away
from me! People love it!" He laughed, and I laughed.

"Yeah," he said, "there aren't many good stories like that."

Crawling
Backwards

THE FIRSTBORN OF MY FAMILY was never born.

And then I came along.

There was another baby on the way, a year before me, but one day my mother felt a sharp pain and, within minutes, Mike the First expressed second thoughts about his much-anticipated debut on Earth, shouted "Check, please!" and was out of the uterus before the audience with their applause decided who was Queen for a Day.

This sudden and unfortunate development greatly saddened my mother. So to console her, my grandmother took her on a pilgrimage to Canada to beg for mercy from the Patron Saint of Women in Labor, the mother of the Virgin Mary herself, Saint Anne. Saint Anne is also the patron saint of Quebec, and a shrine had been built in her honor at the Basilica of Sainte-Anne-de-Beaupré in the province of Quebec. This holy site contained some of the saint's actual bones plus other holy items encased in the Holy Stairs on the grounds of the shrine. It was said that if you climbed these stairs on your knees, the mother of the Blessed Virgin would help you do what virgins don't do, which is to conceive.

33

And so my mother ascended each of the twenty-eight stairs on her knees—and within weeks, as sure as God is both my witness and fertility specialist, I was conceived on a hot July night, first as an idea and then...well, the rest I'll leave to your imagination. Suffice it to say that within nine months the fertilized egg grew into a fetus and that eventually became an eight-pound-twelve-ounce baby boy that was born with the body of a linebacker and the head of Thor.

They knocked my mother out cold so she wouldn't have to experience firsthand the miracle of life. Me, I wasn't so lucky. They poked and prodded and pushed and, instead of letting me get around to the business at hand in my own goddamned time, they grabbed me and yanked me out into a world of bright lights and strangers wearing masks, obviously to conceal their identity from me.

And before I could feel the love in the room, they gave me a serious 1950s old-school wallop on the behind. Yeow! "WAAAAAAAHHHHHHHHHH!" That *fucking* hurt. And then, get this—they severed my most important organ— *the feeding tube to my mother!* They just cut me right the fuck off from her! I could see this was not a world that believed in prior consent or my necessity for a nonstop 24/7 supply of *fundamental nourishment.*

After permanently separating me from the only person who ever loved me (a good and decent woman who was drugged, then mugged, and was still out cold a half hour later), it was now time for the comedy show. The nurse joked that she thought I was "big enough to be twins." *Laughter!* The doctor remarked that at least five of those nearly nine pounds had to be in my head. *Huge guffaws!* Yes, these guys were a *riot!*

I'll admit I had an unusually large-sized head, though this was not uncommon for a baby born in the Midwest. The craniums in our part of the country were designed to leave a little extra room for the brain to grow should we ever have a chance to learn anything outside of our rigid and insular lives. Perhaps one day we might get exposed to something we didn't quite understand, like a foreign language, or a salad. Our extra cranial area would protect us from such mishaps.

But my head was different than the other large-headed Michigan babies — not because of its actual weight and size, but because *it did not look like the head (or face) of a baby!* It looked as if someone had Photoshopped an adult's head onto a baby's body.

The hospitals in the 1950s saw themselves on the cutting edge of post-war modern society. And they convinced the women who entered their establishments that to be "modern" meant to *not* breast-feed your baby — that breast-feeding was passé and trashy. *Modern* women used *the Bottle!*

Of course, *modern* was the wrong word. Try *evil*. They convinced our mothers that if a food item came in a bottle — or a can or a box or a cellophane bag — then it was somehow *better* for you than when it came to you free of charge via Mother Nature. There we were, millions of us in diapers and blankies, and instead of being placed on our mother's breasts, bottles were inserted into our mouths, where we were expected to find some sort of pleasure from a fake rubber nipple whose coloring resembled that of a loose stool. Who *were* these people? Was it really that easy to con our parents? If they could be fooled so easily on this, what else could they be convinced to try? Creamed corn in a can? Chemlawn? A Corvair?

An entire generation of us were introduced in *our very first week* to the concept that *phony* was better than *real,* that something *manufactured* was better than something that was *right there in the room.* (Later in life, this explained the popularity of the fast food breakfast burrito, neocons, Kardashians, and why we think reading this book on a tiny screen with three minutes of battery life left is enjoyable).

I spent a full week in the maternity ward at St. Joseph Hospital in Flint, Michigan, and let me tell you, from some of the conversations I had with the other newborns, *no one* was digging the fake rubber nipple — and this made us a miserable, cynical bunch, with most of us looking forward to the day when we could strike back at this generation with our long hair, crazy-massive amounts of premarital sex, and Malcolm X. The Bottle created Woodstock and flag burning and PETA. You can quote me.

On the day of my release from St. Joe's, I was taken outside for the first time and the sun hit my face and it was good. It was a rather warm day for Michigan in April, but I didn't seem to mind, all wrapped up in a comfy new baby-blue blanket, content to be in my mother's arms. She and my dad got into the front seat of their two-tone 1954 Chevy Bel Air sedan. My dad started the engine. My mother said she was feeling "too hot." Me, I was fine.

She suggested that he open up the fresh air vents to cool down the car. And when my dad obeyed, all the gunk that had built up during the winter came spewing out of the vents, and a black, sootlike substance spread all over my baby-blue blanket and me. My little face was now blackened, and I started to cough and wheeze and cry. *Take me back to the hospital!* My mother let out a yelp of horror, and my dad quickly turned off the fan and began to assist in my cleanup.

Within twenty minutes we were at my first home, a tiny, two-bedroom apartment upstairs over Kelly's Cleaners, a dry-cleaning establishment in downtown Davison, Michigan. Davison was a small town, five and a half miles from the city limits of Flint. My mother's family had lived in the Davison area since Andrew Jackson was president—in other words, since pretty much before anyone, save the native people. Hers was one of the first families that founded the local Catholic parish. My father, who came from an Irish-American family on the east side of Flint, enjoyed the quiet, homespun nature of Davison, a far cry from the hardscrabble existence he was used to in the city. His only prior experience with the town of Davison was when his Flint St. Mary's High School basketball team came out to play the Davison High School Cardinals, and the crowd started taunting the players with anti-Catholic slurs ("Hey, fish-eaters!" was the main insult being hurled by the Davison fans). That was enough for Father Soest, St. Mary's pastor. He stood up, pronounced the game over, and hauled his team out of the gym and back to Flint. Other than that, my dad liked Davison.

The store that housed our apartment was owned by my mother's father, my grandfather Doc Wall, who, for a half century, was known as the "town doctor" of Davison. Doc Wall, and his wife, Bess, lived in the two-story white house that my mother was born in, just two doors down from us. Every day the good doctor would climb the twenty-one stairs up to our apartment to see how his grandson was doing. I think he was also intrigued by the new device sitting in our living room: a Westinghouse nineteen-inch television set, and he would spend the occasional hour or two watching it. My grandmother would comment that I was already taking after him, and he liked that. He even had his own name for me — "Malcolm" — and he would make up songs and sing them to me (*"He's a nice little fellow, and a fine little lad, and we fixed up his buggy, with a nice little pad"*). He would pass away before my third birthday, and I have only two vivid, but wonderful, memories of him: him building me a tent made of blankets in his living room, and the lively music he played for me on his Irish fiddle while I was perched precariously on his bouncing knee.

It has been reported that my first few hours in my new home were uneventful. But as the evening wore on, so did I, and thus began a nonstop crying jag that, despite the best intentions of my mother to comfort me, did not cease. After an hour or so of this, she became worried that something might be wrong and phoned over to her parents for advice. Grandmother Bess came right over and, after inspecting the crying baby with the adult-sized head, she asked, "When was the last time you fed him?"

"At the hospital," my mother replied.

"Why, that was hours ago! *This baby is hungry!*"

Thank you, Grandma Bess, for saying the words I did not yet possess in my vocabulary.

My mother found the baby bag they gave her at the hospital and looked inside for the bottle — but there was none to be found. No bottle, no formula. But, wait a minute... *isn't there a breast in the room?! Helllooo!*

My mother must have heard me, and so she attempted, with her own mother's instruction, to breast-feed me. But either the plumbing wasn't working, or I was already hooked on the Carnation Sugared Milk-Like Fatty Liquid Yum-Yum Substance, because I was having none of it. The crying continued, and Bess instructed her daughter to wake up my dad (who was already asleep; first shift at the factory began at 6:00 a.m.) and send him into Flint to get some formula at the only all-night drugstore.

As for me — *I was convinced these people were trying to starve me to death!* And I didn't know why! The wailing continued. Dutifully, my dad put on his clothes and took the two-lane road into Flint to buy some formula and a bottle. He returned an hour later, and they quickly prepared it and gave it to me. I grabbed at it with what little strength was left in me. And I didn't stop gulping until it was all gone.

For some reason, I never found my way to the path called "normal," and it was a good thing that science and business had not yet conspired to invent ways to sedate and desensitize a little soul like mine. It's one of the few times I thank God for growing up in the ignorant and innocent fifties and sixties. It would still be a few years before the pharmaceutical community would figure out how to dope up a toddler like me and have the teachers and parents send me off to the "timeout room." I have often imagined what the pediatricians of today would have done to me had they lived back then and witnessed my bizarre behavior.

For instance, the way I would transport myself in my initial years. Crawling and then walking, like most babies did, wasn't good enough for me. I had other plans. To begin with, I refused to crawl. I would not crawl for anyone. My parents would set me down on the floor and I would go on strike. Motionless. "I'm not going anywhere. You can stand there and look at me *allllll* you want 'til the cows come home, but I ain't movin'!"

After a while I could sense their disappointment, so around my ninth month I decided to crawl—backwards. Put me down and I would just go in reverse. Never forward, only backwards. And I mean as soon as I hit the floor I would shoot in the opposite direction. But I never ran into anything. It was weird, like I had eyes in the back of my diaper. My little body was somehow stuck in reverse, and if you wanted me to come to you, you had to point me in the opposite direction so I could back my rear end toward you.

This became a source of amusement for the adults—*too much amusement,* I thought, as people were now stopping by just to see the backwards-crawling baby—so I decided to change it up. I began slowly, methodically, crawling forward. Not all slaphappy-forward like most babies. Just a very determined, thoughtful, one hand in front of the other—and not before feeling the texture of the floor first (a little here, now a little there) and then picking just the right spot that was acceptable to my aesthetic and my taste. And then I would crawl. If I felt like it.

Walking seemed overrated, and as I watched the other toddlers in the neighborhood lifting themselves up and hanging on to furniture and pant legs in order to steady themselves before crashing down a few hundred times, I preferred to wait out this phase of my life.

It became quite the standoff in the household. There was already another baby on the way, and even after Anne, my sister, was born and ready to crawl herself, I still hadn't walked. Why? Why did I need to expend useless energy? I could already see what most of life involved: A third of it was lying in a bed, sleeping. Another third of it was either standing on your feet in one spot all day on an assembly line or sitting at a desk. And the final third of the day was spent sitting either at the dinner table or on a couch watching TV. And why did a baby need to walk as long as there were strollers, scooters, walkers, bouncy walkers, tricycles, and parents to carry you? Give me a break! Plus it wasn't like I had anywhere to go or someplace to be.

This attitude was not winning me any praise from my parents. A one-and-a-half-year-old needs love and adoration, and these seemed to be quickly fading away. So one day, in my seventeenth month, I thought it best to rise up and show them what I was made of. I leapt off the floor like an East German gymnast and walked straight as an arrow over to the fan and tried to stick my tongue in it. The parents were overjoyed and horrified.

You want me walking? This is what it looks like!

My mother knew that I was different, and so she decided to share a secret with me when I turned four. She taught me how to read. This little bit of empowerment was not supposed to take place for a couple of years, and for good reason: If you could read, you knew shit. And knowing shit, especially in the 1950s, was a prescription for trouble.

She began with the daily newspaper. Not a kid's book (of which there were plenty in the house), but the *Flint Journal*. She first taught me to read the daily weather box. This was useful information, and I appreciated knowing something the other kids didn't, like whether it was going to rain or snow tomorrow. I also was fixated on the pollen count. I would proudly tell whomever I saw on the street what today's pollen count was. I believe Davison became the most pollen-proficient town in the county thanks to me. To this day, you go to Davison, Michigan, and ask anyone, "Hey, what's the pollen count?" and they will happily give it to you, without hesitation or prejudice. I started that.

After the weather box and pollen count, it was on to teaching me to read the front-page headlines, and after that, the daily astronomy forecast, followed by the sports scores. My mother didn't teach me the ABCs. She taught me words. Words connected to other words. Words that had meaning to me and words that had me stumped but eager to learn what they meant. Every word on the page became a puzzle to solve — *and it was fun!*

Soon, we were going to the library once a week and I would always check out the maximum limit — ten books. Usually I would try to slip an eleventh into the pile, and it was my good fortune that the kindly librarians were either poor at math or, more than likely, they saw what I was doing — and the last thing they wanted to do was discourage a kid who wanted to read.

Now here's where the child abuse came in: *my parents sent me to school!* I was instantly bored outta my cotton-pickin' mind — but I was careful not to let on to the other students that I could already read and write and do math. This would have been the kiss of death, especially with the boys who would have constantly beaten me up; for safety, I tried to sit by the smart girls like Ellen Carr and Kathy Collins. If the teachers suspected anything, they would have issued an Inquisition to find out who was teaching me all of this OUT OF ORDER.

So I played along, and picked up an additional skill set: acting. As the other kids sang "A-B-C-D-E-F-G," I "struggled" right along with them, while secretly reading Dr. Seuss under the cover of my desktop. *Oh, the places I would go, as long as Sister Mary didn't know!*

"Where did you get this book?" the friendly nun asked me the day she caught me.

"A third grader let me look at the pictures," I said, with a face so straight it would've made Beaver Cleaver proud.

But the nuns were on to me, and yet far from condemning me for being literate, they did the only reasonable and nurturing thing they could do.

"Michael," Sister John Catherine said to me one day before the morning bell rang, "we've decided that you already know what we're teaching you in first grade, so beginning today we're moving you to second grade."

My eyes widened with victory.

"Now, you know, if we put you in second grade, you won't be the smartest boy in the room like you are here. Do you think that will be OK?"

"Does this mean I won't have to sing the 'ABCs' anymore?"

"Correct. There will be no more 'ABCs.' In fact you'll have to learn cursive penmanship right away. Are you OK with this?"

"Yes, Sister, thank you!" It was like the warden telling a prisoner that he's being moved from solitary to, I dunno,

Disneyland? I couldn't wait to get home to tell my parents the good news.

"They did *what?*" my mother quietly shouted, not believing she had just heard what I told her.

"They put me in second grade! I spent the whole day in second grade! It was great!"

"Well, you're going right back to first grade!"

"*What? No!* Why?!"

"Because I want you to be with children your own age."

"But they're only a year older!"

"And a year bigger and a year ahead of you, and if you stayed with them you are going to get shortchanged a year in your education."

I could not understand this logic. Years later my sister Anne would say it was because Mom was a traditional Republican and she figured, *I'm paying taxes for a full twelve years of schooling, I want my kid to get the entire twelve years!* But we paid tuition to go to a Catholic school. Had I known anything then about family finances, I would have pointed out to her that skipping me a grade meant that she'd be *saving* a whole year's tuition! Regardless, she didn't want the older kids beating me up.

"I'm calling the Mother Superior," she announced, as she headed toward the phone in the kitchen.

"No, Mom— Wait! I can't stand first grade! I already know everything they're teaching. Sister will tell you!"

And now for the trump card, my final hope:

"The Catholic Church says I should be in second grade! You have to obey the Church!"

She stopped and turned around for a split second and shot me the look of "you've got to be kidding me" and proceeded into the kitchen. She picked up the phone on the wall, asked the neighbor who was using our party line to please get off, and then she shut the sliding door and dialed the convent. I listened through the door while she respectfully, but forcefully, informed the Mother Superior that I was *not* to be moved up a grade. There were long pauses during which the nun was obviously making the SANE and CORRECT case to her as to why I was bored and getting into trouble and how I should have been in second grade (if not *third!*).

My mother replied that her mind had been made up and that was that. She closed the conversation by politely asking the Mother Superior not to make any other "unilateral" parenting decisions without her in the future. I didn't quite know what that meant, but I knew what it felt like. Ouch. You don't talk to the Mother Superior this way. I would pay for this, for sure.

Idle minds are either the work of the devil or the handmaiden of revolution. Although I was loved by all my nuns and lay teachers, they would be the first to tell you that I was also a bit of a handful. I had my own ideas about what the school should be doing and how it should be run. I would crack jokes in class and play pranks when necessary. As an altar boy, I would make faces at people during Communion while I held the gold plate under their chin so they wouldn't drop the Lord. One time, Father Tomascheski caught me doing this and he halted the Communion and told me in a loud voice for the whole congregation to hear: "Wipe that smirk off your face!" It was the first time I heard the word *smirk*.

I had my own pretend TV show at school (complete with theme song), and I would involve the other kids in it as characters (I would tell them that hidden cameras were filming the show). I started my own paper and I wrote poems and plays. In eighth grade, I volunteered to write the Christmas play for the school pageant. When the authorities saw the dress rehearsal, it was decided that the show would not go on. In the play's key scene, all the nation's rodents came to St. John's school in Davison and held their annual convention in our aging parish hall. The rodent situation was so bad in this place that in second grade, a mouse ran up the habit of Sister Ann Joseph — which jolted her out of her chair and had her doing the Watusi in order to shake the mouse out of her. So I thought it would be funny to write about this. In the final act, the parish hall collapses and kills all of the rats. The students and the nuns rejoice. Good triumphs over rodent. Joy reigns throughout the land.

The priest suggested the eighth grade just stand there and sing Christmas carols on the stage instead. I got most of the boys to join me in protest by not singing the first song. We just stood there, mouths shut, looking straight ahead. That was a bad idea because we stared straight into the Fear-of-God glare emanating from the Mother Superior. We were all singing by the next song, to be sure.

My mother should've just let me skip a grade. There would've been much less trouble for all concerned.

Search Party

FEW STREETS IN AMERICA are structured so that no matter whether you make a right turn or a left turn, you end up at a dead end.

Such was the street where I lived and grew up: East Hill Street, a one-block-long dirt and gravel lane with two dead ends. The only way to get onto this double-dead-end street was by taking *another* dead-end dirt lane known as Lapeer Street. Lapeer stretched from the railroad tracks on one end to smack dab in the center of Hill on ours, forming a T and thus our own little tucked-away neighborhood. Beyond Lapeer Street was a field that led to the town's lone movie palace, the Midway. Behind Hill Street was an adventure-filled swamp and a large, mysterious forest.

In the early 1950s, old Mr. Hill sold off his farmland, and it was turned into this plat of twenty-seven homes on these two mostly invisible and nondescript streets. The houses were primarily of a post-war Levittown nature: small, quaint, necessary. They were filled with the families of the new middle class. There was hope and hostility in these 900-square-foot structures. There were big backyards that, in the early

years, all blended into each other, but eventually had to be
sectioned off with wood fences and thick hedges. "We" became "me" in less than a decade, but for a while the entire
neighborhood felt like one big summer camp.

At each dead end of Hill Street lay an open field. In the
field to the west we would have "dirt clod" fights: the goal
was to pick up hard-packed pieces of earth and hurl them
into the eyes of your friends. Each spring we would take my
dad's riding lawn mower and carve out a baseball diamond,
where we would meet every day of the summer and play
baseball until sunset. The field on the east end of the street
was where we would set up "camp" with makeshift tents of
our dads' discarded tarps and blankets, the neighborhood
headquarters where all things delinquent were planned.

The forest behind our houses on Hill Street was vast and
seemed to extend so deep that none of us ever found the end
of it, no matter how many hours we trekked through its tall
pines, thick maples, and white birches. The "woods," as we
called it, was an amusement park of nature where we could
fish, hunt, trap, camp, get lost. To get to these woods you
had to cross through the open backyards of four neighbors
and none of them ever seemed to mind. A large swamp separated the yards from the woods, and the swamp itself held
much sway over us. We learned to leap from one fallen tree
to another to avoid getting a "soaker." The water wasn't more
than knee-deep, and there were no critters that might cause
us harm. There were hundreds of frogs, though, and we did
our best to catch them, though usually the frogs were faster
and smarter. There were flowers of all kinds and a requisite
number of mosquitoes that appreciated our presence as little
walking blood banks for their dining pleasure.

After crossing the swamp you found yourself at the foot of a hill that, frozen in the winter, became our sledding playground. At the top of the hill began the footpath that took us deep into the infinite woods. We would hike for hours, though no one used the word *hike,* as that implied a planned activity. None of what we did in our free time as kids was ever planned or structured in any way. It just *was.* An hour of homework and then "git outside and git the stink blown off ya!" were the orders from our dads.

We stalked deer and rabbits and coons; we had BB guns and bows and arrows, and occasionally the boys next door brought out their bird gun so we could shoot pheasants. And we were ten. Heaven. The adults left us alone, and we went on many expeditions in those woods, packing lunches of Spam, which we would cook on our "buddy burners," empty tin cans with a wad of cardboard tightly stuffed inside and covered with the wax we would melt and drip over it. Later, we would light our buddy burners, and the waxed cardboard would burn slow enough to grill our Spam. More Heaven.

Girls were excluded from all these activities, except the sledding. Our parents would make us take them up the hill and force us to ride the sled down the hill with them. After all, who but a boy was qualified to do the steering? We actually enjoyed this immensely, as we were able to scare the bejesus out of the girls by pretending to steer the fast-moving sled into a tree—but pulling out at the last instant. Usually. There was the occasional crash and crying baby sister, but even that brought us great happiness.

Other than these sledding memories I have no recall of

ever seeing any of the neighborhood girls anywhere, and if you were to press me I could make the case that there were, in fact, no girls at all in the neighborhood. Years later, it would turn out, we learned they had spent a lot of time reading, and playing instruments, and making things, and telling stories to each other and to Barbie. This would serve them well once they left childhood behind, but for now they were invisible to our existence, and I guess we thought we were all the better without them. Boys will not only be boys, but boys like to be with boys. And some boys like to be with certain boys a lot.

Sammy Good was different. In 1965, you could be different—*to a point*—and that was considered OK. For instance, you could have blue eyes while the other kids had brown eyes. Your hair could be a rusty color while others' may be sandy or dark. There were tall kids, short kids, kids who rode on bikes, fat kids, skinny kids, even kids with chicken pox (and, yes, they all loved hot dogs).

What there *weren't* were boys who fell in love with other boys.

Of course, there were those boys, but we didn't know that in fifth grade. It's not that anyone was opposed to homosexuality; it's just that there was no need to oppose it because *it just didn't exist!* It would be like opposing unicorns or Atlantis or men without nipples—I mean, you couldn't hate what isn't real.

This made it all the more critical that if you were a boy who liked boys (or a girl who liked girls), you had better guard that secret like it was your own personal Fort Knox, sealed airtight and impenetrable. You had to behave knowing you were an alien who landed from another planet, but in human form. No one knew you were an alien, and if they ever found out who you really were, they would annihilate you. The knowledge that you were not "like others" was so scary to possess that if you came across another boy-loving alien, you could not let on to that homosexual who you really were.

But, of course, the other alien would know. Yet you dare not risk making contact with each other, for if you were caught by the Normal People, they could ruin you. Sometimes you had to turn in one of your own just to prove you weren't one of "them." It was an often devastating existence to be gay in the fifties and sixties (and seventies and eighties, and…), and it made you sometimes do very cruel and unnecessary things to yourself and to others.

Such was the case with the boy three doors down from us on Lapeer Street. The Good family seemed like educated people, which immediately made them stick out. There were many fathers in the neighborhood with no college education and some had even barely gone to high school. But in those days, being educated or smart was not considered a drawback. It was something that was admired, respected, even aspired to.

Also in that time, the educated and professional class was not separated from the lowly wage earner and the factory serf. As their income differential was negligible, they lived among each other and shared their knowledge. The college professor down the block tutored the neighborhood kids in math, and in turn the garage mechanic father would be "over in a jiff" to fix the professor's carburetor. The dentist was available to pull an emergency tooth for the plumber's kid, and the plumber was on call to fix the leak in the dentist's house on a Sunday night. That's just how it was.

And so on our two democratic, egalitarian dirt streets, this was who lived there, going from west to east: Presbyterian minister, manager of the five-and-dime, spark-plug assembly-line worker (our dad), steelworker, postmaster, shirt salesman, the osteopath and his mother. On the other block: truck driver, retired couple, department store manager, high school teacher, janitor, disabled elderly person, grocery store checkout-line bagger, retiree, city councilman, single mother with son, banker. It was the American middle class. No one's house cost more than two or three years' salary, and I doubt the spread in annual wages (except for the osteopath) exceeded more than five thousand dollars. And other than the doctor (who made house calls), the store managers, the minister, the salesman, and the banker, everyone belonged to a union. That meant they worked a forty-hour week, had the entire weekend off (plus two to four weeks' paid vacation in the summer), comprehensive medical benefits, and job security. In return for all that, the country became the most productive in the world, and in our little neighborhood it meant your furnace was always working, your kids could be dropped off at the neighbors without notice, you could run next door anytime to borrow a half-dozen eggs, and the doors to all the homes were never locked—because who would need to steal anything if they already had all that they needed?

But, dear reader, before you start playing Stephen Foster and "The Star Spangled Banner," I need to remind you what you may already know: This idyllic existence (so aptly documented on shows like *Donna Reed* and *Father Knows Best*) had its dark side. Beyond the fact that women were still years away from a liberation movement, and beyond the fact that had a single black person moved into this neighborhood the FOR SALE signs would have grown like poisonous weeds, there was the insurmountable fact that you simply could not love who you loved if who you loved possessed the same genitalia as you. You didn't even *exist* to begin with, so therefore you became either very quiet or a very angry actor performing each day on the heterosexual stage.

Mr. and Mrs. Good had three children: Sammy, Alice, and Jerry. If you wanted to pack up a family and send them around the world so people in other lands could see what a nice American family looked like, the Goods were it. Mr. Good was the manager of the local department store. Sammy was the oldest child, about four years ahead of me in school. He had been adopted when the Goods did not know if the stork would come with any of their own. But then they had Alice, who was my age, and Jerry, who was three years younger.

The Goods lived in a spritely brick ranch house with a large, screened-in back porch and a backyard that stretched a decent 150 feet. Mr. Good's comfortable income, just slightly better (though not by much) than the rest of the street, allowed him to have a maid who came to the house once a week to do laundry, iron clothes, and clean. She was black and took the bus in from the north end of Flint. Her presence did not cause any "discomfort" in the neighborhood other than making most of the women wish that they had one of them, too.

The Goods were not flashy people, and if there was any other sign that they had some extra income it was that each winter Mr. Good had men come and flood his backyard to create a free neighborhood ice rink for all to enjoy, any time, day or night. He had large floodlights that lit the rink, and if you were to ask the neighbors for one of their fondest Hill/Lapeer Street memories, it would be that of a man who turned over his backyard so that anyone could go skating there for hours on end.

Mr. Good always drove a new-model car, usually a Buick. He was friendly but reserved, a bit shorter than the other dads on the street. He was different in two other ways: he had a black mustache on a street devoid of facial hair, and he was a Jew.

Sometime around the summer of 1964 a sound started coming out of the normally staid Good house. It was a thumping noise, a low, vibrating thump that occurred in a repetitive rhythm, sorta like the beat to a song, but no song any of us were familiar with. *BOOM-boom-boom, BOOM-boom-boom, BOOM-boom-boom, BOOM-boom-boom.*

It could have been Mr. Good working on something with his new Craftsman tools. It could have been a new kitchen they were putting in. Maybe Hamaad, the local exterminator, had been called in to root out some pesky termites or a possum that got under the crawl space.

But no, it was none of that. It was black people's music. Specifically, the Supremes, a group none of us had heard of. The song was "Where Did Our Love Go," and where it went was across the three backyards of Lapeer Street, in through our living room window, and straight into my tapping toe.

Sammy Good had been given a record player for Christmas — yes, the Goods celebrated Christmas, their house beautifully decorated with colorful outdoor lights and blinding white angels with trumpets. The coolest thing about having your dad working at a department store was that you got all the greatest, newest gadgets first—the first Admiral dryer with separate settings for different clothing, the first Westinghouse frostless refrigerator, and the first Silvertone reel-to-reel tape recorder (which was my gift from Santa that Christmas).

When the winter snows subsided in May of '64, Sammy moved his stereo out to the screened-in back porch along with some 45 rpm records. The label on the record said "Motown." Each record had one song on the front and one on the back. Motown had many labels and artists, including the Miracles and the Marvelettes, the Vandellas and Little Stevie Wonder. Sammy said they all lived near us, in Detroit, a place we knew from driving to Tigers ball games and movies at the Music Hall Cinerama.

We would look across the yards and see him on the back porch every day after school, playing his Motown records and…dancing. We had seen this kind of dancing on TV, on *American Bandstand* and *Shindig*. But we had never seen it in person. And there he was, dancing up a storm, in a world of his own, Sammy Good's Afternoon Dance Party, Live from Lapeer Street.

This created enough curiosity among the rest of us boys in the neighborhood that we would wander over to watch and to listen. The music was catchy, but it seemed exotic, almost…alien.

And thus it was the sounds of Motown and their girl groups that outed Sammy to the older boys who knew exactly what his deal was. He soon began to feel the occasional shove or bump or trip in the hallway at school. And that only intensified. But Sammy's dance party carried on. A bloody nose wasn't going to stop in the name of love.

Sammy invited us in one day, something we didn't expect. The older boys in his age group, the seventh and eighth graders, usually wanted nothing to do with us unless we were needed to fill out two teams for a game of baseball. Sammy showed us his stack of records and some fan magazines that had pictures of the singers and groups. It was a foreign world to us younger boys, but for Sammy it was Dreamland. As he would tell us about this land of Oz called "Motown," his hands would make these exaggerated motions, as if they were catching air and waving it like streamers, so that we would understand not just its importance but also its *beauty*. And if we didn't, we'd be dismissed with the quick flop of the hand, as if his wrist had gone into instant catatonia. "*Shoo, shoo,* you li'l brats," he would say when we were too stupid to understand what he was conducting. He tried to school us on what it all meant, how it was all about "the beat" and "the look" and "the style," and why everything was "fabulous" to him.

So whenever we heard the music we would come running over to be part of his dance party. No girls were allowed, which was just fine with us. Soon he had us dancing with him and with each other, and probably around the time he brought out his mother's rouge and eyeliner to show us how we could "do ourselves up," the older boys in Davison, who had been keeping a wary eye on these proceedings from afar, had decided they'd seen enough. It was time to shut this dance party down.

The boys in town stepped up their ground assault on Sammy. He became a victim of multiple slappings, punchings, beatings, and "face washings" with dirt or snow.

Sammy did not take kindly to such treatment and would always fight back, something that seemed to catch his fellow junior high students by surprise. First, he would go right for their eyes, like a cat trapped in the wild. He was serious about gouging them right out of their sockets. He was always able to get his longer-than-normal nails implanted into their cheeks and he would scratch and claw until he drew blood. And he would kick, wildly kick, whatever part of the body he could reach. This was not the Sonny Liston fighting style that these boys were used to. His attackers would subdue him in the end, but it did not come without a price. Soon the neighborhood and school bullies considered him to be too much work to put down and not worth the energy (or the scars) to beat him into submission. They also discovered that, for the life of them, they couldn't beat the queer out of him. Surely if one of these faggots was just pummeled enough, like over and over and over, the gay would somehow spill out of them and they would be made Normal. But it wasn't happening, so the bullies gave up and returned to the more entertaining tradition of humiliation via taunting, ridiculing, and calling Sammy names.

All this drove Sammy into a dark place. The phenomenal hate toward him did not, in turn, make him want to love others. And so he took it out on us little ones. We weren't quite sure at our age why the older boys were so mean to him, but we soon learned that Sammy saw us as just shorter versions of his tormentors—and he never missed a chance to give any of us a good vicious slapping.

Anything could set him off—seeing us chew gum, mismatched pants and shirts, forbidden attempts to sing along with the songs on the 45 rpm records—and he grew more violent toward us with his punches and throwdowns. One day he tied little Pete Kowalski to a chair for "being bad," and his mother had to come over and get him released (after giving Sammy a good whack across his face). We quickly stopped going over to the Afternoon Dance Party, but that didn't stop Sammy when he saw one of us on the street. He'd push us down on the ground. Whenever passing by, he'd give us a good slug. After a while, we did our best to steer clear of him. We were kids; we didn't understand the hurt he was carrying and how he needed to act it out. Even the adults seemed incapable of grasping such a concept in 1965.

One Saturday afternoon, I was riding my bike down the sidewalk on Lapeer Street and Sammy was walking toward me. I tried to cross on the patch of lawn between his sidewalk and the street, but when I did he screamed at me to "get off my lawn!" He then took the stick he had in his hand and threw it into the spokes of my front wheel — which caused it to stop suddenly, throwing me into the street. He just stood there screaming at me to "never, ever, even *look* at our lawn" and "don't give me any lip!" Then he started laughing wildly as I brushed myself off and went running home with my bike.

When I got to our house, my Aunt Cindy and her husband, Uncle Jimmy, were there with their sons paying a visit. They were the relatives known as the Mulrooneys, and their brood consisted of three very tough sons, all much older than me. They lived on the east side of Flint, and I am certain these three boys were much feared in their own neighborhood. I myself was scared to death of them — and I was related to them!

I came up the front steps of our house and went inside, my elbows scraped and bleeding, and tears streaming down my cheeks. The cousin-thugs wanted to know what happened. I told them and they said, "Point him out." I looked

out our picture window and there he was, still standing down
the street. "That's him," I said, knowing full well what was
going to happen next. Unfortunately, I felt no remorse, only
a sense of justice. That is, until I saw how justice was being
meted out.

There in the street, the three Mulrooney boys were beating the holy crap out of Sammy Good. They first formed
a circle around him. I knew that Sammy's trapped-animal
instincts would instantly kick in. He threw the first slap, and
with that I couldn't see any more of Sammy. The Mulrooneys
pounced on him like piranhas on raw meat. Let's just say
the Mulrooneys weren't "slappers," and the velocity and fe-
rocity of their fists going up in the air and then slamming
down on him was a fierce sight to watch, something akin to a
National Geographic special. You could hear Sammy's screams
for help, and while my Uncle Jimmy Mulrooney was taking
it in with pleasure, my dad, perhaps later than he wished,
opened up the screen door and shouted for my cousins to
"knock it off!" By that time, Mr. Dietering, who lived next
door to the Goods, had also come out to break things up.
The Mulrooneys put in a few more kicks and then turned
triumphantly in our direction. Sammy lay on the street all
crumpled up, crying.

"Sissy!" "You fight like a girl!" "Go put on your dress!"
were the words they left Sammy with as Mr. Dietering
helped him up. Sammy didn't want any help. He limped back
to his house. I was *pleased* that my cousins had taken care
of him.

My dad was not so happy. "You can't use your cousins to
defend yourself. You need to learn to fight. I'm sending you
down to the Y for boxing class."

What? No! Oh God, I'd rather have taken my sisters sledding—in July! Why was I being punished? Sending me into downtown Flint so Flint kids like the Mulrooneys could beat me up—legally? I begged my mom to intercede.

"Whatever your dad thinks is best" was all she could muster. I can swear to you I had never heard her utter those words before because, in our house, it was always what *she* thought was best, and Dad concurred with that line of authority.

All this because I had to come home crying! Because I saw the Mulrooneys' car there! I wanted revenge. I knew what they would do. The only thing that would have made me happier is if they would have also smashed every single Supremes record in his collection.

About three months later, around ten o'clock one night, there was a knock on our front door. It was Mr. Popper, a large but soft-spoken man who lived across the street from the Goods.

"Frank, the Good boy's gone missing. His parents think he mighta been kidnapped. Taken out to the woods. They called the police but we thought we'd go searching for him. Can you come?"

"Sure," Dad said, though it was already past his bedtime. He went and got our large flashlight and a baseball bat.

Within minutes most of the men from the neighborhood had gathered on our lawn, each of them with flashlights and sticks or clubs and wearing the kind of hunting jackets one wears in the late Michigan fall. My sisters and I, already in our pajamas and in bed, came out to the living room and watched this scene unfold. What was going on? Kidnapping?!

We got instantly frightened. It was the only crime against a child short of murder that they would arrest you for in those days. There was no such thing as "child abuse," or "neglect," and nearly all children were accustomed to a healthy dose of spankings and whoopin's — and worse. Even the school sanctioned it, and teachers were allowed to use a large wooden weapon against the area known as your rump.

The one thing you could not do as an adult was *steal* us. If you were not a parent or a relative from the extended family, you could not just take us away without permission. The line had to be drawn somewhere, and this is where it was.

It was believed that Sammy Good had been taken away (lured?) by someone who was "like him" but "older." We didn't know what this meant. Frankly, it was hard to imagine anyone able to pin down and then transport Sammy anywhere, unless they had no use for the eyes God gave them.

It was determined that if someone *was* going to molest him ("Mom, what does *molest* mean?"), it would probably be done in the woods behind our house. And so off the search party went. One thing that struck me about all these men — most of whom probably didn't appreciate the fact that Sammy was the neighborhood homosexual — was how genuinely concerned they were for Sammy's safety and well-being, and how they hoped they would find him alive and well. The mothers had come out, too, in order to comfort Mrs. Good, who was standing in the street fighting back her tears. The men assured her they'd bring him back — after all, he probably just ran away and might even be watching us right now! They said this as they tightly clenched their clubs and baseball bats, either ready to roll into action or perhaps scared themselves of going into the deep, dark woods. Yes, they were willing to put themselves at some risk, and if I could sum up their collective feeling, it was, *Well, he may be a faggot—but Goddamn it, he's our faggot—and nobody better touch a hair on his head!*

As the men left on their search, my sisters started to cry, thinking the kidnappers might hurt our dad, too. Our mother told us to go back to bed and that, with more than a dozen men, no harm was going to come to anyone. At that moment, the police chief showed up with one of his officers and proceeded to catch up to the makeshift posse.

I went with my sisters into their bedroom, which had the best view of the woods. We watched the dads cut through the yards and around the swamp and into the woods, where the silhouettes of their frames disappeared—but the sweeping motion of the twelve flashlights allowed us to know exactly where they were. The movement of those lights looked weirdly choreographed—Sammy would have been proud— as they went up and down and across the trees, crisscrossing each other like the klieg lights at the summer carnival or the Chevy dealer's Fourth of July sale.

After what seemed like hours, the dads returned, dejected and empty-handed.

"He's not back there," we heard Dad tell Mom. "No telling where he is. But he ain't back there."

The cops delivered the bad news to Mrs. Good and she broke down again. Her husband put his arm around her to comfort her, and they walked slowly back to their house, as did everyone else to theirs.

The next day Sammy Good was found near Pontiac, Michigan. He had either hitchhiked or taken the bus. He was wandering the streets and he was hungry and he didn't want to go back home. He was tired of the insults and the bullies and the beatings and the inability to enjoy his dance party in peace. He had made it more than halfway to Hitsville, U.S.A., and it was said later, after he had run away again, that he had wanted to meet the Supremes and help them with their "styling." I'm sure he could have made a significant contribution, and I'm certain that a more open and diverse place like Detroit might have suited him better.

We never saw Sammy again. He went to live with an aunt, and that was the last anyone wanted to discuss the subject. One month before his high school graduation, Sammy made his way to New York City, perhaps a more accepting and forgiving place, and it was where he went for a stroll one night, down West 13th Street to pier 54, and threw himself into the Hudson River.

The Canoe

———

WHEN I WAS YOUNG, my grandmother (my mom's mother), sat me down to tell me the family history. She had an old, musty book of notes and clippings, and stacks of albums with faded photographs. As I was the oldest of the three kids, she wanted me to have this information so that it would be passed down to future generations. But for her, it was not just about handing over the printed material that had been handed to her. It was also about the Irish tradition of sitting the wee ones down and letting them see your face and look into your eyes as you told them "the stories of your people." My grandmother explained that these stories were the closest thing we had to family jewels. They were who we were, where we came from, how our lives and values and beliefs came to be. In the generations that came before us, they understood that their good fortune (or tragedy) was not just a series of random happenings. They were the result of how one behaved, what integrity one had, and how carefully each of them made the decisions they made.

These family stories were told and retold without the benefit of computers and other digital devices. One's history was stored in one's brain. Now memory is kept on a Sony stick. But as technology changes each year (see: Profit), we lose family photos in the numerous transfers along the way. The floppy disk from fifteen years ago, the one you have the family history stored on, is hard to retrieve now, and if you ask a kid to help you, you will be met with a confused look or a quiet snicker. If you "stored it" in 1995, it's already ancient history, its ones and zeroes wiped clean.

Yet, many of the stories told to me by my parents and grandparents are now lost, not because of a misplaced file, but because I wasn't always listening. The TV was on, I wanted a Clark Bar, I wanted to go out and play, what did this have to do with the Tigers' pennant chances? All that mattered was right here, right now, me.

Thus, many stories were, in a single generation, erased through a lack of attention and no sense of duty or responsibility. I long to hear those stories now, and I regret that I did not in my youth respect them for the power and energy and beauty they had. I have tried to piece many of them back together with what my sisters and cousins remember, but I can see they will never truly be made whole again.

But there was one story that stayed with me long after my grandmother passed. It was the story of her grandfather and how he came to be one of the early settlers in the Flint area (Lapeer County, to be exact). It was an area, at the time, inhabited by the native peoples. Her father (my great-grandfather) was one of the first white babies born in the township known as Elba. As I was from one of these first families that settled in this area, I recognized that what Elba, Davison, and Flint became had something to do with what these first people did.

One such person was Silas Moore, my grandmother's grandfather, a man born in 1814, when James Madison was president. One day, in the early 1830s, Silas Moore, then living in Bradford, Pennsylvania, came up with a plan he wanted to share with his father-in-law, Richard Pemberton (Silas was married to Richard's daughter, Caroline). It involved leaving Bradford and moving west, into the wild and unsettled areas of a place called Michigan. It would involve traveling first to Buffalo, boarding a ship, and taking it across Lake Erie and up a river to Detroit.

"We can take the family and our essential belongings by oxcart up through Kill Buck and Springville and then on to Buffalo," Silas explained to his father-in-law. "That should take us almost a week. Then we will sell the oxen in Buffalo and board the steamer that will take us across Lake Erie to Detroit. In Detroit we can go to the land office and buy land to farm for a dollar twenty-five an acre."

"A dollar twenty-five?" Pemberton asked. "That's a mighty steep price for land unseen. What's to say there will be any left when we get there? I hear Detroit is busting at the seams, too many people there as it is."

"Yes," Silas replied. "It's a pretty big place. I hear they have over two thousand people."

"Two thousand?!" Pemberton was beside himself.

"It's a huge territory," Moore reassured him. "There's plenty of land for everyone. We're not the only ones from Bradford that want to go. We could all help each other."

Word had spread through Bradford (a village on the New York State line) as it had through all of western New York State that the Michigan Territory had opened up to homesteaders and would soon be admitted into the Union. Land was cheap in the "West" and mostly unsettled, and for those with the pioneer itch this seemed like an appealing idea.

The Pembertons and the Moores had spent the previous hundred years as westward-moving immigrants, landing in America from Ireland and England and settling in Hartford, Connecticut, and Pawtucket, Rhode Island. A Pemberton relation became an early colonial governor of Connecti-cut. Silas Moore's father had fought with the Vermont bri-gade in the War of 1812. His grandfather had fought in the Revolutionary War, first with Ethan Allen at the Battle of Fort Ticonderoga, and then with George Washington at Valley Forge.

After Independence, the Moores and the Pembertons kept moving west, first to Albany, then Elmira, and finally across the Pennsylvania line to Tioga and Bradford counties in the Allegheny Mountains. They helped to establish settle-ments, and became active politically, but mostly they farmed the land. They believed in cooperating with the Indians, and it was said that they were proud to have "never raised a hand or gun against them."

Both Richard Pemberton (who liked to point out he was born the same year that George Washington became president) and Silas Moore were growing tired of farming in the Alleghenies. They wanted to try their luck in more untamed wilderness, where the land was said to be flat, the soil rich, and the freshwater was as plentiful as any place you could find on earth. Silas and Caroline Pemberton Moore (Richard's daughter) were newlyweds, and that seemed like as good a time as any to put down fresh stakes in a new land, to raise a new family in a new state.

So the Moores and the Pembertons, along with a few of their neighbors, sold their farms, packed up their families, and left. This included Richard Pemberton and his wife, Amelia, and their five other daughters. With their oxen and two carts, they began their slow and strenuous journey in the spring of 1836.

Six days later they arrived in the teeming metropolis of Buffalo. There were people everywhere and so many shops that you could stock up for a year by spending just one day in what was already one of America's largest cities. There was so much activity and commotion, Pemberton encouraged everyone to stay close and keep an eye on their belongings. The Erie Canal had opened in the last decade, and this had brought many settlers and businesses to Buffalo, which was now called "the gateway to the Great Lakes." The canal, which stretched from the Hudson River in eastern New York, now made it possible to ship goods and people from the Atlantic Ocean all the way to the rivers of the West, including the Mississippi River. Silas could not believe the claims made on the posters around town: LEAVE BUFFALO TODAY — ARRIVE DETROIT TOMORROW! They advertised new, large-capacity steamships that could literally whisk you out of New York and have you in the Western Territories by sundown the next day. That just did not seem possible.

The Moores and Pembertons paid eight dollars apiece and got on the first boat in the morning, one of four ships that left every day between April and November. The following day, they arrived in Detroit. Silas and Richard went to the land office to see about purchasing property near Detroit. They were told they could buy the land on a plot called the "Grand Circus" for thirty-five dollars. But when the men went to check out the land, they found it swampy and unsuitable for farming. Instead, they bought, sight unseen, a large parcel near a lake about fifty miles north of Detroit—"the far, far wilderness," they were told—in a place near "Lapeer" (derived from the French word for "flint").

The Moores and Pembertons took a stagecoach to Pontiac, where they purchased oxen and continued on to Lapeer County. Less than eight years prior, there were no white people in the county. Now there were already a few hundred, but not many in the area near the land purchased by Silas Moore. There *were* at least three hundred Indians living nearby. When Silas arrived, he was greeted by the chief of the Neppessing band of the Chippewa Indians. Silas explained how he had purchased some land a couple miles away. The chief and his men, familiar with the white man and his concept for "owning land," showed them the place they were looking for: Lake Neppessing. The chief and his tribe lived on the western side of the lake. There he took Silas to his plot of land. The chief then brought Moore to his village to welcome him. After a while, Silas decided to move to the east end of Lake Neppessing. The idea of living across the lake from three hundred Indians did not seem to worry the Moores.

These early settlers decided to call their village "Elba," after the island in the Mediterranean, off the coast of Italy, where Napoleon had been exiled some twenty years prior. But to these settlers, who valued knowledge and education and taught themselves to read the classics, they also knew Elba as the island in Greek mythology that had been visited by the Argonauts in their search for Circe (Medea had sent them on this journey). To reference the classics like this was not unusual for people from the New England states, where schooling was considered a necessity. Ignorance was frowned upon, and to come to a new territory that had not a single school seemed quite appalling to them (neither the French nor the British thought it necessary to build schools in Detroit or the rest of the territory). But once the Erie Canal opened and brought New Yorkers to Michigan (where they named their settlements "Rochester" and "Troy" and "Utica" after their beloved hometowns in New York), they also brought certain New England sensibilities with them: town-hall democracy, a strong work ethic, and a belief that a "liberal education" was vital to a civilized society. In the oxcarts and in the steamer trunks weren't just pots and pans and family heirlooms; there were also books, many books. Throughout the 1830s and '40s, other radical "New York" ideas began to permeate Michigan, thanks to the new settlers, ideas such as the concept of letting women vote and the abolition of slavery. Their strong Quaker and Brethren traditions, along with their fellow Congregationalists and Catholics, led Michigan in 1846 to become the first government in the English-speaking world to abolish capital punishment. Such was their state of mind.

At the beginning of the summer of 1837, Silas and Caroline announced that they would be having a baby sometime near the end of November. This brought great joy to their family and friends from Bradford, as this would be one of the first non-Indian babies born in the area.

Silas readied his cabin for the new arrival. He had hoped that there would be glass for his windows, but cut glass was scarce and none had arrived from Pontiac for him to use. So, to keep the elements out, a wooden shutter was built.

It was not airtight—the wind would howl and find its way through the cracks—but it suited their needs. It wasn't like they didn't know what winter was, being from Pennsylvania and upstate New York.

On November 30, Caroline went into labor. As Lapeer now had a doctor, Silas decided to go there to fetch him and bring him back to assist with the birth. Caroline's mother and sisters would stay with Caroline until Silas returned with him. It was late in the day, and travel at night could be quite difficult. But Silas wanted to take no chances with his first-born, so off he rode to Lapeer.

Indians passing by noticed that Silas was leaving behind his very pregnant wife. The Chippewa had taken a keen interest in Caroline's pregnancy and would often stop by to offer blankets or herbs or special beads that, they explained, would keep the evil spirits away.

Her labor was accelerating faster than anyone had expected and, with the sun going down, her screams could be heard by the Indians. Within minutes, a group of them were at her door.

"Please," Caroline's sister said, exasperated that she might be the one delivering the baby. "Everything is OK. We don't need any help."

"Wolves," one of the Indians said in his very broken English. "Wolves."

"Yes, wolves. We know there's wolves in the woods. We're OK."

"Wolves smell blood. They come through here," he said, pointing at the glassless window. "Smelling blood. Not good."

He then said something to his two friends and they left. Within minutes, they returned with blankets.

"I put blankets here for you. Wolves then not smell."

He proceeded to affix the blankets tightly around the window and the door so that the wolves would not pick up the scent of blood.

"We," he said, pointing outdoors as they left. "Outside."

The three Chippewa then went out and stood guard in front of the cabin to ensure that the wolves would stay away.

Within the hour, Silas returned and saw the Indians around a fire they had built outside the cabin. The sight of them made him worry that something had gone wrong. He, and the doctor with him, ran into the cabin, just in time for a little boy to be born. They called him Martin Pemberton Moore. He was my grandmother's father.

Caroline told Silas how the Chippewa had stood guard and had placed the blankets over the window and door so that there would be no attack by the wolves.

The following day Silas paid a visit to the chief and thanked him and the members of his tribe for protecting his wife and his newborn son. The chief said it was his duty to protect all life in the area. He gave Silas a wood carving in honor of his son being born. Silas was grateful and again thanked the chief and his men.

Not all the white people in the area maintained the same friendly relations with the Indians as did Silas Moore. Some were downright scared of them and wanted nothing to do with the "red beasts." Others would muse about how much better Elba would be without them. Silas would listen to none of this, and he would get angry at this sort of talk. This, in turn, caused some to be suspicious of Silas, and when the first elections in Elba were held the next year, Silas found himself on the losing side.

The following autumn, the Indians on the west side of Lake Neppessing came down with the measles. If there was one threat the native peoples had little defense against, it was the diseases that the white people brought with them. Measles, mumps, chicken pox, influenza, tuberculosis, smallpox—they killed both whites and Indians without mercy, but by the nineteenth century, Europeans had developed certain immunities within their bodies so that many could withstand a bout of the flu or the measles.

Not so the American Indian. Because there had not been centuries to build up such an immunity, the Indians were quickly felled when a virus spread through their community. When the British, who had a desire to rid the new land of the Indians, saw how easily the Indians would get sick, it was not a violation of their moral code to lace blankets or water with these diseases to wipe out whole Indian encampments.

When word spread through Elba that the Chippewa had the measles, the settlers set up an immediate quarantine and forbade any white person to have contact with any Indian. This did not sit well with Silas.

The Indians would send runners to the quarantine line and beg for help. Their people were dying. They needed food and medicine. They were told by the white settlers that there was nothing the people of Elba could do but pray for them.

Silas believed in prayer, but not in prayer alone. Disobeying the edict, he took his canoe out into the middle of Lake Neppessing. Once there he waved and shouted to the Indians on the other shore. Those who were well enough came out of their lodges and waved back. He motioned for them to come out onto the lake to meet him. Two of the Chippewa, one of whom was the chief, got into a canoe and paddled out to meet Silas. As they got closer he motioned for them to not come any farther.

"I am here to help," he said, his voice raised so they could hear him. "I am here to help. How many of you are sick?"

"Many," said the chief. "Some die. The rest, we need food and supplies."

"I will see what I can do. Meet me here tomorrow at this time."

Silas went back to his side of the lake. He told Caroline of the predicament the Indians were in.

"I'm going to see what I can gather up from the others," he said.

Silas rode around to the families in the Elba area to collect food and provisions to give to the Indians. Most contributed, even those who had spoken ill of the tribe before. There were those who thought Silas was taking an unnecessary chance, and they warned him that if they believed he was coming down with the measles himself, they would send him to the quarantine area to live with the Indians.

The next day Silas paddled out to the middle of Lake Neppessing. Behind him he towed another canoe full of food and supplies. The chief and a half-dozen men were already waiting on the lake.

"I will leave this here. You take everything." The Indians paddled toward it and unloaded the provisions into their canoes.

"In two days, I will bring more food. Our doctor is also bringing some of our medicine for you. You might wish to try it."

Two days later, Silas filled what he could into his canoe and went back out to meet the Chippewa, who had brought the empty canoe back out into the middle of the lake. When Silas got to the empty canoe that sat between him and the Indians, he was very careful not to touch it so as not to contract the disease.

The sharing of this canoe went on for a few weeks. Silas's neighbors pitched in on his farm so he wouldn't fall behind, and most continued to contribute to his efforts to save the Indians. But none would join him in his trips across the lake.

Most of the Chippewa recovered, and for years they would never forget the generosity of Silas Moore. When his son, Martin, was of school age, instead of sending him to the Elba school (which was farther away), Silas sent him to the Indian school that the county had established near his house. In later years, he insisted that Martin and his other four children all go to high school in Lapeer. Martin would go on to college and then return to open a general store in Elba. He would hold many elected positions in the community — clerk, treasurer, supervisor — but it was said that none were more important to him than the post of "overseer of the poor." He would tell the story about the Indians and his father, Silas, to his daughter, Bess, and she would tell her daughter, my mother.

And my mother would tell me.

Pietà

———

I WAS LOST.

I had paused for perhaps too long to inspect the statues in the hallways and the Rotunda, bronzed and marbled rendi-tions of an odd assortment of great and not-so-great Ameri-cans: Will Rogers, Daniel Webster, George Washington, Robert La Follette, Robert E. Lee, Jefferson Davis, Brigham Young, Andrew Jackson.

And then there was the statue of Zachariah Chandler. Not well-known outside the state of Michigan (and not well-known there, either), he was a four-term United States sena-tor representing the Great Lakes state in the mid-nineteenth century. Historians who feel a kinship with the Confederacy credit *him* with starting the Civil War. On February 11, 1861, two months before the rebels fired on Fort Sumter, Chandler gave an inflammatory speech on the Senate floor where he threw down the gauntlet and called for some "bloodletting," to purge the nation of its proslavery sentiments. In other words, once we kill a few of these slave owners, they'll get the message that slavery is over. The South took this as an unofficial declaration of war and they continued to prepare for the bloodletting *they* would initiate.

Chandler is also credited with being a founder of the Republican Party. On July 6, 1854, he led the first effort in the nation to form a statewide antislavery party. He called upon all abolitionists to meet him under a giant oak tree in Jackson, Michigan—and six short years later they saw the Republican candidate, Abraham Lincoln, win the White House.

By the age of eleven I was fascinated with history and politics. For this, along with those too-early reading lessons, I blamed my mother. Her father (my grandfather) was a leader of the Republican Party in our town of Davison during the early half of the twentieth century. Being an immigrant from Canada, Dr. William J. Wall brought with him a Canadian common sense and a keen interest in the "goings-on" of government. He also believed that books and music were necessary companions in the pursuit of happiness.

Born and raised on a farm between Sarnia and London, Ontario, "Will" was one of eleven children. Reaching adulthood, he obtained his own small farm next to his brother Chris's farm, and together they tilled the soil by day and played the Irish fiddle by night. The Wall brothers and their fiddles became much in demand for the local dances and shindigs. Even during their midday break from farming, they would get together and play their fiddles.

Within time, Will, who was well regarded by those in the village, was asked if he would teach at the one-room schoolhouse during the winter months. He accepted the offer and soon grew to like teaching so much that he ceded his farm to his brother.

After a few years of teaching, Will decided he wanted to be a doctor. The nearest medical school was across the St. Clair River in the state of Michigan. In 1898, medical school took one year, as that was all the time needed to teach everything that was known then about healing the human body. After finishing medical school in Saginaw, he traveled through Michigan's "thumb" and happened upon a village called Elba, about thirteen miles east of Flint. He liked the people of Michigan and he liked the Americans, and though he would remain proud of his Canadian roots, he saw America as a place full of curious, inventive, progressive people and ideas. He decided to settle in Elba.

In September 1901, Dr. Wall traveled back to Ontario to visit his family and, at the last minute, decided to take the train over to Buffalo to see the much-anticipated Pan-American Exposition. This Exposition, with its City of Light, was the talk of the nation, as it would be one of the first times such a large area would be lit up with electric lights. There were fascinating exhibits on display, including the first X-ray machine and numerous other turn-of-the-century inventions, that filled the crowds with wonder and excitement. There was even a ride simulating the "First Trip to the Moon."

The Exposition also provided a chance for Dr. Wall to see a president of the United States. And it was there, at four in the afternoon, on September 6, 1901, as my Grandpa Wall waited to get a glimpse of President William McKinley, that a shot rang out in the Temple of Music. An anarchist from Detroit (by way of Alpena, Michigan), Leon Czolgosz, fired two bullets in the ribs and abdomen of President McKinley. McKinley's security guard would later admit (in an early and tragic case of racial profiling) that he had been distracted by keeping his eye on the large black man standing behind Czolgosz. It was that large black man, James Parker, who actually stopped Czolgosz from firing any further shots when he knocked him to the ground.

My grandfather, being a doctor, tried to get through the mob that had descended on the Temple from the fairgrounds when the shots rang out. An ambulance was there within minutes, and though Will announced he was a doctor and could help, they had already placed the president in the ambulance and were rushing him off to the temporary hospital that was part of the Exposition. Although there were electric lights located all around the fair, no one had thought to place any in the emergency room at the makeshift hospital. The surgeons had to operate on the president by having nurses hold metal trays in the direction of the windows in order to bounce enough light onto the president's wounds. Unable to locate one of the bullets, the doctors decided to sew McKinley back up.

Remarkably, as is often the case after an operation, President McKinley recovered rapidly and seemed in good spirits. He was transferred to the home of the Exposition's president so he could recuperate. But within six days, McKinley was dead of gangrene and a build-up of fluid. In spite of the Exposition's heralding of new inventions like the electric vacuum sweeper, the wireless telegraph, ketchup in a bottle, and the X-ray machine, there was not much known about infection and how to prevent it from spreading.

Dr. Wall returned to Michigan. The violence he had witnessed (no Canadian prime minister had ever been assassinated; this was the third killing of an American president within thirty-six years) did not deter him from becoming an American citizen. Like McKinley, he also became a Republican. He met his wife, my grandmother, when he stopped by her father's store to see about renting some space to set up his doctor's office. Martin Moore was happy to oblige, as Elba was in need of its own doctor. He invited Will over to the house for dinner, and when Will came in he saw Martin's daughter, Bess, playing the piano. He asked if she could play along if he brought his fiddle over. She said yes. Within a couple years the two of them were married and moved to nearby Davison.

The walls of their home were lined with books instead of wallpaper. I'm not even sure if there were walls. A piano sat in their parlor, and Will's doctor's office was at the back of the house with its own entrance. By the 1920s, a large radio sat on the floor in the living room, and it was here that the Walls would listen to the music of Caruso and Rudy Vallee, news shows and baseball games and *The Lone Ranger*. As no pictures were provided, they had to invent the images in their heads. Doc Wall loved imagining the streets of New York, the lair of the Green Hornet, or the canyons through which the Lone Ranger and Tonto would ride. Across the street from the Wall house was the local cinema, where the main feature would change two or three times a week. The village doctor made sure he never missed one, and he would sit there always hoping that newborns would be kind enough to take their time until the closing credits.

My grandfather enjoyed being in the thick of politics, and the local Republicans would meet at his house to plan their campaigns. His youngest daughter, my mother, Veronica, was bitten by the political bug and it would never leave her. And thus it was in our garage in the fall of 1960 where I, as a freshly minted first grader, heard my mother and father have their first argument.

"President Eisenhower," my mother said as she handed my dad a box of old clothes to store in the attic, "He won the war and, despite the fact he's not campaigning for him, he does support Nixon. What more do you need than that?"

"Yes," my dad responded, "I like Ike. But Kennedy — *our first Catholic president!*" That was enough for me. But not for my mom.

"He's too young, he's inexperienced — and *he's a Democrat!*"

"That's a plus! We Moores've been voting for Democrats since Roosevelt!"

"Oh! Pshaw!"

Pshaw? Yes, she said "pshaw" a lot. And "ice box" (never "refrigerator"). And "grip" (instead of "suitcase"). The Bible on her shelf, from her mother's side of the family, was from the 1840s. The complete volume of Shakespeare, also from the 1800s, was from her father. Her language and mannerisms were also from the nineteenth century. And clearly her view of the Republican Party was also lodged somewhere in a lost time. My dad was always fond of reminding her which party was in charge when the nation was sent reeling into the Great Depression. She would ignore such slights, as they were irrelevant to her. Her father, being the village doctor, was paid through the Depression with chickens and eggs and milk, not to mention a used sewing machine here or an oil change there. My dad, on the other hand, had memories of much more difficult times, and if there was one thing he was sure of, it was that *he* would be a Democrat 'til the day he died.

And so throughout September and October of 1960 I would listen to this back-and-forth parental sparring during the great Nixon vs. Kennedy presidential election. My sisters and I were with my dad (my youngest sister was only three and a half, so she just nodded when we told her to). I felt bad for my mom, as she was up against not only the four of us but also God—because the Catholic Church was the One True Church. The nuns and priests could barely contain their excitement that 170 years of anti-Catholic bigotry was about to end. We said daily prayers, held rosaries, conducted novenas, and did everything we could to implore the Almighty to put the Catholic in the White House. In the end, the value of Catholic prayer was proven to be quite powerful, and Kennedy "miraculously" became president. It would be another twenty years before my mother would finally toss the Republicans overboard. *"My father would not recognize these Republicans!"* she would say (and for that I have Ronald Reagan to thank).

My mother's love of country, its government, and its political institutions was always evident. She saw it as part of her parental responsibility to school us in the values of a democratic republic, specifically this one: the United States of America.

When I finished fifth grade in the summer of 1965, she loaded my sisters and me into our Buick and drove us to our nation's capital for our summer vacation. While the other kids in the neighborhood got to go "up north" or to Scout camp or to Tot Lot, we were forced to go see the original documents of the Founding Fathers, the first flag sewn by Betsy Ross, the plane that Charles Lindbergh flew across the Atlantic. We took the FBI tour at the Department of Justice, we had our picture taken in front of the Iwo Jima statue, and we knelt and prayed in Arlington at the grave of our fallen Catholic president. We traipsed from one end of Pennsylvania Avenue to the other, climbed all 896 steps of the Washington Monument, and paid a visit to our congressman to shake his hand and let him know we'd be voters someday.

And it was while I was there, inside the Capitol building, that I found myself separated from my mother and sisters and our cousin Patricia. We were on our way to sit in the Senate gallery as the senators were debating a bill that would provide free health care for all the old people in America. But I got distracted by the statues and sharing the life of Zachariah Chandler with whomever would listen.

Eventually it dawned on me that I was all alone and on my own. My mother and sisters were nowhere in sight. I began to panic. *Where did they go? Why did they leave me here?* I may have thought I was a smart kid, but I had no idea where I was, where they were, or how I would find them. At age eleven, the Capitol Rotunda seemed like its own planet to me or, worse, a giant white marble vortex spinning madly and sucking everything into it. I tried to catch my breath and began walking quickly in whatever direction seemed like the way out.

I somehow ended up on the Senate side of the building and went down a staircase, looking frantically for any sign of my family. Realizing I was getting nowhere, I bolted through a pair of elevator doors just as they were closing.

Inside the elevator I began to cry. There was a lone man in the back corner, leaning against the railing, his face covered by the newspaper he was reading. He heard my sniffling and put the paper down to see what the commotion was all about.

As I had been properly schooled in all things political and Catholic, I instantly recognized this man. He was the junior senator from New York, Robert Francis Kennedy.

"What's wrong, young man?" he said in a voice that was comforting enough to stop the tears. After all, no one had ever called me a young man before.

"I lost my mom," I said sheepishly.

"Well, that can't be good. Let's see if we can find her."

"Thank you," I said.

"Where are you from?"

"Michigan. Near Flint."

"Oh, yes. My brother loved that Labor Day Parade. Big parade."

The doors of the elevator opened, and he put his arm on my shoulder and escorted me to the nearest Capitol police officer.

"Seems this young man from Michigan..." He turned to me. "What's your name, son?"

"Michael. Moore."

"Michael has lost his mother, and perhaps we can help him."

"Yes, sir, Senator. We'll take care of it." The officer told the senator he'd handle the matter from here on so that the senator could proceed with his much more important duties.

"Well, I'll stay here for a minute or two to make sure he's OK."

I stood there thinking how stupid did I have to be to get lost, and now I was holding up Bobby Kennedy and the business of the United States Senate so that everybody could go search for my mommy. Jeez-oh-pete, was I embarrassed.

"How old are you, Mike—can I call you Mike?" Kennedy asked.

"I'm eleven. This is my first time in the Capitol," I offered, hoping to make myself seem less like an idiot.

"Well, you got your first ride in the Senate elevator. That almost makes you a senator!" The Irish in him had now kicked in, and he flashed that Kennedy grin. I smiled, too, and joined in.

"Hey, you never know!" I said, then wanted quickly to retract this wise-ass remark.

"Well, we got two good Democrats from Michigan already, Senators McNamara and—"

"—Hart!" I jumped in as if I were on a quiz show.

"You know your senators. Very good! And promising," he added with a wink to the officer.

"We've got his mother," a voice squawked across the police radio the cop was holding. *"Stay there. She's coming."*

"Well, it seems everything worked out OK," proclaimed the senator from New York. "Good luck, young man—and never lose sight of your mother!"

And with that he was gone, before I even had a chance to thank him or wish him well or recite for him my favorite passages from his brother's Inaugural Address.

Within minutes my mother and sisters and cousin arrived, and after a stern look and a word or two, we were off to sit in the Senate gallery and listen to ninety-eight men and two women debate the passage of a new law that would pay for the doctor bills of every single senior citizen, a radical idea to be sure. They called it "Medicare," and the idea seemed to sit well with the doctor's daughter in the gallery. Most senators also seemed to like the bill, though there were some who said it was the first step toward something called "socialism." My sisters and I had no idea what that was; we just knew it was a bad word.

"This law will also help poor people," our mother added, and although that wasn't us, by the tenets of the Church it was considered a good thing, even if it did conflict with the principles of Mom's Republican Party. The bill passed, and one senator proclaimed that the elderly would never have to worry again about going broke because of medical bills.

When we went back a few days later to sit in the House gallery, a new bill was up for discussion: the Voting Rights Act of 1965. From watching the evening news and being taught to read the daily newspaper, I knew that "colored people" were being unfairly treated, even killed. A few months earlier, in March 1965, a white housewife from Detroit, Viola Liuzzo, upset at what she had been seeing on the television regarding the savage treatment of black people, made an impromptu decision to head down to Selma, Alabama, to march with the Rev. Martin Luther King. I knew King to be the Negro man in charge of the civil rights movement, and in the town where I lived his name was rarely mentioned — and when it was, it usually had other words attached to it, none pleasant.

Mrs. Liuzzo, a mother of five children, was brutally murdered by the Ku Klux Klan while volunteering as one of the drivers who ferried demonstrators back and forth to Selma. It was a shock to most of Michigan, and when I heard it being discussed by Jesse the barber, he informed those who were getting their hair cut that day that she was found with "some nigga boy" in the car — a married woman up to no good and "sticking her puss in where it don't belong!" Jesse's Barber Shop was the place you went for enlightenment in Davison, and the place was always full. Jesse was a short man with a short haircut, and there was always a pair of scissors or a long razor in his hand. This was problematic, as he wore thick-lensed glasses, the kind the legally blind wore, and it frightened me when I sat in his chair as he held court, the sharp instruments being used to make various punctuation points in the air.

For many nights after Mrs. Liuzzo's murder I could not sleep, and when I did, I had dreams that it was my mother found dead in the car along the road in Alabama. I told my parents of this, and they suggested I give the news-watching a break, but I continued to tune in to Walter Cronkite each night.

It was confusing for me and my sisters, sitting in the House gallery, listening to men talking about how "it isn't the federal government's business" who gets to vote.

"Why don't they want people to vote?" I asked my mother.

"Some people don't want some people to vote," she said, trying to protect me from the fact that even United States senators could think like the men who killed Viola Liuzzo.

The next day we took an overly long and punishingly hot car ride to Monticello, the home of Thomas Jefferson. This historic site, located about two hours southwest of Washington, deep in the state of Virginia, took us into the beginnings of the "real South," as our mother called it. The tour through Monticello was mostly unmemorable, except for the too-short doorways that indicated people two hundred years ago were not that tall, and the glaring omission of any mention of Jefferson's slaves.

On the way back to D.C. we pulled off the highway for gas and for a trip to the rest room. I walked with my mother around to the back of the station, where there were two doors. One was marked WHITE and the other COLORED (though it looked like someone had tried to scrape that last word off, unsuccessfully). I stood and stared at these signs, and although I knew what it meant, I wanted to hear my mother's explanation of it.

"What is this?" I asked.

She looked at the signs and was silent for a moment.

"You know what it is," she said curtly. "Just go in there and do your business and get out." I went into the "Colored" bathroom and she went into the "Whites." When we came out, she led me back to the car.

"Get in there and stay with your sisters."

She then headed into the gas station with the kind of walk we three kids knew meant that heads would roll. We cranked *our* heads out the windows, hoping to hear what she was saying to the man at the counter, but all that was available to us was the tight-lipped look on her face and the few motions she made with her index finger. He, too, made a few gestures, including a shrug of his shoulders. She came back outside to the car and got in and said nothing.

"What were you doing?" I asked.

"Just mind your business," she said, cutting me off. "And lock your doors." (This would be the only time in my life I would hear such a demand when in the vicinity of all white people.) We never learned what she said to the man, or what he told her, and years later I liked to think she had given him a piece of her mind for her children having to witness such immorality in the U.S.A. that she loved. He might have told her that they just hadn't gotten around to taking it down yet, or had tried (the Civil Rights Act outlawing such things had passed twelve months earlier), or maybe he told her to get her nigger-loving ass out of there. Or maybe she was just complaining that the ladies' room was out of toilet paper. I always meant to ask but didn't. She was no Viola Liuzzo, and for that, I guess, I was thankful, as I liked my mother being alive.

The trip to D.C. to learn how our government worked was coming to a close, but our mother had scheduled a "part two" for our summer trip: we were going to New York City and to the New York World's Fair! When she was eighteen, her parents took her to the 1939 World's Fair in New York, and it was there she first saw inventions like the television and was given a glimpse of the "World of Tomorrow." We would now get a glimpse into our future via this new Fair. Five hours later we arrived at our aunt's house on Staten Island.

The New York World's Fair of 1964–65 was a mind-bursting experience. Located on 646 acres in the borough of Queens, the Fair included over 140 pavilions and exhibits from all over the world. Most of it, for our young eyes, was a thrilling look at what the adults of that day thought the world would look like in the twenty-first century. The IBM pavilion introduced us to what computers could do for us, and while it was never proposed that we would ever own our own computers, it did spike the imagination and create an excitement for the bold world of the coming new millennium.

At the Pepsi pavilion we saw a very entertaining show called "It's a Small World," a precursor to the "We Are the

World" vibe of the 1980s — though Pepsi was less concerned with African starvation than with beating Coke.

There was nothing that came close to the massive building sponsored by General Motors at the Fair. They called it Futurama, and with all of us being from the company's hometown, we were quite proud to enter its doors. They put us in chairs — and suddenly those chairs began to move! They took us on a ride through the Future — flying cars, cities under the oceans, colonies on the moon, and happy people everywhere. It was a world at peace, where everyone had a nice job, and there was no poverty or pollution or anything that might upset us. That was cool. We went on the ride again, and this time I took notes. GM was making a very generous promise, and I wanted to be able to tell the boys back in the neighborhood about it.

Many states and countries also had their own pavilions. New York State had three towers from which you could see the tri-state area. The tallest one had a huge lobby with a million-dollar map of New York laid out with exotic tiles (and a star on the location of every Texaco gas station in the state). At the top of the tower was a revolving restaurant. The new state of Alaska had an exhibit, as did Wisconsin (free samples of cheese!), and the British, French, Canadians, and dozens of other countries were well represented.

But the longest lines were reserved for the Vatican City pavilion. For it was inside this edifice that the Pope had sent abroad, for the first time ever, a work of art from St. Peter's Basilica. Yet this wasn't just any piece of art. This was one of the most famous works of sculpture in the history of the world: the *Pietà*, by Michelangelo.

The *Pietà* depicted the Blessed Virgin Mary, the mother

of Jesus, holding the body of her dead son after he was taken down from the cross. It measured approximately six feet high and six feet wide and was only the third sculpture by a young and somewhat unknown twenty-four-year-old Michelangelo of Florence, Italy.

To view the *Pietà* you had to wait in a long line and, once inside, you were placed on a moving sidewalk where you could view the work at 1.2 miles per hour. No photography was allowed and silence and reverence were expected at all times.

On my pass by the *Pietà* I was frozen in amazement. I had never seen anything like it. Suddenly, all the exhibits depicting the future were a distant memory, because this piece of marble from four hundred years ago had me transfixed. The moving walkway sped by far too fast for me, and as I passed by I cranked my neck back as far as it would go, until the conveyor belt deposited me out of the room.

"I want to go back again!" I told my mom.

"Really? Um, OK. Girls, let's get back in line."

We got back in line, and within the hour, we were on the movable belt again.

This time I locked my eyes in slow motion and soaked up every inch of the *Pietà*. Here was Mary holding her only son—her dead son—but she wasn't sad! Her face was young and smooth and...*content*. What could be a worse moment in anyone's life, to lose one's child? And to have it happen in such a violent, barbaric way—and you, the mother, were forced to watch the whole sickening ordeal? And yet, there was no sign of any violence in the *Pietà*, just a mother gazing down at her son as he slept in her arms. And that was what Jesus looked like—serenely asleep in her arms. No blood from the crown of thorns, no hole in his side from the Roman's spear. It was as if he would wake up at any moment—and she knew it. There was death, but there was life.

I couldn't take it much further than that—I mean, I *was* eleven!—but it was profound and it had my head spinning—*and I wanted to see it again!*

"No, we have to move on," my mother responded to my pleas. My sisters, too, had had it with me, as they wanted to get back over to the more fun parts of the Fair.

"But I want to get a picture! We have to show Dad!"

That won the argument: something for Dad, back home, toiling away in the factory. And fortunately she hadn't seen the No Photography signs. So back in we went for a third time, my mother with the 8mm home movie Bell & Howell, me with the Kodak Brownie in hand.

On the third pass—where we were chastised for the cameras (this disturbed my mother, who did not like to be told to do anything by anybody)—I was now completely focused on the face of the mother Mary. At one point I turned away to look at my mother's face, and I decided that the resemblance was significant enough to warrant better treatment of her in the weeks to come.

Before exiting the Vatican City pavilion, I approached a bevy of monsignors in robes who stood near the Swiss Guards. I had two questions I wanted to ask. A friendly-looking, Irish-accented priest with a nose as red as Rudolph's offered his assistance.

"There was some writing carved into Mary's clothes," I asked, innocently. "Do you know what it says?"

"It says MICHAEL. ANGELUS. BONAROTUS. FLORENTIN. FACIEBAT—'Michelangelo Buonarroti of

Florence Created This.' He carved it in there because when he attended the unveiling of the sculpture he heard people in the crowd give credit to another famous sculptor at the time, saying 'so-and-so must have made this!' It upset him, so that night he came into St. Peter's and carved that inscription across Mary's sash. But when he came back the next day, he saw what that looked like, and he was ashamed and upset that he had defaced his own artwork because of his pride and vanity. He vowed at that moment, as his penance, never to sign another sculpture of his again. And he never did."

I paused to take that in, and it seemed like a good lesson to hear.

My other question was a simpler one. "What does *Pietà* mean?"

"It's Italian," the priest said.

"It means 'pity.'"

———

"I want to see where the Towers stood," she said, and she wouldn't let me talk her out of it. I did not want to take my mother down to lower Manhattan. I did not want this to be her last possible memory of the city she loved, a place that was so much a part of her imagination and memories and a lifelong source of joy for her whenever she stepped onto this island. That magical place was now still smoldering, the fires underground still burning, some ten weeks after the attack. It still felt and smelled of death, and the progress of combing through the 220 stories of twisted steel and pulverized concrete in search of the departed was painstakingly slow.

"I want to see it."

Days before, I went out to LaGuardia Airport in our Volkswagen Beetle to pick up my parents who had flown in to be with us for the Thanksgiving weekend. As I stood behind the newly tightened airport security zone I could see the two of them coming up the aisle of the Northwest Airlines terminal. My mother had not been well, and her health was deteriorating as each month went by. Yet there she was, walking three paces ahead of my dad as if she were twenty years younger, the kind of lilt in her step that only New York could give her. She also spotted me long before my dad did and started waving enthusiastically. I waved back.

Whatever "slowing down" she had done back at home was not evident once she was firmly planted in Manhattan. No longer forced to take the ferry and the bus to get into the city from her sister's house on Staten Island, she was now "sitting pretty," as my dad would say, in our West Side apartment. He would walk into my condo building and, without fail, remark that I was "sure livin' high on the hog!" This was beyond anything he could have imagined on the factory floor of AC Spark Plug, and while he enjoyed the amenities and the view of the city, he remained appropriately skeptical for a man of his means.

The night before Thanksgiving, my wife and I took them over to West Eighty-First Street and along Central Park West so they could see the balloons being inflated for the Macy's Parade the next day. It was cold and we bundled them as best we could, and for a short time they enjoyed being with thousands of New Yorkers marveling at the deflated Snoopy and slightly inflated Bart Simpson lying on the ground (though they had no idea who the latter was). It was a peek behind the curtain, one of many they had been given, due to my Life After Flint—a trip to the Cannes Film Festival with a walk up the stairs of the Palais, a seat at the Emmy Awards next to Sid Caesar the night we won, a chance to have people like Rob Reiner tell them that "your son's film has the impact of an *Uncle Tom's Cabin*"—that alone being worth the price of admission if you're a parent, slightly embarrassing if you're the son.

But now my mother wanted to see Ground Zero, the site of the recent massacre of 2,752 people. I acquiesced and, thinking that Thanksgiving Day would find it the least crowded there, I loaded them in the Beetle and headed down the West Side Highway.

By mid-November of 2001, the authorities had opened up more streets in Tribeca to traffic, and it was possible to drive right up the perimeter of the World Trade Center's former location. The place was every bit the disaster area it had been for the past two months, and smoke could still be seen wafting its way up from the ruins.

I slowed down so they could get a better look. I glanced over at my mother, who was sitting in the front seat with me. There were tears in her eyes, and I would have to go back to the death of her sister to recall such a look of sadness on her face. It was like her facial muscles had just collapsed on their own. She looked down, and then away, and then back again at the destruction. This was not the New York of Ed Sullivan or the Rainbow Room or giving your regards to Broadway.

This was the future not promised, her world of tomorrow, and I was sorry for her to see it.

"Mike! *Mike!*"

I was sitting in the living room of our home in northern Michigan, planning which movie I was going to take the family to in the next half hour. The choice was between *Men in Black II* or *Divine Secrets of the Ya-Ya Sisterhood*. It was the Fourth of July weekend, 2002, and my sister Veronica had flown in from California with her kids to be with my wife and daughter and our parents. It was Saturday, early evening, and we had spent the day on the lake, taking the kids tubing, and giving Mom and Dad a spin on the boat. My mother hung on to her hat and laughed and admonished me to slow down as the kids on the inner tube shouted to go faster.

Afterward, before dinner, I sat with my mom in the Adirondack chairs on top of the small hill beside the lake. She rolled up her pants to get some sun on her legs and closed her eyes, and you could see it all felt good to her.

For the past three weeks I had taken off from work and come to Davison to hang out with them. I took them out for a wedding anniversary dinner, and we did driving tours of all their old haunts from their years of growing up in the Flint area. We visited the graves of all the ancestors, some with birthdates going back to the late 1700s. We planted flowers, we visited the free legal service provide by the UAW (they wanted to update their wills), and we went to a Tigers ball game in Detroit. It was, without a doubt, three of the best weeks I ever spent with them. Though my mother was fading in energy, she participated in everything. But I noticed her time in the bathroom seemed to be getting longer and longer. My dad complained about it, and I agreed we should take her to the doctor and get her checked out.

"Mike! Mike!!" It was my mother's voice, but it wasn't coming from inside the house where the rest of us were. It was coming from the back deck. I went out to see what she needed.

When I came out the door, it was clear she was very, very sick.

"I need to get to the bathroom—" She threw up at that moment, and what she threw up was pitch-black gunk. My dad, by then, had come outside to see what was the matter, and he and I helped her up and took her inside. My wife called the local hospital to see what they suggested.

"Pepto Bismol," my wife said, relaying the message. This did not seem like a job for a pink liquid. My mother continued to throw up. "I think we should take her to the hospital," I said. I did not want to call an ambulance as that would take a long time (the nearest one was at least eight miles away).

We walked her slowly out to my dad's Ford, and my wife and sister made her comfortable in the back seat. I got behind the wheel and headed down our long driveway to the road. We lived deep in the middle of nowhere (in 2002, our road still wasn't wired for cable TV).

As I reached the end of the driveway, I had a quick decision to make: Do I take her to the *nearest* hospital—or do I take her to the *better* hospital? The nearest hospital was in a small town twenty-three miles to the north. The better hospital, the best in northern Michigan, was in the opposite direction, forty-five miles away, twice the drive. So there was the dilemma. Your mother is seriously ill, you don't know why, but it doesn't look good. Do you get her help immediately or, if she's much worse than even you realize, do you drive the longer distance and end up with a better array of doctors and facilities available?

What would *you* do? You'd get her to the quickest hospital, right? *Right?* That's what I did. I chose the nearest hospital.

I got there in record time—less than twenty minutes—and we took her in, told them the problem, and they saw to her right away. There was only one doctor on duty, but it wasn't long before he looked at her.

"It seems that her intestinal tract is blocked. We're going to take some X-rays." And, sure enough, the X-rays confirmed the doctor's suspicions.

They gave her liquids that they said should help. It didn't. They gave her an IV and they said that should do the trick. It didn't. While waiting to see which procedure would get the expected results and then seeing no results, the clock had peeled away the hours; it was well past midnight.

"OK," said the doctor finally. "Here's what we're going to do. We're going to give her a series of four or five enemas and keep her overnight. This should work and she should be able to go home tomorrow."

We went with her to the room they had given her and we stayed until they were ready to start the enema procedures. At that point the nurse suggested, "It's almost three a.m.—why don't you go get some sleep and come back in the morning?"

Our mother agreed. "Take your father home and let him get some rest. I'll be fine. I'll see you in the morning."

For reasons we could never later explain to ourselves, we took her advice and, amazingly—shockingly—left her alone there in this tiny hospital. We went home and crashed quickly—and just as quickly we were awoken a few hours later.

"Is this Michael Moore?" said the voice on the phone. "This is Dr. Calkins, the surgeon here at the hospital. The enemas didn't work on your mother, and she's taken a turn. We need to operate. How soon can you be here?"

In less than twenty minutes we were there. Mom looked embarrassed and sorry to be putting everyone out for the trouble she was causing. "Did you get some sleep?" was all that was on her mind.

"Don't worry about us," I said. "How are *you* doing?"

"Well, nothing seems to be working. They want to operate," she said with a weak voice.

I took the doctor aside and asked him to explain to me what was going on.

"Your mother's intestines are shot," he said matter-of-factly. "We will more than likely need to take a piece of them out."

"Are you sure that's necessary?"

"If we don't get in there, she could go into septic shock. The bacteria trapped in there may have already seeped through the lining of her intestine. This is a common procedure; I've done many of them. Shouldn't take more than an hour or two. She should be fine."

"Fine? How many of these did you say you have done?"

"I do one or two a year—and I've been doing this for thirty-some years. As it is now, I'm all you got 'cause I'm the only one here—and I think we should get going."

We went back in the room and the nurse brought in some paperwork for my dad to sign. She then asked my mother to sign the consent form.

"Would you sign it for me, Frank?" she asked my dad.

He took the clipboard and signed it, slowly. We squeezed my mom's hand and told her everything was going to be OK. She assured *us* everything was going to be OK. I fought hard not to cry. They took her away and we went to the lounge to wait for the hour or two.

Four hours later the surgeon had not come out, and a pall fell over the room. Whatever the news was, it wasn't going to be good.

Finally, the doctor appeared.

"I think it went well," he said. "She's recovering fine now. We had to remove about a foot of her intestine. I'd say the chances for a full recovery are about 90 percent."

Whew. You know how many times you've seen that doctor come through those doors — a thousand times — on TV shows and in the movies and it's rarely good news. He explained to us that she will probably have to stay in the hospital for the better part of the week. He didn't see any seepage through the intestinal lining and her vital signs were all good. In fact, we could see her within the hour as soon as she woke up.

We thanked the surgeon and, with a sense of relief, headed back to the intensive care unit. Well, there was no "unit" or ward at this hospital. They had a small ICU area with two rooms. That was fine, just fine. *She was OK!*

When we went into our mother's room, she was hooked up to all the standard monitors and IV tubes, but she was awake and alert and very happy to see us.

"Here I am," she said, stating the obvious. I liked hearing that: first person, present tense.

"Well, the doctor says you made it through with flying

colors!" I said to her, as I pulled up a chair beside the bed. My sister and wife and father were equally upbeat in their assessments of her condition.

"You're gonna be OK, Mom," Veronica said, giving her a kiss on her forehead. "In fact, you look pretty chipper there!"

Our only concern until this point had been the effects of putting such an elderly person under sedation. We had known of friends with not-good stories of what happened to their parents when knocked out with anesthesia. Sometimes all their memory didn't return, at least not right away. I decided to give her a pop quiz.

"Hey Mom — you know what day this is?"

"Sure," she said, "it's Sunday."

"Where did you and Dad go on your honeymoon?"

"New York. Boston. Albany." (I know. *Albany*. Don't ask.)

And now for the Final Jeopardy question. This was a family that loved to go to the movies.

"Where did you first see *High Noon*?"

"Cheboygan, Michigan. Nineteen fifty-two!" she responded without missing a beat. Wow. Crisis averted, roll credits!

Everyone pulled up a chair, and we spent the next few hours talking about the good times and growing up and Dr. Wall and the time he was "blocked" just before her wedding and how he too had to go to the hospital and almost didn't make it. Never had discussions about enemas been so heartening.

The doctor and nurses on call would occasionally come in to check on her, change the IV bags, inspect the area where the surgery took place. She would doze off now and then, her body wanting to restore itself after the shock of surgery.

By 9:00 p.m. it was decided that we would take shifts and stay with her for as long as she was going to be in the hospital. I offered to take the first shift until the morning. Veronica and my wife took Dad and the kids back to the house. I got comfortable with a book and my ever-present legal pad, sketching out the final fixes I wanted to make to my film before its release in the fall.

Every now and then my mother would wake up and we would talk.

"I'm very lucky to have the family I have," she said.

"We're very lucky to have you," I told her, patting a luke-warm washcloth on her face like she would do for us, so many years ago.

"I'm thirsty," she said. She was not allowed to have any food or liquids, not even water, during these first twenty-four hours. All we could do was to let her suck on a little Q-tip that had a tiny moist sponge on its head. I held one up to her lips, and she sucked on it with some desperation.

"I'm parched." I smiled. No one said "parched" in this century or the last.

"Lemme do this," I said, as I took another one and rubbed it around her lips. Like an infant looking for its mother's nipple, she grabbed at the little stick with her mouth, her tongue, her teeth, wanting more, more.

"Thirsty."

"I think that's all we can do for now, Mom. I'll just sit here with you and we'll do it again in a little bit."

I sat in the chair next to her bed and got comfortable.

"Here," she said, as she lifted her head off her pillows and tried to reach for one of them. "Take one of my pillows."

I could not believe, in the state she was in, that she was

worrying about *me* not having a pillow. And that even in her worst suffering, her instincts were still to be a mother, to look out for her son, to make sure he was OK, to allow him to fall asleep, to sleep peacefully and in comfort. On her pillow.

"That's OK, Mom," I said with a smile, trying to contain a laugh. "I don't need a pillow. You keep it." I arranged the pillow back in place, and her head now nestled in it comfortably.

"I love my kids. I have good children," she said with a sweet, faint smile.

I put my hand on her face and gently combed her hair back with my fingers.

"We love you, too, Mom." I felt lucky to have her as my mother.

A moment later the night nurse came in with an aide and said that she needed to give my mother some potassium in her medicine bag and change the top sheet of the bed. For my mother's modesty and privacy, she suggested that maybe I could "just step out for a few minutes." The nurse had hair fashioned into a long braid that extended down her back, the kind I guess you might see in a religious community. Her glasses were like something from the late seventies, and they framed a face that seemed frozen in time.

I left the room and went out in the hallway to wait. It wasn't long before I heard sheer human panic.

"No—move her over. There! Stop! We've got a problem!"

I rushed back into the room to see my mother in what I later learned was a cardiac arrest. The nurse was panicked and confused and I suggested we get the doctor down here *NOW*.

"Yes, right." She picked up the intercom phone and paged the lone doctor in the ER.

My mother was struggling to breathe—gasping, gasping, *gasping,* her eyes locked on to mine as if to say, *Please help me!*

"Everything's going to be OK, Mom, hang in there!"

I turned to the nurse and demanded action. "We need the doctor in here now! *Do I have to go get him?*"

The doctor walked in and immediately saw what the problem was. "She needs to breathe! Where is the respirator?"

The little ICU at this small-town hospital did not have a respirator machine in the unit at that moment.

"Grab the portable!" the doctor shouted. The nurse went and got a small plastic device that she tore out of a plastic bag, then tried to insert it in my mother's mouth. She had it upside down.

"Here, give it to me!" the doctor demanded. He took it from her, inserted it into my mother's mouth, placing the tube squarely down her throat. *"Here, pump it like this!"*

Jesus, oh Jesus, what the fuck was going on? *He was having to show a nurse how to bring air into a patient's lungs?* This was madness. I wanted to jump in, help, do something, do CPR, something, *ANYTHING, please God this isn't happening!*

While the nurse pumped, the doctor told the aide to go down to the ER and get the hospital's lone ventilator. He worked on my mother, gave her a shot of something, massaged something, and the only good news in this moment was that the heart monitor never went dead, never flatlined. The heart was still beating, there was oxygen getting into the blood.

I picked up my phone and called the house. My sister answered.

"I think you guys better get here now," I said, trying to disguise my panic. "Something's happened. Don't kill yourself getting here. She's alive. But struggling bad. Come now!"

The ventilator arrived with another nurse, and the doctor wasted no time jamming the hose straight down my mother's throat. Her eyes were no longer on mine. They were open, frozen, looking straight up and seemingly unaware of what was happening to her. At that moment a bolt of lightning struck the hospital and it lit up the room. I had not noticed that for the past fifteen minutes a thunderstorm had rolled in and was now in full fury. Deafeningly close thunder exploded, and the lightning continued to flash into the unit. I looked at the clock: 12:45 a.m. For some reason, with all that was going on, it occurred to me that I was born at 12:45 (but in the p.m.). How did I know this? For every year of my adult life, no matter where I was, at exactly 12:45 p.m., my mother would call me to tell me this was the moment she gave birth to me. Now, here I was, crumbling inside, helpless and lost, feeble and useless and impotent in this most critical moment where *I* was responsible for giving *her* life, or at least saving it. The voice inside my head kept pounding: *YOU made the wrong decision!* Yes, I had chosen the closest hospital, *not* the better hospital where I was certain I would *not be* witnessing a Mack Sennett version of intensive care where the Keystone Cops finally find the only ventilator in the mop closet and wheel it out, asking each other if they know how this newfangled contraption works. I was sick, sick, and I wanted to throw up.

I went over by my mother's side and put my hands on her. I whispered in her ear: "I'm here. You're OK. This will be OK. Stay with me. Don't leave me. Dad and Veronica are on the way!"

I bowed my head and said a prayer and asked God to please spare her, to not take her, to let her live. It was not her time! I asked him to take everything from me, everything I had, all my possessions, my career — *anything* — I would give it all up right now just so she could live. It was a crazy, illogical and unnecessary request. God — or nature or my mother herself — were going to decide if her body could carry on. But I meant it nonetheless, and I would be overjoyed if my offer were accepted.

My dad and sister and wife arrived, slightly shaken by what they said was the worst storm they'd ever driven through. They went to her side and spoke to her, and though there would be the occasional twitch in her eyes, there was no guarantee she could hear us.

Her heart beat through the night and into the morning. Our other sister, Anne, rushed to get on a red-eye from Sacramento and would soon arrive there to be with us. Each hour, our mother's vital signs would stabilize, then go slightly downward. The night nurse with the long braid left without a word, and a new day nurse came in. She stopped when she saw me, and she didn't try very hard to contain "that look" I've seen a thousand times from those who would rather not see me. Of course, the other nurses and doctors more than made up for her attitude, and they did their best to make my mother comfortable and to keep the rest of us calm. The doctor on duty admitted that if my mom were stable he'd like to move her to another hospital with facilities that might be better for her. But that kind of travel would be too dangerous at this point, he said. We would just have to play the cards we were dealt.

By two in the afternoon (now twenty-four hours since the surgery), her progress continued steadily downward. The blood pressure read 60 over 35. I called Jack Stanzler, a doctor and friend in Ann Arbor, to get some advice, and he in turn called a doctor friend of his in northern Michigan to see if there was anything he could do. Our mother's eyes remained wide open with little or no movement. We all kept whispering encouraging things to her, hoping it would help.

I took a break for a moment and went out in the hall to the nurses' station, where I encountered the not-so-happy-to-see-me nurse. She looked straight at me, and with a tone of disgust that she didn't even have the decency to hide, she uttered the following:

"Why don't you just knock it off in there? Your mother is dead. And nobody's got the guts to tell you that. She's gone and nothing you're doing is going to bring her back." And then she walked away.

I thought I had suffocated. If I didn't know better, it felt as if the nurse's hand was now on my throat, choking the life out of me.

"Wait a minute!" I yelled, as I found my breath. "*Who are you?!* Why would you say such a thing? You're sick. *Sick!*"

I broke down. The others in the room heard me, and my wife came out. Sobbing, I told her what the nurse just said.

"Your mother's not dead. Those monitors don't lie. I don't know why she would say that. Come back in the room."

Instead, I went to the phone and called the surgeon. I told him what just happened. He told me to ignore the nurse and that the doctor on duty was handling things and that was all that mattered. "And your mother is still alive."

Over the next hour we all took turns spending a few private moments with my mother, saying the things that you would only say if it were just you and your dying mother in the room. Around 4:00 p.m. we all gathered in a circle around her bed, and each of us offered a prayer or a remembrance or a thank-you to this woman who brought us into the world and raised us and took care of us and encouraged us to embrace knowledge and goodness and kind-heartedness and to never back down if we thought that was what our conscience was demanding. No one could get through what they were saying without breaking down.

At thirty seconds after 4:30 p.m. on July 8, 2002, my mother left this world. There was a sharp, profound sorrow in the room, and too many tears to count. We cried for the better part of the next half hour, and one by one, after a long silence, we picked up our things to leave. I was the last in the room. I went over to my mother and held her. She was asleep, her eyes having been closed by the doctor. I kissed her on her head, and when I pulled back I noticed a long gray hair of hers on my shirt. I gently took the hair—the hair that to me was still alive, still full of her DNA, the twenty-three chromosomes that made her who she was, that helped to make me who I am, a piece of *her* (though it was just a simple strand of hair). I tucked the hair into my shirt pocket, looked at her one last time, and left.

To this day, that last strand of gray hair still sits in that same shirt pocket, folded up in a small bag in my old bedroom in the home I grew up in, hidden away, untouched, up on top of the bookshelf, next to a little plastic statue she gave me at the New York World's Fair of Michelangelo's *Pietà*.

Tet

———

I can't quite remember when I turned against the idea of war, but I'm sure it had something to do with the fact that I didn't want to die. From pretty much the sixth grade on, I was firmly, solidly, against dying.

But up until then, I spent many years dying with verve in our neighborhood. The favorite game to play on our street was War. It beat Bloody Murder by a mile because it had *weapons.* Bloody Murder was really just a game of hide-and-seek (when you found the person hiding, you would yell "Bloody murder!" and everyone would try to make it back to touch the home pole before those who were hiding could tag you).

War was the real deal—and girls couldn't play. The rules were simple. A group of boys, ages four to ten, would divide up into two groups: the Americans and the Germans. We each had our own set of toy machine guns, rifles, and bazookas. I was much admired for my fine stash of hand grenades that came complete with the pin you could pull out as you tossed it, accompanied by a very loud "explosion" that would come out of my mouth.

None of us minded whether we were chosen to be a German or an American — we already knew who was going to win. It became less about winning and more about coming up with creative and entertaining ways to kill and be killed. We studied *Combat* and *Rat Patrol* on TV. We asked our dads for ideas but none of us got much help as they didn't seem to want to talk about their war experiences. We all imagined our fathers as well-decorated war heroes, and it was just assumed that if we ever had to go to war we would be every bit the brave defenders of freedom they were.

I was particularly good at dying, and the other kids loved machine-gunning me down. Especially if I was playing a German; I'd stand for as long as I could, taking as many of their bullets as I could, and, long before Sam Peckinpah arrived on the scene, I was going down in a slow-motion agony that gave all the other boys a thrill for offing my sorry Nazi ass. And when I hit the ground, I'd roll over a couple times and, in a fit of spasms, I would expire. As I lay there, eyes open, motionless, I felt a strange sense of satisfaction that I played an important role in seeing one more nasty Nazi bite the dust.

But when I played an American, I would try to stay alive as long as possible. I would find some way to sneak in behind enemy lines, hide in a tree, and then take out as many of the Germans as I could. I especially loved lobbing the grenades from above; it was so upsetting to the "Nazi" boys who could not figure out where all these little bombs were coming from. I would make sure to leave one or two of them alive so they could shoot me. Then I could die a hero's death, cut down in my prime, maybe taking one last "Nazi" with me as I fell on them, pulling the pin off my final grenade, blowing both of us to bits as we hit the ground.

But by 1966, as the pictures on the evening news seemed nothing like what we were acting out on our little dirt street, "playing" war became less and less fun. These soldiers on TV were really dead—bloody and dead, covered in mud, then covered by a tarp, no slow-motion heroics provided. The soldiers who remained alive, they looked all scared and disheveled and confused. They smoked cigarettes, and not one of them looked like he was having much fun. One by one, the boys in the neighborhood put away their toy guns. No one said anything. We just stopped. There was home-work and chores to do, and girls seemed distantly interesting. The Americans won The Big War That Counted, and that was enough.

By the summer after seventh grade our family left the dirt street and moved on to a paved one—the very street that we lived on when I was born. I started to think a lot about the Vietnam War that summer, and most of what I thought about wasn't good. I did the math and I realized I was just five years away from draft age! And it was becoming clear that this war was not going to be over anytime soon.

Mrs. Beachum was our afternoon lay teacher in eighth grade. Because our nun was also the Mother Superior for the school, she taught us only in the morning. Her afternoons were spent on her administrative duties and doling out the necessary disciplinary measures to the fallen ones among us.

Mrs. Beachum was black. There were no other black

teachers and only three black kids in the entire school—
and perhaps because their last name was JuanRico, we somehow convinced ourselves they weren't *really* black, probably
Cuban or Puerto Rican! One of the boys was called Ricardo
and the other was named Juan. See—not Negro! They were
popular, and their parents were at every event helping out in
any way that they could.

But Mrs. Beachum was definitely black. There was no
getting around it. Her skin was nearly as dark as coal, and
she spoke in a Southern dialect none of us were familiar
with. Not a day would pass where she wouldn't say to one
of us in her distinctive Southern black accent, "Don't be facetious, child!" We had no idea what that meant, but we just
loved the sound of it. She had a body that was not covered
by a nun's habit, and I would not be surprised if, in 1967, I
wasn't the only boy in our class whose first "dream" had the
good fortune of Mrs. Beachum playing a significant role in it.

But in our waking hours we did not sexualize her, as none
of us wanted to deal with that in the confessional booth. Plus,
the Mother Superior kept a strict and watchful eye on our
puberty and its progress, and she made sure to spend time
reminding each gender in the class just how much we could
trust the other gender—which was, to put it simply, not a
lot. Since fifth grade, the two genders of our class did their
best to put down or ridicule each other, and by the time
we were thirteen or fourteen, we had developed enough
of a vocabulary and a streak of meanness to slice and dice
the opposing side with plausible gusto. The girls were most
fond of pointing out the boys who had hygiene issues, and
they would anonymously leave a can of Ban deodorant on
the locker of the offending boy for all to see. The boys had

already picked up on the girls' sensitivity to their growing (or not-so-growing) breasts. One boy had swiped his older sister's falsies and they were thus left on the desks of those girls who had failed to blossom rapidly enough to match the ones we saw in Mike McIntosh's *Playboys*.

This was how we spent our mornings in eighth grade, fighting back the heat inside with some church-sanctioned cool cruelty—all done with the good intention, I am sure, to keep us out of trouble and way out of wedlock.

After lunch, though, it was all jazz.

Mrs. Beachum would have none of this "boys versus girls" stuff. She believed in "love" and "being in love," and though we couldn't quite put our finger on it, years later we knew she was also the only teacher in the school making love (or so we wanted to think). When she taught us history, she made the characters come alive.

"What do y'all know about Teapot Dome!" she'd say, never meaning it as a question. We had no thoughts about Teapot Dome, but we knew we were going to hear a sassy story about it.

"Warren G. Harding—uh-huh! He sure was sumpin'! Scandal? Lordy, he wrote the book on it!"

Every class was like this.

"Lemme hear some sweet poetry today, children! Who's written a poem just for me?" Oh, believe me, we were all writing poems. She had us rhyming and she taught us rhythms, and sometimes she would take our poem and sing it back to us. Every once in a while, the Mother Superior would stick her head in to see what was going on. She didn't object, just as long as the boys were still sitting on one side of the room and girls were on the other. Her tacit approval of Mrs. Beachum's methods made us less worried for her, and it relaxed the room to the point where on the day Mrs. Beachum proposed her Big Idea, there was surprisingly little objection among us.

"I think it's time to teach y'all a little *manners!* You ever hear of 'etiquette'?"

We had heard of it but certainly had never been practitioners of it.

"Well, boys and girls, I think it's time we all went out to dinner with each other and learn how *proper people* do things! Boys, I want you each to pick a girl to be your dinner partner. Then for the next three weeks we'll all learn proper table manners. When we're ready, we'll go to Frankenmuth for one of those famous fried chicken dinners!"

Of course, what she had in mind wasn't "learnin' manners" or "etiquette." She was going to teach us how to *date.* I'm sure she had to sell this idea to the authorities without saying the word *date,* and I guess they saw nothing wrong with us knowing which one was the salad fork and understanding how the releasing of toxic gasses during a meal was not how God expected us to enjoy the fruits of his earth.

The twenty-seven of us in Mrs. Beachum's class had just been told that nature's gates could now be opened. For a few minutes we all giggled and twitched and — *and, dang, we liked this idea!* It was remarkable how quickly we each took to this concept of "going out" with someone else in the classroom who didn't have our specific reproductive organs. (In years hence, I've wondered what this must have been like for the nonheterosexuals in the room — finally a chance to acknowledge sexual feelings! — *but, damn! With the wrong gender!* For them, I guess, it became an early lesson in faking it.)

The proper order of the world fell into place quite perfectly as each boy in the room rushed over to ask out the girl
who was "appropriate" for him. The basketball star asked out
the softball whiz. The piano player asked out the dancer.
The writer asked out the actress. The boy from the trailer
park asked out the girl from the trailer park. The boy with
the hygiene issues asked out the girl with the hygiene issues.

And I asked out Kathy Root. I'm not quite sure how to
explain the matchup, but perhaps the easiest way is to say
she was the tallest girl in the class and I was the tallest boy.
For my part, I couldn't have cared less about our height—I
had not taken my eyes off her for the past three years. She
had long tan legs and a constant smile and was truly nice to
everyone. And she was whip-smart. She was the girl most of
the other boys would be too afraid to ask out—including
me—so she made it easy on me and came across the room
to where I was, frozen and petrified at my desk.

"Well, I guess it's you and me," she said gently so that I
wouldn't collapse into my pants.

"Sure," I responded. "Yeah. For real. It'll be fun."

And that was that. I had the catch of the room. The girl
who in high school would be elected our homecoming queen
was going to be my "date" at our "etiquette" dinner.

By the next afternoon, though, tragedy struck.

"Michael," Mrs. Beachum called out to me in the hallway
after lunch. "Can I have a moment with you?"

She led me to a corner so that no one could hear us.

"I just want you to know that you're probably the only
boy in the class to whom I could ask this favor."

She had the most encouraging eyes. Her hair made it
seem as if she were the fourth Supreme. Her lips...Well, I

didn't know much about lips at thirteen, but what I did know, now standing closer to her than I ever had before, confirmed to me that there were no more inviting lips than those that Mrs. Beachum carried with her.

The lips parted, and she began to speak.

"I've already talked to your date, to Kathy Root, and she said it was OK with her if it's OK with you."

Yes, go on. Please. Don't let the twitch on the left side of my face distract you.

"There are thirteen boys and fourteen girls in the class. So all the girls have a date except Lydia."

"Lydia" was Lydia Scanlon. "Lydia the Moron" was the name most of the boys in class called her. Lydia was the class cipher. No one sat by her, and even fewer knew anything about her. She never spoke, even when called on, and she hadn't been called on since fifth grade. There is always that student or two whom the teachers have to decide whether to fish or cut bait—there are only so many minutes in the school day, and if they won't talk, you have to move on and teach the others. Five years of working on her to participate were apparently enough, and so most of us didn't even know she was still in our class, although she was there every single day, in the last seat in the row farthest from our reality.

Lydia's Catholic schoolgirl uniform was ill fitting, most likely the result of having been worn by two or three other girls in the family before her. Her hygiene was said to be worse than a boy's, and her hair was cut... well, at least she had access to a mirror while she was cutting it.

It was no surprise that not one boy had made a beeline to her to ask her to be his date.

"I need you to ask Lydia to be your date for the dinner," Mrs. Beachum said.

"Huh?" was all I could mutter. There was an instant lump in my throat because she was asking me TO GIVE UP THE BRONZE-LEGGED FUTURE-HOMECOMING-QUEEN BEAUTY AS MY DATE! I had won the Gold Medal, and now I was being asked to *give it back!* Just like Jim Thorpe! You cannot do this!

Without saying any of the above, Mrs. Beachum could read it on my face.

"Look, honey, I know you wanted to go with Kathy — but I know you know that no one will ask Lydia, and there's just sumpin' not right 'bout that. She's a nice girl. Just a little slow. Some people fast, some people slow. All God's children. All. 'Specially Lydia. You know that, don't you?"

"Yes, Mrs. Beachum." Yes, I knew that, and I actually even believed it. But weren't the longest tanned legs in the school *also* something worth believing in?

"I knew that would be your answer," she said proudly. "Couldn't ask this of the other boys. No sir! Only you. Thank you, child."

Ugh. Why not? *Why not ask them?* Why me?

"Plus, I figured seeing how you are thinking of going to the seminary next year, you won't really need many of these 'manners' I'm teaching you, now will you?"

Apparently the Mother Superior had shared my thoughts about becoming a priest with Mrs. Beachum. And, of course, what use does a priest have for sex, much less "manners," much less those pink-black engorged lips you're using to hand me the worst news of my life?

"Sure. It's fine. But what about Kathy?" I asked. Yes, *what about Kathy?* You're not considering the *grief* she's going to experience not being able to be *my* date!

"Like I said, I already talked to her. She was very happy to do this special thing for Lydia. Said you would be, too."

I decided to give it one last shot. "But, but then Kathy will be all alone at the dinner!"

"No, child, here's what we do. Lydia will sit across from you. Kathy will sit with the both of you, next to Lydia. So in a way, Kathy will still be there as sorta your date, too."

Sorta. (This will become the story of my dating life. More later.)

"But you'll officially be there with Lydia and you will pull her chair out for her and order for her and talk to her and make her feel that she, that she…is…"

A hint of tears began to make their way to the front of her eyes, but she blinked fast enough to catch them and wick them back behind her sockets and finished her sentence.

"That she is wanted. Can you do that, Michael?"

That this had suddenly been elevated beyond an etiquette lesson, beyond a date, to a call for mercy and possible sainthood—well, that was all I needed to hear.

"Yes, I can do this. I *want* to do this. You can count on me! You're right, I won't have any use for girls after this year anyways!" Exactly! Mrs. Beachum, you'd just be wasting all these lessons on me. I'm off to be a monk for life!

I had a pain in the pit of my stomach.

I went into the classroom and asked Lydia to be my date. Though I tried to say it soft enough so none of the other boys would hear me, it wasn't long before word got out that I had given up the top prize for the Loser Lydia—and these little men in their high-waisted pants spent a lot of time on the playground scratching their butch-cut heads and trying to figure out exactly what had happened to me.

"Don't make sense, Mike," Pete said, shaking his head. "How are you even gonna *stand it,* being *next* to her?"

"I dunno" was about all I could muster. How *was* I going to sit next to her? Ewww.

The big night came to go to Frankenmuth, and Lydia was all freshly scrubbed and her dress was plain but pretty. I opened the door for her, let her take my arm, pulled her chair out for her and, in a momentary act of rebellion against my impending lifelong celibacy, I pulled Kathy's out for her, too. Kathy talked to Lydia, then I talked to Lydia, and Lydia talked back to us. We heard the story of how her brother had died and how her dad was working two jobs because her mother had health problems and how she spent her time in her room writing poems. Lydia was shy but *not* a cipher. She was funny, and she had a snorty laugh that after a while was cute and catchy. The other classmates looked down the table to see what the three of us were up to, and a couple of the boys joined in to talk to the newly interesting Lydia. This gave Kathy and me a chance to talk, also a new thing for me, for up until now she had just been an object to observe as often and as vigorously as possible.

"You were a good guy, Mike, to do this," she whispered to me.

"Really? Um, well, you know I'm going to the seminary?"

"Sure. I heard that."

"So, you see, this class wasn't really for me."

"Well, it was fun, don't you think?"

"Sure. Can I have your pie if you're not gonna eat it?"

After our class's First Date Night at the Frankenmuth Bavarian Chicken House, there was no going back to the War of the Sexes. Thanks to Mrs. Beachum, we all discovered that we liked each other — a lot. And while others contemplated their next moves in the dating life, I had time to ponder such things as what kind of trouble would Mrs. Beachum be in for having upended the Puberty Retardation Policy that the Church had implemented. Boys stopped picking on girls, and girls stopped laughing at boys. We helped each other with homework. We let the girls throw the basketball around. Everything felt better and we were grateful to Mrs. Beachum for her enthusiasm and her desire to teach us more than just the capitals of all fifty states. We looked forward to our afternoons with her; it was the best part of every day. So when we came back from lunch for our afternoon with Mrs. Beachum on February 5, 1968, we were surprised to learn that she had not shown up to school. She did not show up the next day, either. Nor the next day. We were told that no one knew where she was, that she was missing. At first, we hoped that maybe she had overslept and just not shown up for work for a few days. The Mother Superior filled in for her. But as the week went on, the look of worry and concern on Mother Superior's face was evident, and her attempts to follow Mrs. Beachum's lesson plans were awkward, as she was surely distracted. She offered no information, and by the fifth day of Mrs. Beachum's absence, enough of us had complained to our parents and asked them to please get to the bottom of just what the heck was going on.

The nightly news on TV that week was grisly. It was the Vietnamese New Year ("Tet") of 1968, and though this was the first time any of us knew the Vietnamese got a second New Year, the only reason we knew this was by way of Chet Huntley and David Brinkley explaining to us why the Viet Cong and the North Vietnamese had launched their biggest offensive of the war. NBC News was especially graphic (in those days, TV showed the war uncensored). Their camera caught a South Vietnamese general grabbing a Viet Cong suspect on the street, putting his gun to the man's temple, and blowing his brains literally out of the other side of his head. That made the Swanson Salisbury Steak TV dinner go down easier.

The Tet Offensive of 1968 sent a shock wave through the American public because, opposite of everything we had been told about the United States soon "winning" the war — "We can see the light at the end of the tunnel!" — in fact, Tet showed just how powerful the other side was and how badly we were losing. The Viet Cong were all over Saigon, even at the door of the U.S. embassy. We were nowhere near to winning anything. This war was going to be with us for a very long time. I stared at the TV, and I was happy I was going to the seminary next year. If you were in the seminary, they couldn't draft you. One more reason not to need Mrs. Beachum's dating service.

Word eventually filtered through the parents that Mrs. Beachum had indeed vanished. There was no official word from the parish, but this much was said:

"Mrs. Beachum's husband is missing in Vietnam and presumed dead. Nobody knows where Mrs. Beachum is, but she has probably left and gone home to be with her family."

We never heard from Mrs. Beachum again. No one did. It was said she was too distraught to talk to anyone at St. John's and, if she had, no one would have quite known what to say to her. Others said she had a complete nervous breakdown when she got the news about her husband and she went off, to be far, far away, to be by herself and shun this cruel world. One parishioner said she took her own life, but none of us believed that because if there was one person who was thrilled about being alive, it was Mrs. Beachum. We finished out the year with an afternoon substitute teacher who did his best, but he never asked us to sing him a poem.

It was then, in the spring of 1968, after the deaths in Vietnam of Sergeant Beachum and a boy from the high school, plus the assassinations of King and the sweet man in the Senate elevator who helped me find my mother, that I made up my mind: under no circumstances, regardless of whatever amount of coercion, threats, or torture leveled at me, I would never, *ever*, pick up a gun and let my country send me to go kill Vietnamese.

And if anyone would ever ask me why I felt this way, I'd just look at 'em and say, "Don't be facetious, child."

Perhaps Mrs. Beachum is reading this. If so, I want to say: I'm sorry for whatever it was that took you away from us. I'm sorry we never had the chance to say good-bye. And I'm so sorry I never got to thank you for teaching me all those wonderful manners.

Christmas '43

MY DAD HAD NOTICED for some years that I no longer wanted to shoot guns. He had taken note of when we boys in the neighborhood had stopped playing War. I didn't know much about his time as a Marine in the South Pacific during World War II. The only clues my sisters and I got was when he would name our dogs after battles he was in: Peleliu, Tarawa, etc. In our attic he kept some war souvenirs: a Japanese flag, a sword, and the gun he had taken off a Japanese soldier. One day, without explanation, Dad decided he no longer wanted these items in our house. He quietly went and got a shovel out of the garage, gathered together the Japanese spoils of war, and went out to the large weeping willow tree in our backyard. He dug a hole — a very, very deep hole — and buried the gun and the sword and flag under the shade of that tree. When it was all done and the earth had been restored, he stood there alone, looking down, deep in thought or prayer or who knows what. I watched from my bedroom window.

"I want to tell you a story from the war," he told me one day. "I want you to know why every day is precious and why I am thankful each day to be here."

My dad was one of seven children, and they lived in twelve homes over eighteen years. They moved around a lot, dodging landlords who came to collect the rent they couldn't afford to pay. The Great Depression had not been particularly kind to the Moore family of Kansas Avenue/Franklin Avenue/Kensington Avenue/Bennett Street/Kentucky Street/ Illinois Street/Caldwell Avenue/Jane Street and other thoroughfares on the east side of Flint, Michigan.

Francis (or Frank, as he was known) was the fourth child of the family, and now, suddenly, at the age of twenty-two, his whole life—*falling down the coal chute at two, clinging on for dear life at four while stuck on the running board of his dad's car, getting cut from the high school basketball team the game before the state championship so that the coach could make room for a younger player coming in next year, getting fired the first day of driving the Coca-Cola delivery truck because he admitted he "didn't much like the taste of Coke," being placed by his mother temporarily at the age of ten in an orphanage along with his brother because she simply couldn't afford to take care of seven children*—**all of this** flashed before him as he lay exposed on top of Hill 250 on some miserable piece-of-shit island in the South Pacific, watching as the tracer rounds came out of the plane above, firing directly at him and his fellow Marines on Christmas Day, 1943. Except the planes, like him, were American.

How Frank came to find himself on Hill 250 on the island of New Britain made about as much sense to him as the fact that his own side was now trying to kill him with such ease.

To begin with, no one ever explained to him how these hills got their names; it wasn't as if there were 249 other hills he had to climb to get to Hill 250. In fact, to even call them "hills" seemed like some War Department cartographer's idea of a joke. Maybe by calling them hills they would make an American Marine feel more like he was home—and that if he were going to die for this *hill,* then, well, at least he'd feel like he was dying for…home. Home had hills. Hills with trees and wildflowers with names like Yellow Lady Slippers and Jack in the Pulpit and Shooting Stars. Hills with pleasant hiking paths. Hills to hide out in. Hills to pick berries from. Hills where hobos could find a peaceful night's rest. Hills where you and yours could find a small, quiet space to build a quick fire and make love beside it.

What led Frank to this particular hill was a worldwide war that had nothing in particular to do with *his* world. His world was one of hard work and sports and Saturday nights at the Knickerbocker Dance Hall. Though they lived the shared poverty of many in the worst days of the Depression, the Moore brothers—Bill, Frank, Lornie, and Herbie—each took extra care to always have a clean, well-pressed suit, a sharp haircut, and enough coin in their pockets to buy a pretty girl the first drink, if not the second.

They took dance lessons upon leaving high school, somehow figuring out that the fairer gender liked to go dancing. Because the other young men in town were slightly less adept at picking up on this, the Moore boys were always the first ones out on the dance floor, and this impressed the ladies. If nothing else, it showed the girls that they were fearless, and that in and of itself was quite attractive. Lornie, sixteen months younger than Frank, became known as the king of the dance floor and soon found himself teaching dance in a downtown dance studio. It dawned on him that he was in fact helping out the enemy by teaching other men how to dance a cool jitterbug, but Lornie had a gentle soul and a generous spirit, and he was just happy to see more people dancing the night away.

Things had been looking up in Flint by 1941. The Roosevelt policies of putting everyone back to work, plus the beginning of industrial production in anticipation of American involvement in a war that had started two years earlier in Europe and the Far East, was enough to prevent a factory town like Flint, Michigan, from collapsing entirely. Bill and Frank and Lornie all had WPA jobs right out of high school (a fact they tried to hide when speaking to girls). By the summer of '41 Frank had already held down numerous jobs from hawking flyers for a local grocery store to driving an egg truck to (briefly) driving a truck full of the maximum-size (6 oz.), green-tinted Coke bottles. Each of the boys eventually landed the coveted General Motors assembly-line job. Frank, not looking forward to the monotony and repetition of placing the same nodule on an AC Spark Plug 4,800 times a day, took a night class to learn how to type, hoping to get a clerk's job in the factory's office. But he couldn't type as fast as the girls, so he was relegated to Plant 7, line 2, spark plug pin insertion.

Eventually his three brothers saw a bigger world in their future and quit the factory ("Sales, Frank — that's where the money is!"), and their combined incomes in 1941 were enough to pay the rent on their mother's home and cease the constant upheaval of being two steps ahead of the landlord and his good friend, the county sheriff.

And after the rent and the food and the coal bills were paid, there was enough left over for the bus ride to the Knickerbocker. Or, if it was a special weekend, to the Industrial Mutual Association auditorium where the likes of Tommy Dorsey and Frank Sinatra would play as they passed through the Midwest. It was, for young working men, a version—a *version*—of paradise.

So it came with some disappointment that the Emperor decided to interfere with their lives on the morning of December 7, 1941. The attack, the elimination of nearly the entire Pacific fleet, came as a shock to the nation. The following day, even as President Roosevelt issued his call to arms, young men flocked to recruitment centers like the one in Flint, Michigan, which had been hastily set up in a large grade school on the near east side of town. The Brothers Moore, though, would not be among those signing up that day, or the next day, or the next week or the following month, or the month or two or three or six after that. It wasn't that they weren't upset at Hirohito or any less patriotic or any less eager to go kick some Axis ass. After all, they weren't known at St. Mary's High as "dancers." They were Irish, and they never shied away from a fight.

It's just that this new war was, well, poorly timed. Bill had just gotten married, and Frank was sweet on a girl who had been the valedictorian of her class at Flint Northern. She planned to go to Ann Arbor, to the University of Michigan, to study medicine, which in those days meant she would become a nurse. Frank had some ambition for further education, but the recent union victories at GM meant that he was making good money, and Ann Arbor might as well have been on the moon. Nonetheless, the valedictorian seemed worth pursuing, so this war was unwelcome at best.

Frank's father had served in the Marines in World War I, and his uncle Tom had been a doughboy in the trenches in France during that same war. Having been gassed by the Germans, Tom was of ill health and thus lived with Frank and the family in Flint. Frank got to see up close the effect that nasty war had on these two good men. Neither could explain to Frank why America had gone to war in 1917, and so when the drums began to beat again, Frank wanted to know exactly what this one was all about. Yes, it was enough that the nation was attacked — but was there something else we should know? Anything? Something? OK, well, those bastards destroying our fleet was certainly good enough for Frank. He was ready to go fight.

He waited until the last minute, until the draft notices started to arrive in July 1942. He decided he didn't want to be drafted into the Army — "every man's for himself in that operation," he would say — and so on the first of August, 1942, Frank went down to the recruitment center at the large grade school and signed up to be a Marine. A Marine? "The Marines fight as a team," he told his friends. "They look out for each other." But his brothers (all of whom would soon enlist themselves: Bill in the Air Force, Herbie in the Navy, and Lornie in the paratroopers, where he would die from a sniper's bullet in the last months of the war) told him, "Marines are sent into the worst of situations. You'll get killed in the Marines."

"Perhaps," said Frank, "but the Marines never leave a man behind." After thirteen years of crushing Depression, Frank had had enough of being left behind.

The enlistment officer asked him when he could get his affairs in order to ship out.

"What's the last possible date I have?" Frank asked.

"August 31," the recruiter replied.

"I'll take that day."

Frank spent that final month enjoying the life he had: working, going to Knickerbocker's, helping his mother. On the day he packed his duffel bag, he left quietly and went down to the bus station by himself. When he arrived he found himself waiting on a bench with fifteen other Marine recruits. A photographer from the *Flint Journal* snapped a picture of them and captioned it "READY!" The look on Frank's face in the photograph was anything but READY! and apparently this wasn't noticed by the copy editor, who let the ironic caption go through and be printed on the page the next day. By that time, Frank was on a train, on his way to basic training outside San Diego, California.

The delay in enlisting not only had bought Frank a few extra months of peace, it caused him to miss the first large Marine amphibious landing in the war—on the island of Guadalcanal. Over 7,000 Marines and soldiers would be killed, along with 29 ships sunk and an amazing 615 planes lost. Frank would not arrive in the South Pacific until the end of the Guadalcanal campaign, and thus he avoided one of the worst massacres of the war. But there would be plenty of other opportunities to die in the next three years.

"Private Moore," the sergeant whispered. "Cap'n wants ya."

It was sometime around 11:00 p.m. on Christmas Eve, 1943. Frank Moore wasn't sure if it was Christmas Eve or

Christmas Day, and he didn't care much for this thing called the International Date Line that meant he was always a day ahead of his life, the life he left back home. Instead of trying to do the math, he just decided to keep himself on "Flint time." Easier. Friendlier.

He and a thousand other Marines had bunked down early on this night on the transport ship as it headed toward the battle on New Britain, an island that was part of Papua New Guinea, a few hundred miles off the coast of Australia. There wasn't much Christmas celebrating going on, though there were, no doubt, many, many prayers being said. Because at 0700 hours they would be loaded into amphibious assault vehicles and lowered into the Pacific Ocean just a mile off the coast of Cape Gloucester, New Britain. But for now, Captain Moyer wanted to see Frank.

"I hear you can type," Moyer said to the young private.

"Yes, sir, sorta," replied Frank, not quite understanding what typing had to do with killing Japanese or Christmas.

"I want you to stay behind here on the ship," Moyer said. "I need someone who can type up the casualty reports."

"But sir…"

"Listen, this is important. We need to be accurate and we need to be accountable. If not to HQ, at least to the families of these men."

This was, Frank realized, a free Get-Out-of-Dying card being offered to him. Stay behind on the boat. Don't die in the wave of bullets and mortars that will spray across the chests and the necks and the heads of his friends and fellow Marines. Live for another day. But there were no guarantees of living in the days or weeks ahead.

He had figured out in the previous months of fighting on

New Guinea that the South Pacific theater was a slaughter-house. He wondered: If he had joined the Army instead of the Marines, would he be somewhere in the Mediterranean right now? He figured there was no way that Italians and Germans were fighting tooth-and-nail like these Japanese. Sure, the enemy in Europe wanted to win, but not at the expense of everyone in their unit dying. After all, what's the point of winning if you're all dead? He would like to ask a Japanese soldier that question, but never really got the chance as none of them were into being captured, or worse, surrendering.

The offer from Captain Moyer seemed mighty tempting, but Frank knew that staying behind on the ship was only delaying the inevitable. If your time is up, you might as well go on Christ's birthday.

"Captain, I'd rather stay with my battalion. If it's OK with you, sir, let me stay with my buddies."

Moyer had been impressed with Private Moore and how he had volunteered to help the chaplain during Mass, serving as his "altar boy." Though Moyer was Episcopalian, he often attended the close-enough-to-count Catholic services and observed how reverently Moore treated the whole ceremony, even if it was being said on the stump of a fallen coconut tree. He thought he'd give Moore a chance to live another day, but the kid wasn't biting.

"OK," he told the private, "you're dismissed. Get some sleep."

"Thank you, sir." Frank returned to his bunk and for the first time in a long time had no problem falling asleep.

At 0500 hours the booming sounds of the artillery guns from the nearby American destroyers made Frank stop and wonder if he had made a mistake turning the captain down.

Someone mentioned that Moyer and a reconnaissance party had slipped down into the bay two hours earlier with the intent of landing before the invasion, under cover of darkness, in order to find out just what the First Marine Division was about to face.

Tucked tightly into his amphibious lander with thirty or so other Marines, Frank said one final prayer before the door came down and deposited everyone into the slosh of chest-high saltwater. They were nothing more than the fish in the Japanese shooting barrel. The first thing Frank noticed was that it was nearly impossible to walk, that it was impossible to fire his gun, and although he was a human target for Japanese snipers in need of some early-morning target practice, Frank's focus was on some very short-term goals: one foot forward, now the other foot. Keep gun above head so it doesn't get wet. Now one more foot forward. This seemed like it took an hour or more (it took less than five minutes), and Frank kept wondering how it was that he was still alive. Dumbroski, a sergeant who had been the big, tough bully of the unit until this moment, was frozen in place, weeping. Keep moving. Leg. Foot. Rifle. Dry.

And then suddenly he was on the beach. A beach of black volcanic sand. Red blood on black sand made for an odd mixture; both caught the light of the morning sun and glistened with more life than they deserved. The brush of the jungle was just a few yards away and appeared to offer the best chance for cover from the incoming shells being fired from a cliff about a mile away. Within a couple hours most of the Marines had landed and the casualties were not as great as anticipated. The Japanese had decided not to fight this battle on the beach, perhaps because the Marines had set off enough smoke bombs so that the enemy had difficulty seeing the invading Americans.

Frank's battalion moved out on the left flank to head toward higher ground, while other battalions pushed straight through the jungle. Frank and his men were again surprised at the absence of Japanese gunfire or resistance. Within the hour, moving fast, they began to climb Hill 250. It seemed too easy.

They were right.

For some reason they had found a magical crack in their own front lines and, without realizing it, slipped right through it with no one noticing. They were now in Japanese territory, a good thousand yards ahead of what everyone believed were the front lines of the United States Marine Corps.

Their map indicated it might be Hill 250. It is generally believed that during a battle, it is better to be on top of the hill than at the bottom. You don't need to be a West Point graduate to understand that. So Frank and the others began to make their way up the hill. The Japanese at the top of the hill didn't want any company that day, so they lobbed everything they had on the lost battalion. Then, out of nowhere, a monsoon rain erupted, making it impossible to see more than a few yards ahead. That gave the Marines the cover and the advantage they needed, and they quickly made their way up Hill 250. With grenades, 37mm machine guns, and sheer force of will, they took the hill. The Japanese on top of the hill had no way of knowing that this was just a small unit of Marines; they assumed that they were facing an invading horde of hundreds, if not thousands, of Americans. So they retreated down the other side, where the larger force of their Japanese army lay in wait.

As the Marines secured the ridge, the rain stopped. This first victory felt good—not exactly flag-planting good (they had barely advanced onto the three-hundred-mile-long island) but good enough—and there were remarkably no casualties.

It was then they heard the sound of airplanes. This was a welcome sound, as it was the sweet hum of a Wright Cyclone engine on a B-25, the sound that said, *Here we are, boys! The Cavalry to the rescue!* The grunts on the ground had cleared the hill—now it was time for the flyboys to swoop in and take out the valley!

But as Frank squinted at the planes backlit against the now-punishing tropical sun, he saw a plume of smoke coming out of one of them. The plane had been hit. How could that be? They were coming from behind, coming from American-held territory—who would have shot at an American plane from back there?

In fact, it *was* Americans back on the beachhead who had actually fired on the American planes, thinking (wrongly) that they were Japanese bombers. The American planes, in turn, thought that the Japanese had hit them (two of the B-25s went down in flames), and so when they looked down on Hill 250 and saw the "Japanese" whom they thought fired on them, well, it was payback time.

But, of course, these were not Japanese on Hill 250; these were the men of my dad's unit.

Swooping in at almost treetop level, the B-25s strafed Hill 250 with their bullets. Frank and the men had no time to signal that they were on the same side. There was nowhere to run for cover. They threw themselves down and prayed for the best. Frank could see the tracer rounds coming from the planes straight at them. He accepted that this was the end of his life, and he closed his eyes as that life, with all of its scenes of joy and poverty and family, sped by him in an instant. He knew that the next instant would be his last.

When Frank opened his eyes, his life was not over. But the scene in front of him was one he had never wanted to see. Lying beside him was one of his friends. His face was gone. Frank looked up and over the body to see a dozen or so of the men in his unit lying there, riddled with bullets, many crying out for help, some alive, some perhaps dead, their uniforms beginning to stain broadly with the blood that was oozing out of the numerous wounds. In all, fourteen Marines were hit and one was dead. Only Frank was alive and untouched. For a moment he was convinced that he must be dead, too, as it was simply not possible to survive that many bullets fired from so low, bullets that not only penetrated the bodies of his comrades but also chewed up the volcanic rock all around him. How could this be? Why was he untouched? And why in God's name did this good Marine next to him die at the hands of other Americans?

Frank had little memory of what happened next. Apparently the Marines on the front lines behind him had witnessed the whole stunning incident. They reached Frank and the others as Frank was trying to administer first aid to his buddies. Medics and stretchers were called in, and after the wounded were attended to, Frank was brought back down to the staging point near the shore.

"I'm OK," Frank said after a few hours of rest. "I'm ready to go back."

"It'll be night soon," a corporal told him. "I think it's OK if you stay here with us."

He thought perhaps someone would want to talk to him, to file a report or something. But there was a war, a real war, going on, and after he asked one lieutenant why this tragic mistake had happened, he was told this happens in war all the time. "You just have to move on and win." After that, Frank never asked about it again.

The following day, he got word that Captain Moyer and the five men with him had all been killed on their recon mission. He could see that this was the way it was going to be. Death, then more death. Soon another captain from the front line appeared with two privates who had "cracked" under duress.

"These guys are my wiremen," he told the officer in charge. "They're no good to me now. Trade me these for one of your guys."

The lieutenant looked at Frank.

"This guy's a machine gunner. I'll trade you him."

"Don't need a gunner, need a wireman. Someone who can carry spools of radio wire, run fast, and duck."

"This guy knows how to duck. Believe me."

"A wireman?" Frank asked. "Carry and run the radio wire from the front lines back to the command post?"

"Yup."

"No more firing a gun?"

"Nope. You can't fire a gun and carry wire at the same time. But they will fire at you. They go after the radio guys first so we can't talk to HQ. You take this job, you better have some guts and know some fancy dance moves to dodge those Japs."

Guts? Dance moves? Why didn't he say that in the first place?

"I was a wireman for the rest of the war," my dad said as he finished his story. "I would never carry a machine gun again. I would be shot at over and over, but I couldn't shoot back because I had to carry the spool of wire. It was kind of a crazy decision."

I thanked him for telling me all this, but I was thirteen and, by the end of it, I was fidgeting around and checking the clock. I wanted to go outside and hang with the guys. My dad noticed none of that, as his mind was still back in 1943.

"Every Christmas I think about that day. I got to live, somehow…lucky, I guess…," he said, his voice trailing off.

"Dad, um, can I go, now? Maybe you can tell me another war story later?"

It would be years before I heard one again.

A Holy
Thursday

"Don't just stand there, the niggers are comin'!"

Walter was twelve, and he was only trying to be helpful.

"Whaddaya mean?" I asked while standing in his driveway with my baseball glove and a bat, hoping to get a game going before sundown.

"The niggers in Detroit are rioting! My dad says they're on their way *here* right now! We're headin' up north!"

And sure enough they were. They were wasting no time hurriedly jamming their station wagon full of food and supplies and shotguns. Walter's mother, Dorothy, was shouting orders to her six boys about what to load and what to leave behind. I stood there in awe of the precisionlike nature of this operation. It was as if they had run this drill many times before. A few doors down, I noticed another family doing the same thing. I started to get scared.

"Walter, I don't understand. Why are you guys doing this? Are you going to come back?"

"Don't know. Just gotta git. Dad says the niggers from Detroit are on their way here and will be here any minute!"

On their way to where? *Here?* They're coming to *Hill Street?*

"Walter, I think Detroit's a long way away from here."

"Nope, no, no, it's not! Dad says they could be here just like that!" Walter snapped his fingers, as if by doing so he could magically make a Negro appear to prove his point to me. "They're going to get together with the niggers in Flint and then come 'n' kill us all!"

Although I had never heard anything this fantastical before, I was *not* unfamiliar with the attitudes in the town of Davison when it came to the issue of the Colored People. Black people — niggers, as many wistfully called them — were simply not welcomed. There was not, to my knowledge, a single black person living among the 5,900 people who inhabited the city of Davison. Considering we were just outside Flint, a city with fifty thousand black people, this was not an accident. Through the years, realtors knew what to do if there were any inquiries from Negroes looking to move out of Flint and into Davison. And the unwritten, though not always unspoken, agreement among the city residents was to never sell your house to a black family. This kept things nice and orderly and white for decades.

This attitude did not exist a century before. In the 1850s and 1860s, Davison was a stop on the Underground Railroad, a series of secret destinations that stretched from the Ohio River Valley north through Indiana and Ohio and into Michigan, all the way to the Canadian border, where escaping black slaves would find their freedom. There were over two hundred secret stops along the Railroad in the state of Michigan. Members of the new Republican Party in Michigan worked extensively on the Underground Railroad, assisting the runaway slaves, giving them safe passage, and hiding them in their homes.

But bounty hunters from the South were allowed by federal law to come into states like Michigan and legally kidnap any slaves they found and bring them back home to their masters. This was one of the many compromises the North had made over the years to keep the slave states happy and in the Union. Thus, a slave was not free by simply escaping to a free state; he or she had to make it all the way to Canada.

So it was with some risk that hundreds of Michiganders set about to protect the victims of this cruel and barbaric system. One such person owned the home on the corner of Main and Third streets in Davison, a mere fifty-nine miles to the Canadian border. It was said in later years that the family in this house had a hiding space in their cellar and that the townspeople kept this secret from the marauding bounty hunters. (This house would eventually become my grandparents' home.)

It became a sense of pride in Davison that the village was participating in something important, something historic. Many of the boys in the area would soon be off to the Civil War, and when slavery ended, the people of Davison were proud of the small role they played in making this happen.

Such was not the mood on a sweltering August day in the summer of 1924 when twenty thousand people gathered at the Rosemore racetrack in Davison to attend a rally of the Benevolent Knights of the Ku Klux Klan. Looking at the photos from that day, with thousands of citizens in white robes, one wonders how hot they must have been, especially with those pointed hoods! Many, though, did not wear the hoods, as there really was no reason to hide their identities because it seemed that everyone and their third cousin was a member of this fine organization dedicated to terrorizing and lynching black people.

But in the summer of 1924, it wasn't so much the Negroes in Flint (most of whom had learned to know their place and remain quiet) that were the issue. No, the problem confronting the Klan on this Sunday afternoon was the "Papists"—the Catholics. Catholics, it seemed, had starting running for office. They were moving into neighborhoods meant for white Protestants, and this did not seem like the natural order of things. Catholics had also started to intermarry, something that created a deep, sick feeling among the gathered faithful. Marriage, as you were supposed to know, was to be between a Protestant man and a Protestant woman (and, yes, it could be between a Catholic man and a Catholic woman—but not between a Catholic and a Protestant).

My mother's dad (Grandpa Wall) did not understand such rules (and he was to be forgiven as he was, after all, from Canada). In 1904 he, an Anglican, married my grandmother, a Roman Catholic. For his troubles, the Klan burned a cross on his front yard in Davison.

"It wasn't much of a cross," my grandmother would later remark. "You'd think we'd rate more than a four-foot-high cross!"

Throughout the 1920s and 1930s, Davison and other parts of Michigan were hotbeds of enthusiastic bigotry. From Father Charles Coughlin railing against the Jews each Sunday on his nationwide radio show from Royal Oak, to the Sunday Klan rallies in Davison (and Kearsley Park in Flint), there

was enough to be ashamed of and enough to wonder about
how far the state had drifted from the days of the loving
humanity of the newborn Republican Party, a party that not
only ended slavery but also the death penalty and sought to
give women the right to vote. Now what we had were scenes
like Henry Ford getting medals from Hitler.

It was the last week of July 1967, and all that was on my
mind was that we were soon moving six blocks away to a
paved street! But down in Detroit, some sixty miles away, the
city was indeed in flames. It had been on the news the night
before. From what I could gather the police had tried to arrest every black person at an after-hours club that was holding a party for two returning Vietnam vets. This offended
the neighborhood and triggered immediate protests, which
then turned to violence. The National Guard was called in
and much of southeastern Michigan was convinced that the
race riots that broke out in Watts two years prior—and in
Newark, just two weeks earlier— were now in full bloom
in our state.

What was not understood at the time was that, in fact,
this was an *uprising* of Detroit's poor—and those poor found
the police and the Guard going berserk and gunning down
any suspicious person with black skin.

Up in Flint, though, things were different. The year before, the city had elected the country's first black mayor,
Floyd McCree. McCree was a beloved figure in Flint, a city
that was still nearly 80 percent white. Flint's voters would
also soon pass the country's first open housing law, making
it illegal to discriminate when renting or selling a home.

Although Flint's neighborhoods were by and large still seg-regated, there seemed to be some sort of desire to "fix things" when it came to the issue of race.

Which made Walter's family and their crazed fleeing seem all the more absurd to me as I stood in their driveway. Flint was not going to explode, and the black people there were not going to kill me. I didn't even need to check in with a parent to confirm that. Actually, my biggest fear was that my mother might have heard Walter saying "nigger," a word that was never spoken and specifically forbidden in our household. I would suffer some embarrassment if she yelled out to me to get back in the house, but there was nothing to worry about, as she and my dad were busy planning our move to Main Street.

The station wagon was filled to the brim with provisions and paranoia, and so off they peeled down the street, their tires kicking up the gravel as they fled to safety.

Flint did not riot, but Detroit raged on for a week. Each night on the local news, war scenes from Vietnam were re-placed with war scenes from Detroit. It jolted the entire state. Detroit, this beautiful, bountiful city, would never be the same again. In later years it would be hard for anyone to understand what that meant, but those of us who grew up within a stone's throw saw Detroit as our Emerald City, this place so full of life, its sidewalks packed with people, its stores the envy of the Midwest, its universities and parks and gardens and art museum (with its Diego Rivera mural), the Detroit of Aretha and Iggy and Seger and the MC5, Belle Isle and Boblo, and the twelfth floor of Hudson's, where the *real* Santa sat on his throne and promised us a gift-wrapped fu-ture of endless possibilities and eternal cheer, *on Comet and*

Cupid and . . . Donner . . . and . . . Blitzen . . . and . . . and . . . and in the blink of an eye, it was gone. All gone. It wasn't like we didn't know where it went or that we couldn't remember why it went. We knew *when* it went; we knew the exact moment *when* it went. It went up Woodward and down Twelfth Street, over to Grand River and down past Tiger Stadium and it didn't stop until it took our last morsel of optimism with it. And then *we* ran, *da-doo-run-run,* to get away from *them* to leave *them* behind, to let them suffer and wallow in the misery they'd never really climbed out of since we, the Michiganders, led the charge to free them. President Johnson sent the 82nd Airborne Division into Detroit on the fourth day, complete with tanks and machine guns a-blazing, the Vietnam War finally at home. When it was over, forty-three people were dead and two thousand buildings had been blasted apart or burned to the ground, and our spirit was buried deep under the rubble.

It was in this backdrop that my dad took the family to a Tigers ball game in Detroit just a couple weeks later. The tickets had been purchased at the beginning of the summer, and although my mother voiced her concern over the wisdom of such a "trip" to Detroit at this time, I suppose they decided that to throw away tickets they'd paid for was a worse crime, and so off we went.

It was a Thursday night, an unusual time for us to drive to Detroit to see a ball game. My dad preferred to drive there during the daytime; all previous excursions were made to day games on Saturdays or Sundays. But this was a game against the Chicago White Sox, who that year had Tommy

John and Hoyt Wilhelm pitching for them, and former Tiger Rocky Colavito in the outfield. My dad thought this would be a good game, as both teams were in a tight pennant race.

It wasn't. The Tigers lost, 2–1. But it was my first night game, and it may not make me sound like much of a sports guy, but it was truly a magical moment for me to see that historic field bathed in such a bright light, as if it came from the heavens, or at least a nearby Fermi nuclear plant.

When the game was over, there was a tension in the crowd as people exited into the neighborhood that bordered the riot area. It was the March of the Frightened White People, a kind of walk-run people do when they hear the sound of a tornado siren. Walk, don't run — but run! *Run for your life!*

We got to our car, a '67 Chevy Bel Air, which my dad had parked in a paid lot instead of on the usual free side street. Saving money on parking in this post-riot month was not on anyone's mind. Getting out alive was.

We pulled out of the lot off Cochrane Street and headed down Michigan Avenue until we came to the right turn that would take us onto the Fisher Freeway north. As we approached the expressway ramp, steam began coming out of the hood of our car. Thinking there might be a gas station on the other side of the entrance ramp, my father continued on the overpass and into uncharted territory. It was there that the Chevy simply died. I looked up at the street sign. We were on Twelfth Street, ground zero for the riots. I pointed this out to my dad, and he became agitated in a way I rarely saw.

"Everybody just stay calm," he said in a voice that was nothing resembling calm. *"Lock the doors!"*

We obeyed immediately, but our father saw the growing terror on our faces, and he took this as a lack of faith in his ability to get us out of this mess.

"Dammit! I don't know why we came down here! Wasn't anyone paying attention?!"

That he could be both philosophical about why we were in Detroit *and* accusatory over an accidental breech in engine fluids was impressive, I thought.

My mother and sisters got very quiet. I was sure I could hear the thumping of our hearts, but the actual thumping was being caused by a black man knocking on our window.

"You need help?" he asked, as panic filled the Chevy's interior.

My dad answered, "Yes."

"Well, let's take a look at what the problem is," the black man offered.

"Just stay inside," my dad said. "I'll handle this." He did not look like the guy who wanted to handle this.

I looked out the back window to see that the man's car was parked behind us. And in the car was a woman and two or three kids.

"You at the ball game?" he asked my dad, as they met at the steaming hood.

"Yes."

"We were, too! Came down from Pontiac. Man, that sure was some sorry game!"

The two dads lifted the hood and poked around and soon figured out the problem.

"We got a bum radiator hose," my dad shouted back to us. The black man went back to his car and opened the trunk.

He brought out a jug of water and gave it to my dad to pour into the radiator.

"This should get you a few blocks to the gas station," the stranger said. "But I'd go back in the other direction."

My dad thanked him for his kindness and offered to pay him something, but the man would have none of it.

"Just glad I could help," the man said. "Hope someone would do that for me if I needed it. You want me to follow you?"

My dad, probably still wondering if we would indeed have stopped for him if *he'd* been in trouble, said, no, we'll be fine, we'll just head back to Michigan Avenue where surely someone would be open.

And someone was. The gas station attendant replaced the radiator hose, filled the radiator up, and we were on our way.

"We were lucky," my dad said somewhere around Clarkston. "That was a good man we ran into. And that was the last night game we're going to."

Eight months later, and just six days before the Opening Day of a new Detroit Tigers season (one in which they would go on to win the World Series), Holy Week was approaching. It was Easter time, and this year the nuns thought it would be a good idea for us to see where the original "Last Supper" on Holy Thursday came from.

"The apostles and Jesus were Jews," Sister Mary Rene told us. "They were not Christian or Catholic. They were Jews and they observed Jewish traditions. And so during this week, Jesus had come to Jerusalem to celebrate the Passover, the Jewish feast commemorating the time Jews were told by God to smear lamb's blood on their doorposts in Egypt. This was done so that when the Angel of Death was making his rounds to kill all the firstborn sons of the Egyptians, he'd know where the Jewish houses were so he could skip them. This was God's way of sending a message to the Pharaoh: let Moses and the Jewish people go or I'll fuck you up some more."*

OK, well, whew, that was some story, and as I was the first (and only) son in my family, I found it mildly interesting if not creepy. God, in the Old Testament, seemed to have some sort of chip on his shoulder. He was constantly whacking whole tribes or tossing guys inside whales' stomachs. Real attitude problem, I used to think. And why wasn't his Angel of Death smart enough to know which ones were the Egyptian homes and which were the Jewish homes without having to mess up the Jewish front doors with difficult-to-remove bloodstains? Couldn't he just tell them apart from the different styles of architecture each group employed — the Egyptians with their split-level colonials, and the Jews with their fixer-upper slave huts? Plus, wouldn't that blood on the door make the Jews less safe, especially considering the next morning, all the Egyptians are going to wake up to find they've got a dead kid in the house and then they're like, "Let's go get the Jews!" But then someone says, "How the hell will we find them?" and then someone else runs in and says, "Hey, they've all got blood out on their porches! Just burn down the huts with the lamb's blood!"

Sister Mary Rene, like Sister Raymond and the other nuns, took great pains to let us know that, contrary to what

---

* She did not use the F word. I just thought it would be cool if she did.

we may have heard, the Jews did not kill our Lord and Savior. The Romans did. Jesus was Jewish, was born Jewish, and died Jewish and he'd be very upset if he thought we blamed his own people for his demise — which was supposed to happen anyway so that he could rise from the dead and start our religion! Yay!

The nuns contacted one of the three synagogues in Flint and asked if they could bring some seventh- and eighth-grade students over for a Passover dinner so we could learn the Jewish tradition of this time of year. The rabbi was more than happy to accommodate and we spent a week learning to sing "Hava Nagila" as a sort of thank-you to them.

I didn't remember much about this event they called a seder, other than someone asked four questions and we couldn't put the chocolate cake on the dish that had what passed for beef.

It was one week from Holy Thursday, 1968, the Thursday before Palm Sunday, the day that Jesus would enter Jerusalem and prepare for what would be his last Passover on the following Thursday. At St. John's during Lent there was either a Lenten service or Mass on each weeknight. I was asked to be an altar boy on this particular Thursday. There were gospel readings and Communion and the consecrating of the altar with incense.

I was given the silver censer that held the burning coal onto which you placed the incense and then swung it around the altar and throughout the church. This had all of my favorite activities rolled into one: fire, smoke, and emitting a strange odor.

When Mass was over, one of my duties was to take the censer outside the church and dispose of the smoldering incense and coal onto the ground, putting it out with my foot.

It was a chilly evening on this early April night, and the vestments that I wore over my clothes were not enough to keep out the piercing wind that was blowing up into my black robe and making me want to get back inside as quickly as possible. I emptied the remnants of the incense out onto the still-frozen ground and rubbed them around, pressing hard with the heel of my shoe, until they were extinguished. It was then that a man in the parking lot, a parishioner who had gone out early to his car to warm it up, had heard a news bulletin on the radio as it came on. Excited, he wanted to share it with everyone as they were departing the church. With his car door open, he stood up on the floorboard so all coming out of Mass could hear his joyful announcement:

"King's been shot! They've shot King! Martin Luther King!"

At that moment—in what I will recall for the rest of my life as one of the most depressing things I would ever witness—a *cheer* went up from the crowd. Not from everyone, not even from most. But from more than a few, a spontaneous joyful noise came out of the mouths that had just held the body of Christ. A whoop and holler and a yell and a cheer. I was still processing the stunning and tragic news about Reverend King I had just heard—heard from a man who said it with such surety that all would be well now, this Negro, this nigger, this terrorist, was somehow no longer going to bother us anymore. Hallelujah.

I jerked my head in the direction of the church door to see who in God's name was celebrating this moment. Some people had smiles. But most were stunned. Some remained silent, while others rushed to their cars so they could turn on their radios and hear for themselves that this troublemaker was no longer with us. A woman began to cry. People passed the news back inside the church to those who had not yet come out. There was much commotion, and all I could think about was that stupid Angel of Death — and who the hell forgot the lamb's blood tonight in Memphis? There would be no pass over.

What was special about this night? Every Easter, from then on and for the rest of my life, I would know the bitter answer.

The Exorcism

"KICK OUT THE JAMS, motherfuckers!" I shouted up the stair-well. O'Malley, my bully of a roommate, slapped me hard across the face.

"Shut the fuck up! Father Waczeski is right there!"

I turned quickly around to see if the priest had heard me, but there was no priest anywhere to be found. O'Malley, who was a year older than me, just wanted to slap me. He laughed his usual sinister laugh, and hit me again.

"Stop it," I said. "I was just singing that new MC5 song."

"Then sing the *clean* version, the one they play on the radio—'Kick out the jams, *brothers and sisters.*'"

What the fuck did he care about a "clean" version? O'Malley was the opposite of anything clean. He was more a version of every mother's nightmare. What was a thug like him doing at the seminary?

When I was fourteen I decided it was time to leave home. Mostly bored with school since the first grade, but politely biding my time to keep everybody happy, I realized I could do more good for myself and the world (wherever that was) if I became a Catholic priest. I'm not sure of the day when I got

155

"the calling," but I can guarantee you there was no vision or voice from above, no burning bush or Virgin sighting. Most likely I was just watching the news, probably saw one or both of the Berrigan brothers, the radical Catholic priests, breaking into a draft office and destroying the records of young men who were to be sent to Vietnam, and I said to myself, "Now, *that's* what I wanna do when I grow up!" I liked the idea of the Action Hero Priest, and I thought I could do that. I liked seeing priests marching with Rev. King and getting arrested. I liked priests helping César Chávez organize the farmworkers. I wasn't completely sure what it all meant; it just seemed like a decent thing to do. It was pretty basic: you had a responsibility to help those worse off than you. I was never going to play for the Pistons or the Red Wings, so the priesthood seemed like a good second choice.

But first I had to convince my parents to let me leave home. They did not like this idea. These were the people who wouldn't let me skip first grade, and they were definitely less inclined to let me skip town. But I told them I had "a calling," and if you were a devout Catholic in those days and your kid told you he had "a calling," you had better not risk getting in between the Holy Spirit and your only begotten son. They consented, reluctantly.

The seminary training would take twelve years before I could be ordained a priest. Four years of high school, four years of college, and four years of theological training. The high school part was optional, but for those who had the calling, there were two seminaries in Michigan for high school students: Sacred Heart in Detroit and St. Paul's in Saginaw. It was less than a year after the Detroit riots, so Sacred Heart was out of the question for my parents. St. Paul's it was.

On the first night after my mother and father dropped me off at the seminary in September 1968, I instantly began to question the wisdom of my decision. My doubts were not driven by the strict rules I had to follow: Up at 5:00 a.m. for prayers, long periods of enforced silence, barred from your room from 8:00 a.m. to 8:00 p.m., difficult studies (nine weeks spent dissecting just one Shakespeare play), hard labor and chores, and severe punishment for violating any of the rules. Freshmen were prohibited from watching any television or listening to the radio for an entire year. You were strictly confined to the campus—with the exception of 2:00 p.m. to 4:00 p.m. on Saturdays, during which time you could walk two miles to the strip mall, grab a Whopper, and rush back.

But I was OK with all of that. My trouble was not with the system (at least not at first). It was with the two roommates I had been assigned to share a room with. Mickey Bader and Dickie O'Malley. Mickey and Dickie. "The Ickies," as I called them (but only to myself). The problem with them being there at the seminary was that neither of them wanted to be a priest. No way. They were into girls, and partying, and smoking and sneaking off campus whenever they could. And pushing me around. They were what the adults referred to as "juvenile delinquents." They were rich kids, the sons of important men in their communities, and it seemed as if at least Dickie already had a number of run-ins with the law. Their parents decided that perhaps the seminary could straighten them out, and how they got through the intense interview process I had to go through to get into this place was beyond me. I came to the realization that their fathers had probably bought their way in, and the priests were obviously in need of any "charity," wherever they could find it.

Discovering that this was both a seminary *and* a reform school did not sit well with me, and it was clear to me that I was going to have to endure the constant harassment of Mickey and Dickie if I wanted to be a priest. When they found out I really believed in all this "religion crap," they were relentless in mocking me as I said my prayers, did my chores, practiced my Latin. They smeared applesauce over my sheets, placed *Playboy* centerfolds in the toilet bowl, and entertained themselves by seeing if a pair of scissors could alter the length of my pants. Although I was bigger than them, I did not want to resort to violence in order to have some peace and quiet, so I kept my distance from them.

There *were* two rules I decided early on that I just couldn't follow at the seminary, and I knew God would forgive me. In October 1968, the Detroit Tigers were headed to the World Series, and as part of our penance for being freshmen, we were not allowed to watch or listen to the games. I was convinced that this edict did not come from the Almighty, and so I snuck a transistor radio into my room and hid it inside my pillowcase. At night I would lie in bed and listen to the games, muffled as they were, through the pillow's duck feathers. The day games I missed.

The other rule was that you could not have any food in your room. As they were more interested in feeding our souls than our bodies, I decided to take care of the latter. That year, science had invented the *Frosted* Pop-Tart ("Proof of God's existence," I would say). I smuggled in boxes of these heavenly items and I would toast them by placing a sheet of paper on top of my lamp and sitting the Pop-Tart on it. I was eventually discovered by a priest who caught a whiff of burnt strawberry out in the hallway. I was given extra kitchen duties for a week and lost my Saturday afternoon escape privileges for a month.

The other thing I enjoyed doing was hanging out with the senior boys. They had a knack for coming up with ingenious pranks that they loved to play on the holy hierarchy. My contribution to this club was to concoct a powder that replaced the chapel's incense. It was called a "stink bomb," and when the altar boy put a scoop of this "incense" onto the hot coal in the censer, it let off the most god-awful stench, a combination of rotten egg odor and a locker room fungus. It cleared the church within minutes.

The other prank, for which I became legendary (but only as "Anonymous," as I was never discovered), involved an "entry" of mine in the school's annual science fair. Of course, I had no interest in science (unless science could make a chocolate fudge Pop-Tart, which it eventually did), but I did have an interest in pulling off the best stunt ever.

About an hour before the doors to the seminary's science fair were to be opened to the public, I quietly entered the exhibit hall and placed my "science project" on one of the tables. It was a simple, plain test tube that contained a clear liquid (in reality, cooking oil). I set it on its stand and placed a placard in front of it. It read:

NITROGLYCERINE:
DO NOT TOUCH OR WILL EXPLODE

It was five minutes before the opening, and I hid nearby so I could watch people's expressions when they saw the test tube of danger. At that moment, the science teacher, a short nun with thick glasses and in her seventies, came in to make a final pass through the fair to make sure everything was in place and all set to go. She came upon my addition to the fair and was surprised to see something on the table that she hadn't placed there. She took her glasses off and cleaned them, not exactly sure what this was she was looking at. As she bent over to read the card, she let out a scream and quickly waddled over to the fire alarm box, broke the glass, and pulled the lever.

I was mortified.* This had gone too far. I got out of there as fast as I could, and as the fire trucks arrived I watched the firemen go inside and retrieve the tube which they could tell was not nitroglycerine. The nuns and the priests apologized—and issued a fatwa on whoever was responsible for this. They never caught the culprit.

There are two types of fear: normal fears that are primal (fear of pain, fear of death), and then there is the fear of Father Ogg.

Ogg taught Latin and German at the seminary. The Church had also christened him with special powers, and he was the only one at the seminary to hold these powers. One night, he gathered together a few of us boys and asked us if we would like to see how these powers could be used. We were already scared of Father Ogg, but no one was going to admit that, and so we all agreed to let him show us.

He took us down into the "catacombs" of the seminary (a series of tunnels under the building) to perform a ceremony

---

* Yes, in the more violent future that lay ahead of us, this sort of thing would have resulted in my expulsion and jail time. But in 1969, it was just funny.

only he was allowed to perform. It was called the Rite of Exorcism.

Father Ogg was an exorcist.

It would be another three years before Hollywood would make Linda Blair's head spin in the William Friedkin film, so all we knew of exorcism was that it was a series of prayers and rituals performed over the body of someone whom Satan had possessed. The devil would be cast out and the victim would be saved. We were told by Father Ogg that he had a "one thousand percent batting average" when confronting Lucifer.

"I always win," he said.

He told us that he would show us the ceremony but it would only be "pretend," as none of us had shown any signs of being consumed by evil.

Yes, but wouldn't this be better, I thought, if there were someone here at St. Paul's who actually *was* evil? Of course it would! And of course there was.

"Father," I said with fake sincerity, "before you start, I think Dickie O'Malley is going to be really upset that we left him out of this. He keeps saying he doesn't believe you're an exorcist and that he'd like to see you try it out on him. Can I go get him?"

"Sure," Ogg said, somewhat miffed that anyone would question his devil-disappearing powers. "But make it quick."

I ran back upstairs and found Dickie where I thought he would be—outside the gym door having a smoke.

"Dickie!"

"Yeah, fuckface, whaddaya want?"

"Father Ogg says he wants you right now!"

"Yeah, well, tell him you couldn't find me."

"He said he saw you come out here to smoke, and that if you came now he wouldn't turn you in."

Dickie considered the offer of leniency carefully, took his last couple of drags, gave me a tap across the face, and followed me inside and down into the catacombs.

"Welcome, Dickie," Father Ogg said with a sly grin. "Thank you for volunteering."

Dickie looked at him with smug-filled puzzlement, but sensing that he was not going to be in trouble if he went along, he stepped forward, unaware of what was to happen next. I could only hope that in about twenty minutes from now there was going to be a new Dickie.

Father Ogg had brought an ominous black duffel bag with a red coat of arms on it and words embossed in Latin that I didn't understand. He reached down in it and pulled out a shaker filled with holy water, some holy oil, about a half-dozen dried-out olive branches and, um, a leather rope.

"Now, normally, Dickie, I would tie you down so you wouldn't be able to hurt me," Father Ogg said to the snickers of those present.

"I ain't gonna hurt you, Father!" Dickie protested. "And you ain't gonna tie me up. I was only smoking."

"Yes, sometimes smoke comes out of the possessed," Ogg said. "A few have caught on fire. But I don't think you have to worry about that tonight."

The exorcist then launched into a bunch of mumbo-jumbo, words and language I had never heard. To see this jabber coming out of his mouth a mile a minute gave me goosebumps. This was the real deal! It scared Dickie, too, and he stood there dumbfounded at what he was witnessing.

"*Exorcizo te, omnis spiritus immunde, in nomine Dei Patris omnipotentis, et in nomine Jesu Christi Filili ejus, Domini et Judicis nostri, et in virtute Spiritus Sancti, ut descedas ab hoc plasmate Dei Dickie O'Malley, quod Dominus noster ad templum, sanctum suum vocare dignatus est!*" Father Ogg continued, spraying holy water all over Dickie. Dickie did not like that.

"C'mon, Father! What is this?!"

"Be still. I am casting Satan out of you!"

I thought, with that, Dickie would bolt. Priest or no priest, he was not going to stand there in front of a bunch of other students and be humiliated. Or have it implied he was in cahoots with the devil.

Instead, Dickie didn't move. He was intrigued with the possibility that his accomplice was the mother of all hoodlums, Beelzebub himself. A sinister smile came across his face.

Father Ogg took the cap off the holy oil and smeared it on Dickie's forehead, cheeks, chin. He then took Dickie's head and placed it between his two hands and pressed it like he was in a vise.

"Oowww!" Dickie screamed. "That hurts."

It was nice to see Dickie hurt.

"*Silence!*" shouted Ogg in a voice that I swear wasn't human.

"*Ephpheta, quod est, Adaperire. In odorem suavitatis. Tu autem effugare, diabole; appropinquabit enim judicium Dei!*" he continued in some ancient tongue, or perhaps no tongue at all. I'm not even supposed to be sharing this with you, and to commit these words to paper makes me want to go and check the lock on my door (I'll be right back).

It was time for the olive branches. We were each given one and told to hold them out over Dickie—but not to touch him. Ogg then took his branch and started to wail on poor Dickie, careful not to whip him anywhere that might hurt.

"Christo Sancti!" Ogg yelled, causing Dickie to turn to me—the one who brought him into this—and scream, "Fuckin' moron! I'm gonna kill you!"

"Don't make me have to tie you down!" Ogg shouted. *"Abrenuntias Satanae? Et omnibus operibus ejus?"*

And at this moment, Dickie started to cry. Father Ogg, a bit surprised, stopped.

"Hey, hey, it's OK," the exorcist said in a comforting tone. "This isn't real. It was just a demonstration. You don't have the devil in you."

At least not now, I thought. I prayed that this exorcism, albeit a "practice" one, would have a real effect on this miserable bully.

But, alas, such was not the case. The next day I found my transistor radio in the toilet and my underwear all gone. One of the nuns would find them later that night in her own drawer, with the words, in magic marker, on each waistband: PROPERTY OF MICHAEL MOORE. I did not want to take the punishment for finking on Dickie, so I took the extra week of garbage duty instead and said nothing. Frankly, it was worth it just to have the extra time to myself so I could replay in my head Dickie being whacked with an olive branch, olive oil dripping from his face, and the Devil departing his miserable body.

Not all the time at the seminary was spent on my knees or observing strange rituals or playing pranks. I actually had one of the best and most challenging years of education I would ever have. The priests and nuns loved to teach literature and history and foreign languages. The class I had the toughest time with was Religion. I had a lot of questions.

"Why don't we let women be priests?" I asked one day, one of the many times that everyone in the class would turn around and stare at me as if I were some freak.

"You don't see any women among the apostles, do you?" Father Jenkins would respond.

"Well, it looks like there were always women around — Mary Magdalene, Mary, Jesus's mother, and his cousin what's-her-name."

"It's just not allowed!" was the end-of-discussion answer he would give to most of my questions — which included:

- "Jesus never said he was here to start the 'Catholic Church,' but rather that his job was to bring Judaism into a new era. So where did we get the idea of the Catholic Church?"
- "The only time Jesus loses his temper is when he sees all these guys loaning money in the Temple and he smashes up their operation. What lesson are we to draw from this?"
- "Do you think Jesus would send soldiers to Vietnam if he were here right now?"
- "In the Bible, there's no mention of Jesus from age twelve to age thirty. Where do you think he went? I have some theories…"

On the first day of English Lit class, Father Ferrer announced that we would spend nine weeks dissecting *Romeo and Juliet,* word by word, line by line—and he promised us that by the end of it, we would understand the structure and language of Shakespeare so well that for the rest of our lives we would be able to enjoy the genius of all his works (a promise that turned out to be true).

I have to say that, in retrospect, the choice of a heterosexual love story with characters who were our age and who were *having sex* was a bold move by this good priest. Or it was sadism. Because if we were to become priests, there would be no Juliet (or Romeo) allowed in our lives.

I devoured every line of *Romeo and Juliet,* and it spun my head and hormones into a wondrous web of excitement. Unfortunately, I had not read the rulebook before signing up for the seminary, and here's what it said:

YOU CAN **NEVER** HAVE SEX, NOT EVEN ONCE IN YOUR LIFE. ESPECIALLY WITH A WOMAN.

Now, had I read that in eighth grade, I'm not sure I would have understood all the ramifications of agreeing to this prohibition. By the time it was explained to me in ninth grade at the seminary, something seemed oddly wrong with this rule. Call me crazy, but I kept hearing voices in my head:

Mmmmmm . . . girls . . . gooooood . . . penis . . . haaaaappy.

The voices intensified on Tuesday and Thursday afternoons. That was when they bused the few of us seminarians who played a musical instrument into the Catholic high school in nearby Bay City to play with their school band. There were not enough of us to make up our own orchestra at the seminary, and the priests, who enjoyed culture and the arts and would often sit around and have conversations with each other in Italian, did not want those of us who were musically inclined to miss our "other callings."

I was placed in the clarinet section next to a girl named Lynn. Did I mention she was a girl? At the seminary I spent 1,676 hours of every week around only boys. But for these two glorious hours, I was in the vicinity of the other gender. Lynn's long, deft fingers that she used on her clarinet were a beauty to behold (as were her breasts and legs and smile— but I only wrote *smile* just in case one of the priests is still alive and reads this story because, truth be told, while her smile was pleasant, I have no recollection of it as it was obscured by her breasts and legs and anything else that didn't resemble a seminarian). Being in a coed Catholic high school band literally drove me insane.

I tried my best to think about The Rule and to offer up this desire as penance for even wondering what might exist under her Catholic schoolgirl uniform. But there is just so much penance a now fifteen-year-old can do, and one day I asked one of the other seminarians on the band bus "Who the hell made up this rule?!" He said he didn't know and that "it was probably God." Right.

One weekend, I reread all four gospels and nowhere— *nowhere!*—did it say that the apostles couldn't have sex, or get married, or be happy with their penises. As my after-school job was working as an assistant in the library, I did my own research. And here's what I found: The priests of the Catholic Church for the first one thousand years were married! They had sex! Peter, chosen by Jesus to be the first Pope, was married, as were most of the apostles. As were thirty-nine Popes!

But then some Pope in the eleventh century got it in

his head that sex sucked and wives sucked worse, and so he banned priests from marrying or having sex. It makes you wonder how all the other great twisted ideas throughout history got their start (like who came up with the card game Bridge?). They might as well have made it a sin to scratch when you have an itch.

I began spending a lot of time on the job in the library going into the basement level where all the old magazines were stored. The cultured priests subscribed to *Paris Match,* and let's just say that in France in 1969, women were inclined to "stay cool" in the summertime. All my first loves could be found right there, in the periodical archives of St. Paul's Seminary.

As we drew near to the end of our study of *Romeo and Juliet,* Father Ferrer announced that there was a new movie in the theaters based on the play and that we would be taking a field trip to see it. This version was by the Italian director Franco Zefferelli, and little did the priest know (or did he?) that his group of fifteen-year-old boys would be exposed for the first time to fifteen-year-old breasts, namely those on the body of the actress playing Juliet, Olivia Hussey.

That night, after seeing *Romeo and Juliet,* the freshmen moaning up and down the hallway sounded like a cross between a lost coyoté and a choir trying to tune itself. I will only say that I became on that night a grateful fan of Miss Hussey's—and a former seminarian to the Catholic priesthood. Thank you, Shakespeare. Thank you, Father Ferrer.

To Dickie's and Mickey's credit, they had no interest in using Shakespeare to inspire their male hormones as they were already "in country." They had little interest in wasting their seed on a cheap seminary bedsheet. Not when there were so many available girls in the greater Tri-City area.

I'm not sure when they began sneaking out at night, or when they found time to sneak the girls in, but these two Montagues obviously were in much demand. On the upside, this did give me the room to myself on a number of occasions. On the downside, once the priests were on to them, they thought I, too, was in on the sex ring. How little they knew me! I was far too busy trying to keep my focus on Vespers and Vietnam rather than Lynn the clarinet player, who was doing just fine in an imaginary state with me, the two of us, frolicking, on the Côte d'Azur.

On this particular night, I decided to take the suggestion of fellow seminarian Fred Orr and try some Noxzema Original Deep Cleansing Cream to help get rid of a few teenage zits. I rubbed the white cream all over my face and went to sleep facing the wall, not wanting Mickey and Dickie to ever catch me with this girl-stuff on my face.

"WAKE UP! I SAID, WAKE UP!!" Father Jenkins shouted, forcing me to tell Lynn in my dream that I'd be right back. I awakened from this pleasant sleep and saw two priests, Father Jenkins and Father Shank, shining police-size flashlights directly into my eyes.

"WHERE ARE THEY?!"

Obviously it was a raid, a surprise assault on the two active and public penises on my floor.

I looked over at their beds and saw that they were made up to look like someone was sleeping in them. Clearly, neither of the Ickies was home.

"Uh, I dunno," I replied, trying to sound awake.

"When did they leave?" Father Shank asked.

"How long have they been gone?" Father Jenkins added.

"I dunno," I repeated.

"Are you sure?" Jenkins asked pointedly. "There's no good that can come from you covering for them."

"The last thing I would do would be to cover for those two punks," I said, surprised at my un-Christian-like language.

"You've never left here with them?" Jenkins continued with his interrogation.

"No. I don't do what they do. I'm guessing they don't go to Burger King."

"How many times would you say they've done this?"

"Father, I don't mean to be disrespectful, but if you're only busting in here tonight for the first time, you clearly have no idea what's been going on."

"I don't like your tone," Jenkins replied.

"I'm sorry. It's my middle-of-the-night tone."

"What in God's name is that stuff on your face?"

Oh. Damn. "Just something the nurse told me to try."

"Where do you think they are?" Father Jenkins asked.

"You can follow their scent to the nearest place where girls are known to exist."

Giving the priests this much lip was not wise, but I didn't care. I, too, had discovered girls, and there was now a part of me that admired Mickey and Dickie for acting on their very normal feelings. Though I did feel sorry for whatever girls they were with.

By this time they had turned their flashlights off—and that one act would end up doing the Ickies in. Not able to see from the outside hallway that I had visitors, the boys quietly opened the door to our room—and were instantly startled, not just by the sight of the priests, but by the mass of white goo covering my entire face. They tried to run, but the priests quickly grabbed them and dragged them down the hall and out of my life forever.

The next morning the parents of my two roommates came to my room and cleaned out their sons' belongings. When I returned that evening I had the privilege that only a senior had—*my own room!* There was only a month left in the school year, but it was sublime. I held parties. I began to grow my hair longer for the first time. I acquired a peace sign and put it on my door. I had made the decision that the seminary wasn't for me, although I had learned much that would remain with me for a long while.

Three days before the semester ended, I made an appointment with my class dean, Father Duewicke, so I could go in and tell him of my decision to not pursue the priesthood.

I walked in and sat down in a chair in front of his desk.

"Soooo," Father Duewicke said in a strange, sarcastic tone. "Michael Moore. I have some unpleasant news for you. We have decided to ask you *not* to return for your sophomore year."

Excuse me? Did he just say what I thought he said? Did he just say they were...*kicking me out?!*

"Wait a minute," I said, agitated and upset. "I came in here to tell you that I was quitting!"

"Well, good," he said with a smarmy tone. "Then we're in agreement."

"You can't kick me out of here! I quit! That's why I wanted to talk to you."

"Well, either way, you won't be gracing us with your presence in the fall."

"I don't understand," I said, still hurting from the rug being pulled out from under me. "Why would you ask me not to come back? I've gotten straight A's, I do all my work, I haven't been in any serious trouble, and I've been forced to endure living in the juvie room with those two delinquents for most of this year. What grounds do you have to expel me?"

"Oh, that's simple," Father Duewicke said. "We don't want you here because you upset the other boys by asking too many questions."

"Too many questions about what? What does that mean? How can you say such a thing?"

"That's three questions right there in less than five seconds, thus proving my point," he said, while giving a mock look at his nonexistent watch. "You do not accept the rules or the teachings of our institution on the basis of faith. You always have a question. *Why's that? What's that for? Who said?* After a while, Mr. Moore, it gets tiring. You either have to accept things, or not. There's no in-between."

"So, you're saying—and, sorry, I'm asking another question, but I don't know any other way to phrase this—that I'm somehow a *nuisance* just because I want to *know* something?"

"Michael, listen—this is never going to work for you, being a priest…"

"I don't want to be a priest."

"Well, if you *did* want to be a priest, you would cause a lot of trouble for both yourself and for whatever church you'd be assigned to. We have ways of doing things that go back two thousand years. And we don't have to answer to anybody about anything, certainly not to you."

I sat and glared at him. I felt indignant and deeply hurt. This must be what it feels like to be excommunicated, I thought. Abandoned by the very people who are here on earth representing Jesus Christ and telling me that Jesus would want nothing to do with me. *Because I asked some stupid questions?* Like the one that was passing through my head, supplanting the fleeting thought of choking the smug out of Father Duewicke.

"You mean like why does this institution hate women and not let them be priests?"

"Yeeeesss!" Father Duewicke said with a knife of a smile. "*Like that one!* Good day, Mr. Moore. I wish you well with whatever you do with your life, and I pray for those who have to endure you."

He got up, and I got up, and I turned around and walked the long walk back to my room. I shut the door, lay down, and thought about my life — and when that became pointless I reached under the bed and consoled myself for the next hour with the latest issue of *Paris Match*.

Boys State

I HAD NO IDEA why the principal was sending me to Boys State. I had broken no rules and was not a disciplinary problem of any sort. Although I was a high school junior, it was only my second year in a public high school after nine years of Catholic education, and not having nuns or priests to direct me still took some getting used to. But I thought I had adjusted quite well to Davison High School. On the very first day of my sophomore year, Russell Boone, a big, good ol' boy who would become one of my best friends, took his fist and knocked the books out of my hands while I was walking down the hall between fourth- and fifth-hour classes.

"That's not how you hold 'em," he shouted at me. "You're holdin' 'em like *a girl*."

I picked up the three or four books and looked around to see if anyone had stopped to laugh at the boy who carried his books like a girl. The coast seemed clear.

"How'm I supposed to carry 'em?" I asked.

Boone took the books from me and held them in the cup of his hand with his arm fully extended toward the floor, letting the books hang by his side.

"Like this," he said while walking a manly walk down the hallway.

"How was I holding 'em?" I asked.

"Like this," he barked as he mocked me, holding my books up to the center of his chest like he was caressing breasts.

"That's how girls do it?" I asked, mortified that for the first half of my first day in public school, everyone had seen me walking around like a pansy.

"Yes. Don't do it again. You'll never survive here."

Check. So, half a day impersonating a girl. What else had I done to deserve Boys State?

Well, there was that time a few months later on the band bus. Boone had fallen asleep with his socks and shoes off. Honestly I can't say he had socks. But there he was, barefoot, his leg propped up on the armrest of the seat in front of him. Larry Kopasz had his cigarettes with him and it was decided that in order to solve the riddle "How long does a cigarette take to burn all the way down if being smoked by a foot?" he lit one and placed it between Boone's toes to find out. (Answer: seven and a half minutes.) Boone let out quite a yell when the hot cinder of the Lucky Strike reached his toes, and he didn't miss a beat from dreamland to wrestling Kopasz to the floor of the bus, which caught the attention of the driver. (In those days, as most adults and bus drivers smoked all the time, student smoking often went undetected because their smoke simply went into the same smoky air we were all breathing.) Somehow I got implicated in this brawl, as Boone held us all collectively responsible. (On that same overnight band trip, we snuck into Boone's room to run another science experiment: "Does placing one's hand while asleep in a warm bowl of water make one piss himself?" Answer: yes. And this time we took a Polaroid so we'd have proof to hold against him should Boone, the bedwetting tuba player, turn us in.)

But that was it. Seriously. I got good grades, was on the debate team, never skipped school and other than a skit I wrote for Comedy Week about the principal living a secret life as Pickles the Clown, I had not a smirch on my record.

As it turned out, Boys State was not a summer reformatory school for hoodlums and malcontents. It was a special honor to be selected to attend. Each June, after school ended, every high school in the state sent two to four boys to the state capital to "play government" for a week. You were chosen if you had shown leadership and good citizenship. I had shown the ability to come up with some very funny pranks to play on Boone.

Michigan's Boys State was held three miles from the Capitol Building on the campus of Michigan State University (the girls held a similar event called Girls State on the other side of the campus). Two thousand boys were assembled to elect our own pretend governor of Michigan, a fake state legislature, and a made-up state supreme court. The idea was for us boys to break down into parties and run for various offices in order to learn the beauties of campaigning and governing. If you were already one of those kids who ran for class office and loved being on student council, this place was your crack house.

But after campaigning for "Nixon-the-peace-candidate" as a freshman, I had developed an early allergy to politicians, and the last thing I wanted was to be one. I arrived at the Michigan State dormitories, was assigned my room and, after one "governmental meeting," where a boy named Ralston talked my ear off about why he should be state treasurer, I decided that my best course of action was to hole up in my room for the week and never come out except at feeding times.

I was given a small single room that belonged to that floor's resident advisor. He apparently had not moved all of his stuff out. I found a record player and some record albums sitting near the windowsill. I had a few books with me, plus a writing tablet and a pen. It was all I needed to make it through the week. So I essentially deserted Boys State and found refuge in this well-stocked fifth-floor room in the Kellogg Dorms. The album collection in my room included James Taylor's *Sweet Baby James,* The Beatles' *Let It Be,* the Guess Who's *American Woman,* and something by Sly and the Family Stone. There was a big coin-operated snack machine down at the end of the hall, so I had everything I needed for the week.

In between listening to the records and writing poems to amuse myself (I called them "song lyrics" to make them seem like a worthwhile endeavor), I became enamored with a new brand of potato chip that I heretofore had not encountered. The snack machine offered bags of something called "Ruffles" potato chips. I was amazed at how they were able to put hills and valleys into a single chip. For some reason, these "hills" (they called 'em "ridges") gave me the impression that I was getting more chip per chip than your regular potato chip. I liked that a lot.

On the fourth day inside my NO POLITICS ALLOWED/FIRE AND RAIN bunker, I had completely run out of Ruffles and made a run down the hall for more. Above the snack machine was a bulletin board, and when I got there I noticed someone had stuck a flyer on it. It read:

BOYS STATERS!

SPEECH CONTEST

on the life of

ABRAHAM LINCOLN

Write a speech on the life of Abe Lincoln

and win a PRIZE!

Contest sponsored by the

ELKS CLUB

I stood and stared at this flyer for some time. I forgot about my Ruffles. I just couldn't get over what I was reading.

The previous month, my dad had gone to the local Elks Club to join. They had a golf course just a few miles from where we lived, and he and his linemates from the factory loved to golf. Golf, the sport of the wealthier class, was not normally played by the working class in places like Flint. But the GM honchos had long ago figured out ways to lull the restless workers into believing that the American Dream was theirs, too. They understood after a while that you couldn't just crush unions — people would always try to start unions simply because of the oppressive nature of their work. So the GM execs who ran Flint knew that the best way to quell rebellion was to let the proles have a few of the accoutrements of wealth — make them think that they were living the life of Riley, make them believe that through hard work they, too, could be rich some day!

So they built public golf courses in and around the factories of Flint. If you worked at AC Spark Plug, you played the I.M.A. or Pierce golf courses. If you worked at Buick you headed over to the Kearsley course. If you worked at the

Hammerberg Road plant, you played at Swartz Creek. If you worked in "The Hole," you played the Mott course.

When the factory whistle blew at 2:30 p.m. every day, our dads grabbed their bags from the car and started whacking balls around (they'd play nine holes and be home for dinner by five). They loved it. Soon working class became "middle class." There was time and money for month-long family vacations, homes in the suburbs, a college fund for the kids. But as the years went on, the monthly union hall meetings became sparsely attended. When the company started asking the union for givebacks and concessions, and when the company asked the workers to build inferior cars that the public would soon no longer want, the company found they had a willing partner in their demise.

But back in 1970, thoughts like that would get you locked up in the loony bin. Those were the salad days (though I'm certain it was illegal to offer a salad anywhere within a fifty-mile radius of Flint). And the guys in the factory grew to believe that golf was *their* game.

The Elks Club owned a beautiful course that was not as crowded as the Flint public courses, but you had to be a member. So it was with some disappointment when my dad went out to the Elks Club to join that he was confronted with a line printed at the top of the application:

CAUCASIANS ONLY

Being a Caucasian, this should not have been a problem for Frank Moore. Being a man of some conscience, though, it gave him pause. He brought the form home and showed me.

"What do you think about this?" he asked me.

I read the Caucasian line and had two thoughts:

1. Are we down South? (How much more north can you get than Michigan?)
2. Isn't this illegal?

My dad was clearly confused about the situation. "Well, I don't think I can sign this piece of paper," he said.

"No, you can't," I said. "Don't worry. We can still golf at the I.M.A."

He would occasionally go back to the Elks course if invited by friends, but he would not join. He was not a civil rights activist. He generally didn't vote because he didn't want to be called for jury duty. He had all the misguided racial "worries" white people of his generation had. But he also had a very basic sense of right and wrong and of setting an example for his children. And because the union had insisted on integrating the factories as early as the 1940s, he worked alongside men and women of all races and, as is the outcome of such social engineering, he grew to see all people as the same (or at least "the same" as in "all the same in God's eyes").

Now, here I was, standing there in front of this Elks Club poster next to the vending machine. The best way to describe my feelings at that moment is that I was seventeen. What do you do at seventeen when you observe hypocrisy or encounter an injustice? What if they are the same thing? Whether it's the local ladies' club refusing to let a black lady join, or a segregated men's club like the Elks that has the audacity to sponsor a contest on the life of the Great Emancipator, when you're seventeen you have no tolerance for this kind of crime. Hell hath no indignation like that of a teen-ager who has forgotten his main mission was to retrieve a bag of Ruffles potato chips.

"They want a speech?" I thought, a goofy smile now making its way across my face. "I think I'm gonna go write me a speech."

I hurried back to my room, sans the bag of Ruffles, got out my pad of paper, my trusty Bic pen, and all the fury I could muster.

"How dare the Elks Club besmirch the fine name of Abraham Lincoln by sponsoring a contest like this!" I began, thinking I would lead with subtlety and save the good stuff for later. *"Have they no shame? How is it that an organization that will not allow black people into their club* **is** *a part of Boys State, spreading their bigotry under the guise of doing something good? What kind of example is being set for the youth here? Who even allowed them in here? If Boys State is to endorse any form of segregation, then by all means, let it be the segregation that separates these racists from the rest of us who believe in the American Way! How dare they even enter these grounds!"*

I went on to tell the story of my dad going to join the Elks and refusing to do so. I quoted Lincoln (my mother's con-tinual stops at Gettysburg whenever we drove to New York would now pay off). And I closed by saying, *"It is my sincere hope that the Elks change their segregationist policies—and that Boys State never, ever invites them back here again."*

I skipped dinner, putting the final touches on the speech, rewriting it a couple times on the pad of paper, and then fell asleep listening to Sly Stone.

The next morning, all speech contestants were instructed to show up in a School of Social Work classroom and give their speech. There were fewer than a dozen of us in the room and, much to my surprise (and relief), there was no one present from the Elks Club. Instead, the speeches were to be judged by a lone high school forensics teacher from Lansing. I took a seat in the back of the room and listened to the boys who went before me. They spoke in laudatory tones of Lincoln's accomplishments and his humanity, but mostly how he won the Civil War. It was the type of stuff the mayor might say at a town's Fourth of July picnic. Sweet. Simple. Noncontroversial.

Few in the room were prepared for the barrage of insults about to be hurled at the Elks Club. Take William Jennings Bryan, add some Jimmy Stewart, and throw in a healthy dose of Don Rickles, and I'm guessing that's what it must've sounded like to the assembled as I unleashed my invective disguised as a speech.

About halfway through my rant, I looked over toward the teacher/judge. He sat there without expression or emotion. I felt my heart skip a beat, as I was not used to being in trouble — and the last thing I wanted was for my parents to have to drive down to East Lansing and haul me home. I occasionally glanced at the other Boys Staters in the room to see how this was going down. Some looked at me in fear, others had that "boy-is-he-gonna-get-it" look on their faces — and the black kid in the room...well, what can I say, he was the only black kid in the room. He was trying to cover the smile on his face with his hand.

When the speeches were over, the teacher/judge went to the head of the class to issue his verdict. I slunk down in my seat, hoping that he would simply announce the winner and not issue any rebukes.

"Thank you, all of you, for your well-thought-out and well-written speeches," he began. "I was impressed with each and every one of you. The winner of this year's Elks Club Boys State Speech Contest is…Michael Moore! Congratulations, Michael. That was a courageous thing to do. And you're right. Thank you."

I didn't realize it, but he was already shaking my hand, as were about a third of the other boys.

"Thank you," I said somewhat sheepishly. "But I really didn't wanna win anything. I just wanted to say something."

"Well, you sure said something," the teacher replied. "You'll receive your award tomorrow at the closing ceremonies with all two thousand boys in attendance.

"Oh—and you'll have to give the speech to them."

What? Give what to whom?

"It's the tradition. The winner of the Elks Club speech gives his speech at the closing assembly, where they announce the election results and hand out all the awards."

"Um, no, I don't really wanna do that," I said, distressed, hoping he would take pity on me. "You don't really want me to give that speech, do you?"

"Oh, yes I do. But it's not up to me, anyway. You have to give it. That's the rule."

He also told me that for my own good, he wasn't going to mention to anyone the content of the speech before tomorrow. *Oh, yes, that's much better,* I thought. Let them all be hit with it fresh, like a big surprise, the kind which has the speaker being chased from the great hall, his prize in one hand, his life in the other.

After winning the speech contest, my night went something like this: "Fire and Rain," bathroom. "Across the Universe," bathroom. "Hot Fun in the Summertime," bathroom. And when you're seventeen and you don't have a car and you aren't prone to walking long distances—and you live in a state where mass transit is outlawed—there is a sense of imprisonment. That's it—I was in Boys State Prison! By morning, I had said my final prayers and made a promise to myself that if I got out of this alive, I'd never cause trouble like this again.

The time came and thousands of Boys Staters were ushered into the university hall. On the stage sat various officials, including, I believe, the real governor of Michigan. I took a seat near the front, on the side, and quickly scanned the place for guys who enjoyed being white. There was virtually no long hair here in 1971, and way too many of them had that clean-cut, disciplined, aggressive look that would probably serve them well after a year or two in the Hanoi Hilton, if not the U.S. Congress.

You will have to forgive me for the order of what came next because the event became a blur. My basic survival instincts had kicked in, and that was all that mattered. Someone was elected lieutenant governor or attorney general or Most Likely to Be Caught in the Senate Bathroom Someday. Somewhere in the middle of those announcements I heard my name. I lifted myself out of the chair (against the better advice of my excretory system) and made my way to the stage. The few boys I made eye contact with had that bored "Oh, shit another speech" look on their faces. For an instant I felt like I was soon going to be doing them a huge favor. This was certainly not going to sound like anything they were used to in third-hour civics class. That much I knew.

I ascended to the stage and walked past the dignitaries

settled in their comfortable chairs. As I looked at them one by one, I noticed a man who was wearing antlers. A hat with *antlers*. It was not Bullwinkle and this was not Halloween. This man was the Chief Elk, the head of all Elks, and he held in his lap the Elks Club Boys State speech trophy. He had a big, wide smile, a smile more appropriate for a Kiwanis or a Rotarian, with more teeth than I thought humanly possible, and he was so proud to see me take the podium. Oh, man, I thought, this guy is about to have a very bad day. I hope they did a patdown.

Unrolling my pages of paper, I peered out at the mass of newly minted testosterone. Sixteen- and seventeen-year-olds who should have been doing anything right now — shooting hoops, kissing girls, gutting trout — anything but sitting here listening to me. I took a deep breath and began the speech.

"How dare the Elks Club…" I remember it was somewhere around that point when I could feel a *whoosh* of tension in the room, hundreds murmuring, snickering under their breath. *Please God,* I thought, *could some responsible adult come up to the podium immediately and put an end to this!*

No one did. I motored onward, and near the end I could hear the cadence in my voice and I thought this wouldn't be half bad if I were singing it in a rock band. I finished with my plea that the Elks change their ways and, as I turned my head to see the crimson tide that was now the face of the Chief Elk, his teeth resembling two chainsaws ready to shred my sorry self, I blurted out, "And you can keep your stinkin' trophy!"

The place went insane. Nearly two thousand boys leapt to their feet and whooped and hollered and cheered me. The hollering wouldn't stop and order had to be restored. I jumped off the stage and tried to get out of there, my escape route having been preplanned. But too many of the Boys Staters wanted to shake my hand or slap my back locker-room style, and this slowed me down. A reporter began to make his way toward me, notebook in hand. He introduced himself and said that he was astonished at what he had just seen and was going to write something and put it over the wire. He asked me a few questions about where I was from and other things that I didn't want to answer. I broke away and headed quickly out a side door. Keeping my head down and avoiding the main campus path, I made it back to the Kellogg Dorms, checked the vending machine for Ruffles, rushed to my room and bolted the door.

The machine was out of Ruffles, but there was the Guess Who, and I turned it up so I could have some time to figure out what in hell's name I'd just done.

At least two hours passed, and it seemed like I was in the clear. No authorities had come to take me away, no Elks militia had arrived seeking revenge. All seemed to be back to normal.

Until the knock on the door.

"Hey," the anonymous voice barked. "There's a call for you."

The dorm rooms had no phones.

"Where's the phone?" I asked without opening the door.

"Down at the end of the hall."

Ugh. That was a long walk. But I needed Ruffles, and maybe they had restocked the machine. I opened the door and headed down the long hallway to the one public phone. The receiver hung dangling by its cord, like a dead man swinging from the gallows. What I didn't know was that on the other end of the line was the rest of my life.

"Hello?" I answered nervously, wondering who would even know where I was or how to reach me.

"Hello, is this Michael Moore?" the voice on the line asked.

"Yes."

"I'm a producer here at the *CBS Evening News* with Walter Cronkite in New York. We got this story that came over the wire about what you did today, and we'd like to send a crew over to interview you for tonight's newscast."

"Huh?" *What was he talking about?*

"We're doing a story on your speech exposing the Elks Club and their racial policies. We want you to come on TV."

Come on TV? There wasn't enough Clearasil in the world to get me to do that.

"Uh, no thank you. I have to get back to my room. Bye."

I hung up and ran back to the room and locked the door again. But it didn't matter. This became my first-ever media lesson: *I* don't get to decide what goes in the morning paper or on the nightly news. That night, I was introduced to the world.

"And today in Lansing, Michigan, a seventeen-year-old boy gave a speech that took on the Elks Club and their seg-regationist practices, shedding light on the fact that it is still legal for private clubs in this country to discriminate on the basis of race...."

The next day the dorm phone rang off the hook, even as I was packing up to leave. I didn't answer any of the calls, but I heard from the other boys that there were reporters phoning from the Associated Press, two TV networks, the NAACP, a paper in New York and another in Chicago. Unless it involved them offering me free food or an introduction to a girl who might like me, I did not want to be bothered.

My parents were waiting outside in the car to take me back home. This much I'll say: my parents were not unhappy with my actions.

When I got home, the phone continued to ring. Finally, a call came from the office of Michigan senator Phil Hart. He wanted to talk to me about coming to Washington. The aide said it was something about a bill that would be introduced, a bill to outlaw discrimination by private entities. A congressman would be calling me about testifying in front of a congressional committee. Would I be willing to do that?

No!! Why were they bothering me? Hadn't I done enough? I didn't mean to cause such a ruckus.

I thanked him and said I would discuss it with my parents (though I never told them; they would have wanted me to go!). I went outside to mow the lawn. We lived on Main Street, on a corner, across the street from the town fire station and kitty-corner from the town bowling alley. Over the din of the mower's engine I could faintly hear the honk of a horn.

"Hey, Mike!" shouted Jan Kittel from the car that had just pulled up to the curb. With her was another girl from our class. I had known Jan since fifth grade in Catholic school. In the past year she and I were partners on the debate team. I loved her. She was smart and pretty and very funny. I waved.

"Hey, c'mere! We heard about what you did at Boys State!" she said excitedly. "Man, that was something! You rocked it! I'm so proud of you."

I was ill equipped to handle the range of feelings and body temperature I was experiencing. I had absolutely no clue where to go with this other than to stutter out a "thanks." They got out of the car and she made me tell them the whole story, complete with the near riot I caused, which resulted in a lot of "right-ons!" and "farm outs!" — and, yes, a big hug for my efforts. They were running an errand and had to get going, but not before she said she hoped to see me again that summer.

"You and I will kick ass in debate this year," she offered, as I glanced in relief at the EMS unit parked in front of the fire station. "It'll be fun."

They drove off and I finished the lawn. It dawned on me that doing something political had brought me both a lot of grief *and* a girl who stopped by to see me. Maybe I was too harsh on the class officer types who populated Boys State with their geeklike love of all things political. Maybe they knew a certain secret. Or maybe they would all just grow up to populate Congress with their slick, smarmy selves, selling the rest of us out at the drop of a dime. Maybe.

The following year was not a good one for the Elks Clubs of America. Many states denied them their liquor licenses (the unkindest cut of all). Grants and funds became scarce. Various bills in Congress to stop them and other private clubs were debated. And then the federal courts in D.C. dealt them a death blow by taking away their tax exempt status. Facing total collapse and the scorn of the majority of the nation, the Elks Club voted to drop their Caucasians Only policy. Other private clubs followed suit. The ripple effect of this was that now racial discrimination *everywhere* in America, be it public or private, was prohibited.

My speech was occasionally cited as a spark for this march forward in racial fixing in the great American experiment, but there were other speeches far more eloquent than mine. Most important for me, I learned a valuable lesson:

That change can occur, and it can occur *anywhere*, with even the simplest of people and craziest of intentions, and that creating change didn't always require having to devote your every waking hour to it with mass meetings and organizations and protests and TV appearances with Walter Cronkite.

Sometimes change can occur because all you wanted was a bag of potato chips.

Zoe

HER BOYFRIEND CALLED ME from the hospital.

"The abortion, Mike. They botched it. We never made it to New York."

Abortion was illegal, a crime, in Michigan in 1971, as it was in most states. If you got pregnant, nine months later you had a baby. And that was that.

I was closer to Zoe than I was to perhaps any other girl in high school. She was what you would call a best friend. She had a big curly fro of hippie hair that landed wherever it damned well pleased. She played piano but was also a prodigy on the violin—which she would only play while barefoot. She smoked pot on occasion in her parents' house, and on rare nights would take LSD "to free myself from the Fascist cop inside me." Zoe was a free spirit, well read, and not afraid to speak her mind. I thought, some day she will change this world.

Which made her choice of a boyfriend in Tucker all the

more puzzling. Tucker was completely clueless and looked like he'd be happiest sticking a blade between your ribs, or drag racing. He was from the "tough neighborhood" in town (such as it was for Davison). His favorite pastime was picking fights, and though Zoe tried to reform him, his love of fisticuffs kept his dance card filled with numerous school suspensions. He treated basic common sense as if it were a "sissy thing," and he knew little of the world outside his trailer park; I'd be surprised if he had ever traveled more than five miles from his home in his lifetime.

But Tucker had the smile of the Sundance Kid and the eyes of James Dean, and Zoe loved him madly. He wore leather shit-kicking boots and had a chain attached to his belt loop—but with nothing on the end of it, as he was too broke to afford a wallet and poorer still to have anything to put in it. A cigarette was always dangling out the side of his mouth, and he had the uncanny knack of being able to inhale and blow out the smoke without ever touching the Camel.

Tucker would wait on Zoe hand and foot, and she was generous with her body in return. This won Tucker the designation by most guys as the Luckiest Dude at Davison High—and he was still a freshman! But not just any freshman: he came in at six-foot-three and weighed 180 pounds. Zoe was a senior, like me, and I was crazy in love with her.

I made sure that she never detected even the mildest inkling of my feelings. And if Tucker ever suspected how I felt I would surely see the sharp end of his jackknife being flung my way. But he had no clue. Either I was that good an actor, or it was just pathetically unbelievable that

someone like me would ever even *think* of having any de-
signs on Zoe. And it was even more implausible that she
would ever see me as anything resembling boyfriend material. After all, I came from the pack of guys who were
usually seen in flight from any oncoming females. I was
no James Dean; I was more Jimmy Dean, the sausage
king. One day, to impress her, I told her I could play cello
when she was putting together a "protest recital" outside the
Army recruitment center in Flint *(how hard could it be—it
had only four strings!)*. I borrowed a cello and used the bow
to run it back and forth at random, and she looked at me
and laughed and accused me later of eating all the special brownies.

Tucker had nothing to worry about with me, and Zoe appreciated having one guy in the school who wasn't hitting on
her. I didn't want to let her down, and there was something
noble about being different (better?) than the other boys in
her eyes. Of course, there was nothing noble about denying
your feelings, sexual or otherwise, but who was I going to
share *that* with? Ann Landers? The cafeteria lady?

Having now admitted to possessing such desire, I will
also admit that having a friend like Zoe was a blessing, a
greater blessing than one could hope for in trying to survive
the misery of adolescence. I could call her anytime, day or
night, and if she wasn't banging Tucker I was free to talk to
her as long as I wanted. I lived in town, so I could easily walk
over to her house anytime—and I was there far more than
Tucker ever was, since he lived out in the country and did
not have a driver's license.

Zoe and I grew very close and shared everything the

way you do with that special friend in high school as you
lie around the rec room—or the bedroom—for all hours
of the day or night, pouring through every subject imaginable: who was "bonin'" who, which classes sucked, ways to
avoid the parents, how to help the kid down the street who
was being punched by his dad every night, how to remove
Nixon from office, playing the new Moody Blues album,
sneaking into an X-rated movie (*Midnight Cowboy*), taking
turns writing verses of poems that would become lyrics to
songs that she would write the music for and sing to me.
Here's how close we were: one day, she informed me that
the lips of her vulva were unlike most women's because her
labia minora was larger than her labia majora, thus causing her inner lips to fold out on top of her outer lips. She
told me this as if she were reading me something from
the *TV Guide,* and the look on my face conveyed nothing more than my desire to watch another rerun of *May-
berry, RFD.*

There were those times that she and Tucker "broke up"
for days at a time—and I would momentarily contemplate
the opening presented to me. And on one such tear-filled
evening, for a second (or maybe the whole night), she "contemplated" it, too.

It was never spoken about again.

Tucker would return and their strange saga would continue, the couple that had nothing in common other than the
perfection of their own bodies.

It was a Sunday night when Zoe called and said she
needed to meet me somewhere private. I drove over and
picked her up and we went for a drive out to the Hogbacks.

"I'm pregnant," she said, as soon as the door slammed shut. I carefully backed out of the driveway, my heart racing, and she started to sob. "I can't believe I was this stupid. I can't have a baby." She then fell onto my shoulder.

"I am so sorry," I said, the way a best friend would say such a thing. And then I paused to catch my breath and do the math. It seemed OK.

"Don't beat yourself up," I said. "This happens. Even to smart people."

Her sobbing continued. I tried to keep my eyes on the road. "Shhhh. Don't cry. I'm here."

She continued to cry and so I pulled over and held her tight, the way a best friend would hold her tight.

"I have to end it," she said, sputtering out the words.

End *what?* I thought. Tucker? *Her . . . life?* Please, God.

"You mean the pregnancy," I said in a tone that did not make it a question.

"Yes," she said. "But how'm I gonna end it?" She looked up at me with those eyes. "How?"

She told me that when she got the pregnancy test at Planned Parenthood, they explained to her that abortion, at least in our state, was illegal.

"Maybe your parents know a doctor who could . . ."

"I can't tell them! I can't let them down like this."

"*Your* parents, more than any others, would understand."

"No. This would crush them. I have to take care of this myself."

"You can't try to abort the fetus yourself," I said.

"I wouldn't do that," she assured me.

"You know," I said, "abortion is legal in New York."

I had no moral conflict in making this suggestion. I knew a fertilized egg wasn't a human being.*

"I will help you, if that's what you want to do," I said.

"Thank you, Mike," she said as she dried her eyes.

"We could drive to Buffalo," I said. "It's probably not that far."

"Uh-huh."

"Or we can go to New York City. I know the city pretty well."

Of course, I was making offers I had no clue if I could deliver on. For instance, how would I get to New York City and not have my parents notice? *That* was never going to happen.

But Buffalo was possible. I started to plot it out in my head. I could leave for school at 7:00 a.m. and we could be in Buffalo by noon. How long would the procedure take? I didn't even know exactly what the "procedure" would be, but let's say three hours, then another five hours back—I could be home by 8:00 p.m.—late for dinner, to be sure, but suffering no more than a stern word or two.

---

* I was a practicing Catholic who went to Mass every Sunday. But this is what I believed: Human life begins when the fetus can survive outside the womb. Until then, it is a *form* of life, but not a human being. A sperm is life (after all, it's not swimming with a battery pack on its back), an egg is life, a fertilized egg is life, a fetus is life—but *none* of these are a human being, none of these are human life—just as a seed or a stem is not a flower. When you are *born,* you are a human being. That's why your driver's license lists your birthday as the day you came out of your mother's womb, not the day you were conceived. Some people, I guess, just like to be the uterus police, the bossypants of other women's reproductive parts. And that has always struck me as really, really weird.

"I have to tell Tucker," she said, as the Bad Idea buzzer rang in my head.

"Yes. Sure. He has to know."

I drove her over to Tucker's trailer and waited outside while she went in to deliver the news. Fifteen minutes later they emerged from his trailer, arm in arm, and I sighed. They got in the front seat with me, with Zoe in the middle.

"Thanks, man, for offering to help," Tucker said as he reached out to put his arm on my shoulder.

"Hey, no problem. I'm sure you guys would do the same for me if I got pregnant."

Zoe laughed. Tucker continued: "I was thinking we should keep the baby," the high school freshman without the driver's license said, loving the swagger and the idea that he had actually produced something in his life.

"Yeah, well, that's not happening," Zoe said, shutting him up and relieving me.

We went over to the A&W for root beers and fries and further planning on how to end the unplanned pregnancy.

In the coming days I did the research and found the most reputable abortion clinics in New York City. I planned out our entire trip—one that we would take with my parents' permission, though they would know nothing about the abortion. We would stay at my aunt's on Staten Island. I told my mother that I wanted to go to New York for the weekend because I was considering going to college there.

"We can't afford that," she replied without shame.

"I've checked into scholarships and I think I might have a good chance. I've looked into Fordham. Jesuits! Good!"

Here I was, playing the Catholic card again, and dang if it didn't always work. Her sister had married a man who went to Fordham, and I told her that would open a door for me. I promised I'd be gone just for the weekend and would miss no school.

"And you'll stay with Aunt Lois?"

"Absolutely."

My parents liked Zoe and, as their radar could detect no carnal scent in either direction, they did not consider her a threat.

I got Zoe and Tucker all excited about the fun time we could have in New York. You would have thought we were going there to have a tooth pulled—and then it was off to Times Square to see *Hair* and the Village to see Joni Mitchell. Maybe I could even score some tickets to *Dick Cavett*.

But my parents had too long to think about this odd trip, and within days the kibosh was put to it. I put up quite a fight, but there was no way to win this one. *And who was this Tucker fellow?*

"Hey," Zoe said, "don't feel bad. You gave it a good shot. Maybe we should go back to the Buffalo plan."

"Sure," I said, somewhat defeated. "Sounds good."

At this point Zoe and Tucker began to realize that in going to get an abortion, three's a crowd, and so they told me they would take over from this point going forward.

I would have said something to them about an umbilical cord being cut here, but this wasn't the time for bad puns, although it certainly was the way I felt. There was nothing I could do other than accept the situation for what it was. Tucker was being very good to her, and she had calmed down and was now pretty matter-of-fact about their trip. I lent them all the cash I had—fifty bucks—to add to the stash of what they were scrounging together to pay for it.

On the day that I knew they were leaving, I went to school as if it were any normal day. But my mind was elsewhere. One's thoughts don't normally drift toward Buffalo, but I couldn't do much else that day but worry about my best friend's safety and well-being.

It was after dinner when the phone rang. My sister answered.

"Mike—it's Tucker."

I went to the phone, knowing that they had returned by now.

"Hey."

"The *abortion*," he said, whispering, out of breath, and, if it weren't Tucker, I'd say he was crying.

"They botched it. We never made it to New York. We didn't go to Buffalo. We're in Detroit."

"Shit!" I said, a bit too loud. "What are you doing in Detroit? *How is she?*"

"Not…not good," he said, now clearly in tears. "*Mike— help me!* She's bleeding pretty bad. I don't know what to do."

"Where are you?" I asked, trying not to scream or cry myself.

"I got her to a hospital…somewhere here in Detroit. It was just awful. Awful. Oh God…I don't want to lose her!"

I was unable to swallow. The lump in the throat grew into a full choke. I cupped my hand over the phone and swung the cord around the wall from the dining room and into the kitchen so no one could hear or see me. I tried to keep it together and figure out what I needed to do.

"What do the doctors say?"

"They say she's lost a lot of blood. She goes in and out. They won't let me in there. I'm fifteen, and I'm sure they've called the cops by now. *I don't know what to do!*" He broke down uncontrollably.

"OK, listen! Pull it together! I'm getting in the car right now. I'll be there in less than an hour. If the cops show up, say nothing. Say you want a lawyer and keep repeating that. And if they'll let you in there, hold her hand and let her know she's not alone—and tell her I'm coming."

"OK. OK. I'm so sorry. This was my idea. We didn't have the money for Buffalo. Someone told us about a safe place in Detroit. Cheap. It was wrong from the minute we got there and I just should've turned her around and left. I'm so sorry. Please…forgive me."

Right now none of that mattered. I shouted upstairs that I was going to go hang out with Tucker and Zoe and I'd be back in a couple hours.

"Back by ten," my mom shouted.

"Yes. Ten. Bye!"

I tore down M-15 to Clarkston and got on I-75 and hit the gas. At times the speedometer read ninety. The V-8 on the Impala had me in Detroit in fifty-two minutes. I followed the signs to the hospital, parked the car in the emergency room lot, and ran in. Tucker was there, his eyes all red.

"It's OK, it's OK," I told him, as I hugged him. I asked the nurse if I could go see Zoe, and she said no. I asked about her condition.

"Are you a relative?" she asked.

"I'm her brother," I said, without thinking.

"And where are your parents?"

"Where are *yours?*" I snapped back at her, realizing instantly that this was not going to serve me well. I changed my tune immediately.

"Look, I'm sorry. I'm upset. I'm nineteen, she's eighteen, and we don't want to involve or upset our parents with this, if that's OK. I hope you understand." The BS flowed smoothly enough, but the tears that had formed in my eyes were real.

"OK, fine," she said, filing away my insult for later retribution. "Just sit over there, and I'll see if a doctor can come out to speak to the two of you."

We waited nearly an hour before the resident came out looking for us.

"Which one of you is family?"

"I am," I said.

"OK. Let me just say this was the stupidest thing you could have done. These back-alley abortionists are not doctors. They have no medical training whatsoever, and they do this only to make money and take advantage of people like you."

"It's all we could afford," Tucker inserted unnecessarily. The doctor paused as he assessed who exactly this hoodlum was.

"It is illegal," he said, hitting every word like he was hitting Tucker's face. "You may have killed her. But you didn't. She's going to recover. You took an enormous risk."

"What exactly is her condition right now?" I asked, hoping to end the lecture.

"She's cut up inside, her uterus and her cervix. It also looks like they used some form of ammonia, so there seem to be burns in there, too. We've stopped the bleeding and are caring for the inner wall linings, and she's in a bit of shock. We have her resting now and sedated, and she's getting the proper attention she needs. Are your parents on their way?"

"Yes," I lied. "They should be here soon."

The doctor shot another look at Tucker. "You care at all to know if she's still carrying the baby?" he said, without adding the implied "punk" at the end of the sentence.

"Yeah, sure," Tucker said without looking at the doctor.

"The baby's gone," he said, using the word *baby* for the second time for effect, to hurt Tucker. It hurt me.

"It's not a baby," I said quietly. "She was ten weeks pregnant. It was a fetus. If Michigan wasn't so backward, she wouldn't be lying in there like that. That's all I'm mad about. Thank you for helping her."

He did not appreciate my diatribe and simply turned away and went back into the ER.

"Are her parents really coming?" Tucker asked, panicked.

"No. But we have to call them. She's going to be here for at least tonight, and they are going to be frightened when she doesn't come home. I'll call them. And I'll try to help when they get here."

I went to the pay phone and called her parents collect. I told them not to worry, Zoe was OK, but she was in the hospital in Detroit as she had come down here to terminate a pregnancy. There was crying and cursing, and I told them I was sorry, I didn't know, I thought Tucker had called them, I drove to the hospital as soon as Tucker called me. I said I would stay with Zoe until they got there.

When they arrived I stood between them and Tucker to ward off any violence, and I asked everyone to try and focus on Zoe and we can yell at each other later. Her mother spoke to the nurse, then the doctor, and they allowed her and her husband back in the room. In a few minutes, they sent for her "brother." I looked at Tucker, who just seemed lost and more in need of a babysitter or a mother of his own at the moment. I followed the nurse into the room, and she pulled back the curtain to reveal Zoe, half awake in bed, her hand being held by her mother, her dad still glancing my way, wanting to punch someone.

"Hi Zoe," I said, and went over to her other side and took her other hand.

"I'm…so…sorry," she mumbled. "We…made…a…m–mistake."

"Don't think about that now. The doctor said you're doing fine, you just need to rest. And your mom and dad are here and everything's gonna be all right."

"Thank…you," she whispered, her throat all raspy. "You're…my…" She broke down crying. There was no real word with which to finish that sentence, none that adequately described our relationship—or if there was, it could not be spoken in this room. I helped her finish the sentence.

"Friend," I said, smiling.

"Yes. Always."

Zoe soon broke up with Tucker. After we graduated, I became consumed with my first year of college and all things political, but Zoe and I still hung out a lot, still listened to music and shared our most intimate feelings with each other. She signed up to go to community college, but halfway through the second semester she dropped out, and she and

her family moved out West. We stayed in touch by writing
letters, but she was into adventure and wandering with hippie friends she met along the way. Soon, there was no contact, and life went on.

I last saw Zoe over a decade ago. She was playing in a recital in Chicago, and she told me how she got part-time work
playing in various orchestras and symphonies (they made her
wear shoes). She had lived in LA for a while and played in
the back-up string sections on pop and rock records. It was
good to catch up and go over old times. The man she was
with seemed nice but of few words. I did notice that he had
the same chain that Tucker used to have, hanging from his
belt loop. I left our reunion feeling good about Zoe and the
life she had carved out for herself, and I was somewhat relieved when I saw that her boyfriend's chain was clearly connected to something substantial in his pocket.

Getaway Car

THE WAR WAS NOW in its sixth year and I was running out of time. I had just turned sixteen, and the possibility of being drafted felt like someone's hot puke breath all over the back of my neck. Nine boys from my high school—*nine*—had already come back from Vietnam in flag-draped boxes. The best thing you could say about that back then was: at least the box was American made.

I had long ago stopped standing for the National Anthem at the Friday night football and Tuesday night basketball games. Fortunately I wasn't alone in this reckless protest. Hippie membership had grown significantly by the fall of 1971 at Davison High School, and the jocks who desperately wanted to throw us off the Main Street bridge and into Black Creek were now outnumbered. But they could still break any of us in two like a matchstick if they got their hands on us. So we hung in packs. If a jock or a redneck wanted to dish out a dose of swift justice to a hippie, he was forced to lie in wait and grab one of us walking home alone after staying late for French Club or choir.

Two of the Davison Vietnam dead lived on my street.

Statistically that had to be an outrageous percentage, considering the residential portion of my street extended for only four blocks. If every four-block street in America was required to cough up two young boys for The Sacrifice, then how many of us across America would be dead by now? Millions, right? I became convinced that my street, South Main Street, was a marked boulevard, singled out by Nixon or that creepy Angel of Death for some reason I couldn't quite comprehend. I was determined there would be no offering made to their cause from my house.

It was back on the morning of May 5, 1970, that I snapped. Earlier in the year, I had convinced my guidance counselor to let me take Government class as a sophomore, a required credit usually reserved for seniors. Mainly, I wanted to get out of gym class. Two years of gym was required to graduate, but I lied and told my counselor that when I was in the Catholic seminary they made us take two gym classes a day so therefore I had, in effect, already taken my two years' worth of gym, see? She approved the waiver to let me take Government class.

On May 4, National Guardsmen at Kent State in Ohio had taken aim on and killed four students while wounding nine others. This unglued me. "OK, so let me get this straight — I don't have to go to Vietnam any more to get killed, I can do that right here at home?"

The next day, our ultracool Government teacher, Mr. Trepus, skipped the lesson plan and had us discuss what had happened in Ohio. Many of the senior boys in class agreed that the future looked mighty shitty. Some were quite angry, and one student suggested a walkout. As I was two years younger than the rest of the room, I kept my head down, doodling in my notebook. On one loose-leaf sheet of paper I began drawing little crosses on graves, the kind I had seen at Arlington Cemetery, just nothing but rows upon rows of crosses, so many crosses that they bled into the horizon.

On one 8½ x 11 sheet of paper I drew 260 crosses in 26 straight rows.

"Whatta you doin'?" asked Bob Bell, the long-haired senior in moccasin shoes who sat next to me.

"I was just wondering how long it would take to draw one of these for every grave of every soldier who's died in Vietnam."

"Ain't that a lot?"

"I think Mr. Trepus said it's like almost fifty thousand."

"Huh. I'd like to see that," he said with a curious smile on his face.

And so I began. I had about a hundred sheets of paper in my notebook. One by one, I drew the little grave crosses. At some point, Mr. Trepus noticed I was doing something and walked down the aisle to see what it was.

"I want to see what fifty thousand dead looks like on paper," I told him, hoping I wasn't in trouble.

He thought about it for a minute. "Good. I'd like to see that, too."

It took the better part of the next couple days to complete my project. When I was done I had 49,193 crosses laid out in neat rows on 188½ sheets of three-hole-punched loose-leaf binder paper. Word spread that I had done this, and many wanted to see it. Others thought it best I eat lunch alone in the cafeteria ("freak!"). Those who wished a peek were treated to me flipping the pages one by one quickly in front of their eyes like a zoetrope machine. The crosses didn't dance or move; it was more like seeing thousands of crosses piling up on top of thousands more. It made one girl in class cry.

"I don't want to end up under one of those crosses," I told her.

The following year, junior year, the war still raging, the hair a bit longer, the anger burning more intensely. With the draft lottery for me now less than twelve months away, it was time for decisive action.

I had heard of guys doing things the night before their draft physical like drinking a gallon of coffee to raise their blood pressure or firing a BB pellet into their groin. That seemed a bit dramatic, and painful. Others forged doctor's notes, some tried to act mentally retarded.

As I saw it, I had but three choices:

1. **Sign up as a conscientious objector.** This would require me not only to denounce all wars past and present but to promise that I would stand by and do nothing as my grandmother was raped and murdered. If they were convinced of my sincerity that I'd remain nonviolent while a ninety-year-old woman was being butchered, I would be assigned to full-time hospital work for two years.

2. **Go to jail.** This made no sense. "So, I'm not going to 'Nam, I'm not going to push a broom in a hospital—I'd rather have the broom handle shoved up my ass." No thanks.

3. **Escape to Canada.** The Canadian government had agreed to give American draft dodgers and deserters a safe haven. This was a remarkable gesture for a country that

spent most of its time trying to be our polite neighbor. We had many things in common, the Canadians and us, but the one place where we seemed to part ways was in the business of invading other countries. For some reason, the Canadians had little interest in imposing their quiet selves onto others. Why some of our hubris hadn't rubbed off on them was a mystery to me, but they didn't want much to do with killing people ten thousand miles away, let alone each other.

Though I lived an hour from the border, I knew little of Canada. I had not spent any time there as a child. My mother's father was a Canadian, but as a young man he left Canada for Michigan, and so our contact with his native land was limited.

Our Canadian relatives would make the occasional jaunt over to see us, and we would go over there less. Maybe our parents were worried we weren't ready for international travel? Maybe Canada didn't have indoor plumbing yet? I dunno. It was a distant land, it was "foreign," and the Queen of England was on their money. Beyond that, we never gave it another thought.

Because borders can't stop airwaves (television used to be transmitted free of charge through the air), we got to watch a lot of Canadian TV on CKLW, Channel 9, from Windsor, Ontario. Most of the programming on the Canadian Broadcasting Channel consisted of nature documentaries and comedy shows in black-and-white with ironic humor we didn't understand. There were Mounties and lumberjacks and lots of shots of prairies. They had a great Sunday afternoon classic movie show, there was the thrilling *Hockey Night in Canada* on Saturday night, and there was the Canadian news.

And it was there, one night as a youngster, that I stumbled across the truth. I paused on Channel 9 as I was turning the dial, and the news was on. They were covering the Vietnam War, but there was something wrong with what they were showing. They were broadcasting images, not from South Vietnam but from *North* Vietnam! The enemy! Why were they doing that? They were showing the destruction caused by our bombing civilian villages. One elderly woman was in tears showing her hut, which "the American planes had bombed." No we didn't! Stop saying that! We're the good guys! They're the Germans!

But not on this night. And I couldn't take my eyes off the CBC after that. And I wasn't the only one. If you lived within sixty miles of the Canadian border and had a decent antenna or set of rabbit ears you could get The Truth about the Vietnam War from the Canadians, right from the beginning. This messed me up a bit because I had no clue that our own government would lie to us. I mean, that would have been un-American. And yet, here was our boring, friendly neighbor whispering across the hedge each night that we were doing a bad, bad thing. I felt like I did when Santa Claus turned out to be just my dad, or when I learned that Cheez Whiz wasn't really cheese—but at least both of those things still brought happiness to my childhood. This revelation was nothing like that. This was a smack across my tender sixteen-year-old face, and I didn't like it one bit.

Thanks to the Canadian channel, I came to fear and hate this war. I felt like I was the only one in the neighborhood who had found the secret key, the buried treasure, and from then on I was hooked on never believing what I saw on

American television, even if I still did dream of Jeannie or cheered for the Fugitive to get away.

By the summer of '71, before my senior year, my mind was made up: if drafted, I would escape to Canada.

How one flees to another country and seeks asylum was not taught in Government class. But I had just attained the rank of Eagle Scout, and with that came the knowledge of many survival skills, earning merit badges in Tracking, Trailing, Animal Stalking, Marksmanship, Basketry, Plumbing, Fingerprinting, Beekeeping, Bookbinding, Signaling, Metallurgy, Masonry, Archery, Fruit and Nut Growing, and World Brotherhood. With a background like this, I could surely find my way across any border, keeping myself alive with a bow and arrow, a beehive, and some semaphore flags.

I had met Joey, Ralph, and Jacko at an antiwar demo I went to within days of receiving my driver's license. Kent State was fresh on everyone's mind, and Willson Park in downtown Flint was the hippie gathering place for rebels and malcontents and monthly draft card burnings. Joey was from Burton Township, where the poor white people lived; suffice it to say you didn't find many of them at orgies of peaceniks. Although I am certain they provided more cannon fodder than any other part of Genesee County (except for the black north end of Flint). They backed the Vietnam War and President Nixon (though he was their second choice for president after Alabama governor George Wallace). Most of Burton Township was populated by families who had come from the southern states to work in the auto factories of Flint.

Moving north did not dissuade them of their racial musings, and if you were not white, you knew it was best not to venture into south Burton after dark.

Joey had somehow escaped most of the attitudinal shortcomings of his neighborhood and yet had retained a pleasant hillbilly charm about himself that the city girls in Flint seemed to take a liking to. He didn't have any particular political leanings, he just felt the war was "stoopid," and he had no desire to see the world beyond the boundary of Maple Road.

Ralph lived in a Hispanic neighborhood on the east side of downtown Flint. His parents were from Mexico where he, too, had been born. He arrived here as a baby while his mother and father were summer crop pickers of sugar beets and blueberries.

Of the four of us, Ralph was the most intense. Angry at an early age from witnessing the treatment of his parents in an urban area that was all about black and white and no real recognition that brown played any role on the color chart. Ralph was also the strongest of us, and though he was the shortest, no one ever thought of messing with him. We assumed he carried some sort of weapon like a knife, but none of us really wanted to ask.

Jacko—we never knew what his given name was—came from a well-off family who lived in the area surrounding the community college and the Flint branch of the University of Michigan. He had hair like Blue Boy, but he was cunning and reckless and had no difficulty finding himself in trouble with the local police from time to time (trouble that his lawyer father had no difficulty making "go away"). If you came up with a crazy idea, Jacko would come up with a way to make it happen—and to top it off, he'd make it even crazier.

And it was one of those ideas that I proposed to them, on a Sunday afternoon in the early fall of 1971, for which Jacko was my perfect co-conspirator. We would call our idea "The Great Blue Water Bridge Escape."

"I was thinking," I said slurping down an A&W root beer that was perched on a tray hanging from the window of my dad's '69 Impala. "If I'm drafted, I'm not going."

"Me neither," said Joey. "No way."

"Well," added Ralph, "they'll never find me. I'll go underground and that'll be that."

"We're not going underground," Jacko shot back. "And we're not going to jail. I've been there. Not for me."

"We could sign up as conscientious objectors," I suggested.

"What's that?" asked Joey.

Ralph interjected. "It means you have to sign a piece a paper saying you're a pussy—and none of us are doing that."

"Yeah, I don't really want to do that, either," I quickly added, though not entirely ruling out the possibility inside my head. "Being a C.O. means giving Uncle Sam two years of your life doing something else for him that doesn't require a gun."

I paused. "How 'bout we escape to Canada?"

"Run?!" Ralph said with surprise.

"No, not '*run*,'" said Jacko. "More like Steve McQueen in *The Great Escape*. Outsmart the bastards. Jump the fence to Canada. Live like kings!"

"Canada doesn't have a fence between us," I said. "It's all water."

Just how much water I wasn't sure, and I didn't want to correct him about Steve McQueen (whose escape attempt on that bike ultimately wasn't successful) because I knew the Canadian plan was the way to go.

Jacko piped in. "I say we check it out. Whadda we got to lose?"

We made a plan for the following Saturday to drive over to the border and assess what our chances would be of getting into Canada. I was in charge of logistics. Ralph would head up what could best be called security ("No Canadian wants to mess with a Mexican," he reassured us). Jacko would get some money from his dad for whatever we needed. And Joey would bring the boat.

"The boat?!" Ralph said. "What's the boat for?"

"Mike said it's all water," Joey responded. "So, my dad and me, we got a small fishing boat we tie onto the back of our car to go up north fishing. It's just sitting beside the garage. I take it out when I want."

Jacko was all smiles. "*I likesy the boatsy!* I can just see us now, bookin' across Lake Huron like James Bond!"

Ralph was not a boat person, but he could see he was outvoted on this. I assumed his opposition was because he couldn't swim and the thought of dealing with any water was not a pleasant one for him.

The next Saturday, Joey arrived at my house. I told my parents I was going to the movies — and fortunately, they never looked out the window, which might have led them to ask why we needed a boat to go to the movies. We headed east out of town on M-21, through Elba and Lapeer and Imlay City, past the church in Capac whose steeple had been built by my great-uncle. I would often pass on these histori-

cal tidbits to my Davison friends at high school who humor-
ously tolerated my I'm-sorry-to-be-so-smart attitude. These
guys from Flint I really didn't know that well, which made
this adventure feel all that more dangerous and alluring.

In a little over an hour we were in Port Huron, Michigan. Port Huron, I had learned in preparation for the escape,
was one of only three border crossings from Michigan into
Canada—the other two were Detroit (which had a tunnel
and a bridge) and Sault Ste. Marie in the Upper Peninsula.
There also appeared to be a boat crossing on the Detroit
River south of the city with a customs station on the Canadian side.

Port Huron was a small city, not known for much in those
days, but all Michigan schoolchildren were taught that it was
where Thomas Edison grew up. Those of us who attended
antiwar rallies knew Port Huron as the place where a bunch
of students from the University of Michigan, led by Tom
Hayden, wrote the manifesto of the Students for a Democratic Society (SDS) called the Port Huron Statement. None
of us had actually read it, but we knew that just the mention
of the letters SDS drove our parents mad, so we considered
ourselves automatic members and prominently displayed
copies of "The Statement" (which we acquired from the local
head shop) in a place where a parent or an assistant principal
might see it and turn red.

I had chosen Port Huron as our escape point not because
of its historical significance but because it appeared to have
the shortest distance of water between the two countries.
The St. Clair River was only about a half mile wide, and on
the Canadian side sat the city of Sarnia, Ontario. But when
we arrived in Port Huron and looked across to Sarnia, it was

truly an ugly site. Taking up what seemed to be the entire riverbank was either an oil refinery or a chemical plant (the large Dow sign, which could be seen across the river, might have been the giveaway).

There had been a point on the drive to Port Huron when Jacko had wondered if we could just swim across to Canada (I think he said this to piss Ralph off). But one look at the St. Clair River dispelled any notion of trying that, if it had in fact been a notion at all. It seemed like if you threw a match into the St. Clair it would light up like Cleveland.

There was only one way to take a car across to Canada, and that was over the Blue Water Bridge. Standing below the bridge we could see what appeared to be serious checkpoints on both ends of the crossing. These did not look welcoming. We decided that the bridge would not work. We would instead use Joey's boat.

Our task then became finding a place to launch the boat to a spot straight across the river in Canada that looked desolate enough for us to not be caught. Immediately north of the bridge Lake Huron began, and it widened out so fast that within two thousand feet there was already at least five miles of lake between the two countries. Just south of Port Huron was a small town called Marysville. We drove there and found a city park with a boat launch on the river. There were no police or immigration people around. There was still a lot of industrial-looking muck across the river in Canada, but just to the north of that appeared to be a long stretch of fields and woods. That seemed to be our best bet.

Joey backed his car down the path of the boat launch to the edge of the water. Ralph was nervous about our chances of getting caught, and I kept my eyes peeled straight across the river looking for Canadians. I could see none, and the late afternoon sun from the west lit up the Canadian shore to reveal absolutely no activity. There were no border guards with binoculars keeping their eyes on us, no patrol boats protecting their sovereign territory. Just a half mile of river lapping up on our land in the same way it lapped up on theirs. Although this was just supposed to be a dry run, there was a part of me that just wanted to take that boat, right then, across the St. Clair and not return.

That was not going to happen. Jocy let out a loud *"Shit!Fuck!Shit!"* and I got out to see what the problem was.

"No fucking motor! My dad took the outboard off! *Fuck!*"

"What the fuck, Joey?!" Ralph kicked the boat's trailer a few times, but neither kick made the outboard motor appear. "How could you be so fucking stupid?!"

The Eagle Scout with the rowing merit badge spoke up. "Hey, it's like two thousand feet of river. There's four of us. Let's just row!"

"We don't have any oars," Joey said quietly, feeling the shame of having wrecked our Great Escape. "My dad musta taken it off to work on it. We just used it last week. Can't believe I didn't see it missing when I left."

"Great. Just great." Ralph was still pissed. "You know I can't swim." We knew.

"We're not swimming," Jacko chimed in. "We're gonna grab a bag of White Castles and hang out here for a while. And I brought 'dessert.'" He was holding a very large and perfectly rolled joint in his hand. This seemed to take the sting out of the situation, and if there was one thing you could count on Jacko for it was the very finest and most expensive marijuana from lands far away.

We headed back in to Port Huron and found a burger joint and took what passed for our picnic dinner to the town's park on the river. There was a big boulder with a plaque honoring Thomas Edison on it. We sat there, with our burgers, staring at it and trying to come up a list of things he invented: Lightbulb. Record player. Movie projector. There was more, but that was enough to make him cool.

"Man," I added, accidentally slipping into know-it-all mode, "a lot of inventors came from our state: Edison. Henry Ford. Kellogg. Dow. Not bad for just one state."

"Well, fuck Dow," Ralph interjected.

"Yeah, fuck Dow!" Jacko repeated.

"Yeah, fuck Dow—fuck Dow royal!" I added, in case it needed emphasis.

"Edison said that of all his inventions, he was proudest of the fact he never invented a weapon, never invented anything for war," Jacko said. We were impressed that he knew something so serious, whether it was true or not.

I was looking up at the bridge above us. Early evening had arrived, and while this adventure was, in spite of its motor mishap, already more fun than anything I had done so far in my senior year, I was still obsessed with not leaving the border zone without a plan on how to escape to Canada. I had to keep this mission on track. Of course, the ability to get the other three to refocus on why we were there was a bit more difficult now, as they were already halfway through the king-size joint.

"C'mon, man, try it," Jacko implored me. "Just once."

I was still a virgin when it came to, well, when it came to everything—but in this instance I was the only seventeen-year-old I knew who hadn't at least tried pot or other controlled substances. I was not against it on any legal or moral grounds, and I was not worried that my first joint would force me to pick up a heroin needle. In fact, I noticed that everyone became nicer and funnier once stoned, and there was certainly nothing wrong with that. My fear was this: To me, I already seemed way too high/stoned/crazy. Or at least I thought I was. I *was* convinced that my natural, everyday altered state did not need any enhancing. I truly believed that if I were to smoke a joint or drop some acid I might not ever come back. I was fine just where I was, thinking up things like sneaking into Canada on a boat without a motor.

"We could always just make a run for it over the bridge," I suggested, knowing that with the joint now finished off, they'd be open to just about anything.

"Whatcha mean, 'make a run'?" Ralph asked in a tone that indicated a rare moment of open-mindedness.

"You don't mean run like run-*run,* do ya?" Joey wondered.

"No, I don't mean literally run across the bridge," I explained. "I mean, let's just get in the car and make like we're going to visit our Canadian cousins. I can speak some Canadian. All you have to do is talk slower and put an extra "u" in some words."

"I thought they spoke French," Ralph interjected.

"They do," I said. "It's like their secret language they go to when they don't want America to know what they're saying. I've already had two years of French, so I'll be ready if they try to pull that trick."

"Good thinkin'," Joey said.

"But we don't need to worry about no French at the American checkpoint," I assured them. "I'll just tell the American border guards we're going over to do some fishing with our Canadian relatives. Then we'll hit the gas and make a run for it to the Canadian side before they figure out none of us look very related."

"Man, I don't know," Jacko said after not thinking long about it. "What if they pull out their guns and start shooting? What if they chase us in some goddamn Army truck or somethin'? Fuck, I dunno."

"Plus," added Joey, "don't forget, we're pulling my dad's boat."

"We could leave the boat on this side and put a note on it," I suggested. "Remember, we're not going over there tonight for good. We're just going to see if, when we do need to escape, we'll be able to do it."

"Well, if it's not for real, then I'd rather we keep the boat with us," Joey responded.

"Makes better sense to have the boat," said Ralph. "That way it does look like we're going on a fishing trip or something."

"OK, we take the boat," I said, feeling like I was talking to Cheech and Chong and Chong. "But you guys are going to have to let me do the driving 'cause you're in no shape to be behind the wheel. And Jacko, make sure you don't have any more drugs on you. *That* will get us in trouble if we get stopped."

"All clean, sir," he replied, cracking up.

"Let's say we do get past the American guards," Ralph wondered. "And we make it across the bridge. When we get to the Canadian side, what do we say?"

"I think we have to say what we're going to say on the real day next year when we have to do this. We have to tell them we are draft resisters and we are here to seek asylum from a peace-loving nation."

"And that's when they take out their Canadian pistols and shoot us," Jacko offered. "Four less bloody Americans! Jolly good job, Jeeves!" he said in his best Flint/British accent.

"They're not going to shoot us, and they're not British," I reminded them. "They just think they are. I don't even think they have guns. But they might take us away for questioning, so I'll just say I was kidding, we're only in high school and we have to get back home tonight 'cause we gotta get up and go to church in the morning."

"Don't lay it on too thick, Mikey," Jacko cautioned. "We don't exactly look like altar boys in this car."

"Look, I think we should give this a try," I pleaded. "We're here. We need to know what we're facing, and, assuming we get past the American soldiers, I think things will be OK."

There was some more mumbling about not wanting to get shot or the car careening off the bridge, but after a few minutes I had them convinced this was the best thing to do. I got in the driver's seat, Ralph rode up front with me, and Joey and Jacko sat in the back trying to sober up.

The Blue Water Bridge, though it crossed only a half mile of water, was an imposing structure. It soared over 150 feet into the air, high above the St. Clair River. This was done to accommodate the huge Great Lakes ships that traveled underneath it. It was the gateway to Lake Huron, and to get on it you had to travel up a long ramp that rose above an old Port Huron neighborhood that once housed the Irish immigrants from my dad's side of the family. As the car climbed up the ramp of the bridge, my heart started to beat at quite a clip. Everyone made their final adjustments to personal grooming as the lone American checkpoint came into view. There was a series of booths for each lane of traffic, some with red lights, others with green, and I thought it best to be in the green-lit lane. There were massive floodlights, and we could see men in uniform inside each guard booth. As we pulled near a booth I issued one final warning.

"OK, keep cool, let me do the talking, and if there's any problem, I'm flooring it. Just keep your heads down in case they start shooting." Pause. "I'm kidding. No one is going to shoot us." Or so I assumed.

The soldier in the booth waved me forward. When I came up beside his booth the window was open—but he wasn't a soldier. He looked more like a school crossing guard volunteer.

"That'll be twenty-five cents, please."

"Huh?"

"Twenty-five cents."

I didn't understand.

"Just a quarter, son."

He wanted money from us.

"Sure," I said. I fished around in my pocket. "Here." I handed him the quarter.

"Thank you."

That was it?

"Is that it?" I asked the man.

"Well, usually people think that's too much! They keep talking about raising it another quarter. I don't think that will sit too well with folks."

"No, I mean, we can just, like, go to Canada now? You don't have to ask us any questions or check us out?"

"Oh Lord, no!" he chuckled. "I'm just a toll collector. They'll ask you some questions when you get over there," he added, pointing to Canada.

"So anyone can just leave America, just like that, no questions asked?"

"Well, I hope so. It's a free country. Say, is there some reason you shouldn't be leaving? Your parents know where you are?"

"Oh no, I mean, yes, no—I was just asking. Our parents went ahead of us. They're waiting for us over there."

"Well, then, you better get going. And now you're holding up traffic!"

I gently touched the gas pedal, or at least I thought I did, and the car jerked forward. At that same instant, a loud whistle went off. I hit the brakes. I was so confused and scared I didn't know what to do. Jacko kept saying, *"Run!"* and Ralph kept saying *"No! Stop!"* I can't quite remember what I did, or what I did wrong, or why someone was blowing a whistle, but I could see in the side view mirror that the old man had left the booth and was approaching my door. I knew this had been a trap! I steeled myself for whatever was to happen. I looked over at Ralph. He had his knife out.

"Jesus, put that—"

The old man was at my window.

"Sorry, son," he said politely and a bit out of breath. "I didn't see the boat you were hauling."

The boat! The boat! *The goddamn boat was going to do us in!* What the *fuck* were we doing with a boat? Oh, shit, what had I got us into?

"That'll be another twenty-five cents for the boat."

Holy shit. Phew!

But at that moment, Jacko, apparently not hearing the man's simple request for an extra quarter, had thrown open his door, jumped out, and took off running across the Blue Water Bridge.

As I handed the man his quarter, he yelled at Jacko.

"Son, get back in the car! There's no pedestrian traffic on this bridge!"

"I'll go get him," I said in a rush. "Don't worry. Sorry!"

I hit the gas and caught up to Jacko in a matter of seconds.

"Get the fuck in here or you'll get us all arrested!" Ralph yelled at him. I pulled over and Ralph grabbed his arm. Jacko snapped back into his senses and got in.

"Jesus!" I said. "That was fucking stupid."

"Hey," he said, "I wasn't taking any chances."

"Jacko," Joey said. "That guy wasn't going to do anything to us. He was *old!* Like fifty or something!"

Things calmed down and we headed across the St. Clair River, leaving the United States behind. At the halfway mark there was a big sign that said WELCOME TO CANADA, and we all let out a big "WOOOO-HOOOO!!"

But now we had to get through the Canadian checkpoint. I pulled the car up to the Canadian booth. This time, it was not a school crossing guard. This Canadian looked official, like one of those Mounties, but not. He waved me to approach him.

"Citizenship?"

That was the only word he said. *Wow,* I thought, *they get right to the point here.*

"Yes," I answered. "Thank you!"

"Citizenship?" he said, louder.

"Yes," I repeated. "We'd like that." I couldn't believe how generous the Canadians were to just, like, right off the bat, offer you citizenship!

The Canadian looked at me. Hard.

"I don't have time to fool around. What is your citizenship and place of birth?"

Oh.

"Uh, Michigan. American."

"And where were you born?"

"Flint, Michigan."

"How 'bout the rest of you?"

"American."

"American."

"American."

"And where were you born?"

"Flint."

"Flint."

"Mexico."

Uh-oh.

"Are you a citizen of Mexico or the United States?"

"Both," Ralph said.

"What's the purpose of your visit to Canada?"

"We just thought we'd come over the bridge because we've never been here," I said.

"What's the boat for?"

"Oh, that's Joey's. His dad just had it attached to the car," I answered, thinking fast.

"How old are you boys?"

"Seventeen." "Seventeen." "Sixteen." "Seventeen."

"OK, pull over in that space over there."

I steered the car over to a small lot in front of a building with official-looking people in it. A man in a uniform came out.

"Please get out of the car, pop the trunk, and step inside."

We got out and went inside the building with the Mountie (or whatever he was). Two other officers started going through the car.

"You two look high," he said, looking at Jacko and Ralph. "Do you have other drugs on you?"

"No sir," Jacko said politely. "And we are *not* high, sir. We're just happy to be in Canada."

Oh, brother.

"What exactly are you boys up to? Do you know your boat has no motor?"

"Yes, sir," I said. "This is Joey's dad's car and boat, and he didn't want us to detach the boat so he said we could just take it with us."

"Uh-huh," the Canadian responded.

"But there is something I would like to ask you," I said, deciding to take the plunge. "Let's say we were draft dodgers, and we wanted to move to Canada—could we do that?"

The "Mountie" looked me up and down, and shouted over to the desk. "Cavity check!"

What???

"This way, please," said another official from the welcome wagon. And then he stopped, and the pseudo-Mounties started laughing.

"Just kidding. We're not like the American border guards. You can keep your pants on for us. We'll just give them a call and tell them you're on your way back." More laughs. I was familiar with this warped humor from watching Canadian television. They needed it to counteract all those dreadful beaver and moose documentaries.

They took us back out to the car where, thankfully, they found nothing but the boat without a motor.

"You can turn your car around now and head back to the U.S.," the head Canadian said.

Pushing my luck, I asked him again. "But, sir—what if we don't want to be drafted someday. Can we come here or not?"

"If you are here legitimately as an objector to the war, the Canadian government will give you asylum, yes. Have you been drafted? Are any of you in the armed services?"

"No."

"Then have a nice night. And be on your way."

We got back in Joey's car and headed back across the Blue Water Bridge to Michigan. The border guards on the American side were, fortunately, in a rush, so they asked the same set of citizenship questions as the Canadians did and sent us on our way. There would be no cavity checks that night. For the rest of the ride home we didn't say much, other than review what we had learned: Canada would take us in if need be, even if we had to endure their Canadian sense of humour.

A fair deal, all around.

In February, my birthday was the 279th date called for the draft lottery, and the year after that it was #115. Both were beyond the cutoff number. I was classified 4-F on my draft card and did not have to learn French, the metric system, or how to soak my fries in cheese curd.

I would remain fond of Canada for a very long time.

Two Dates

THERE WAS LINDA LIMATTA and her sister, Sue, and Mary Powers, Marcia Nastle, and Luanne Turner, too. There was Barb Gilliam, Lisa Dean, Debbie Johnson — it's all true. Denise Hopkins, Cheryl Hopkins, Karen Hopkins, any Hopkins would do! There was Kathy Minto and Kathy Collins, Kathy Root, and Cathy O'Rourke — yes, if her name was Kathy, that just might do. There was Mary Sue Johnson, Mary Jo Madore, Mary Sue Rauschl, and Maribeth Beach. Jill Williams, Diane Peter, Lora Hitchcock, Wendy Carrell, Jeanie Malin, Madeline Peroni, Louise Prine, Suzanne Flynn, and Susie Hicks — and there wasn't *one* of them, not a single one of them, that I had the courage to walk up to and simply ask if they'd like to go out to a movie with me on Friday night.

Well, there *was* Susie Hicks. I was walking down the hall with her between fifth and sixth hour, on our way to student council class. In my last year of high school I ran for student council. I won on a platform of promising to eliminate the homecoming queen contest. This immediately had me crossed off the list of every pretty girl in the school. But I didn't care; I never stood a chance with them anyway.

Susie Hicks was the one exception. She was the vice president of her class, served on student council with me, sang
in the high school musical, and was also a jock. She always
laughed at my jokes and I, of course, somehow misconstrued
that as her giving some thought to me as possible boyfriend
material. I clearly didn't understand that just because a girl
likes you, it doesn't mean that she *likes* you.

Susie and I had three long hallways to navigate before
reaching student council, giving me plenty of time to make
my move. I had worked out my pitch that morning in front
of the mirror. Keep it cool, don't make it sound like you're
asking her to go out on a date, have a backup plan to cover
up my massive hurt and rejection if she says no. With an
optimistic outlook like that, I was sure to score.

I spent all of hallway #1 walking with her and just trying
to calm down and make my heart beat at regular intervals
instead of watching it push its way through my shirt. Hallway
#2 was spent trying to remember my lines—I had forgotten
what to say, what to ask (but not *who* to ask, I knew who to
ask, I was walking with her!). We rounded the bend into the
third and final hallway and, with the last bit of oxygen I had
left, I opened my mouth.

"Su-Susie," I stammered, "I-I was thinking…"

And at that moment an incoming mortar round in the
form of Nick West, captain of the basketball team, president of the class, and possessor of the stolen face of Robert
Redford, flew in between us.

"Hey Susie!" he said, as he went in for a quick kiss. "See
you after council!"

If anything, I was grateful for Nick's interruption. I had
no idea they were going together, and I would have suffered

the worst form of humiliation had I actually been able to get the question out of my mouth. I breathed a sigh of relief. I felt no remorse that the world was an unfair place. To the contrary, I was glad to be reminded that I was not sent to Earth to date homecoming queens. Or at least that sounded good enough to get me through the next hour. (Yes, she became homecoming queen. I admit it—I desperately loved all homecoming queens, each and every single one of them.)

Admission: When it comes to social interaction, I am a shy person. Yes, me. My idea of an exciting Saturday night in high school was staying home and watching *Mannix* and *Mission: Impossible* on CBS (Friday night it was *The High Chaparral* and *Nanny and the Professor*). Occasionally I hung out with my guy friends, and when it looked like the planned activity of the evening didn't involve violating state or federal laws or being driven around by a drunken sixteen-year-old, I was every bit the participant in lighting sacks of dog shit on people's porches, then ringing the doorbell and running like hell.

But girls were far too intimidating to approach, and it was just as well. I had work to do, books to read, and…and…I forgot, but it was important! I was consoled only by statistics and probability: if there were 1.5 billion females on this planet, the chance that at least one of them would want to be with me was something like…100 percent! So, she was out there. Somewhere. Maybe between Bay City and Sterling Heights, please? If it turned out that my one true love had been placed (mistakenly) in Slovenia, then I guess all I could do was sit back and hope that CBS would renew *Mannix* for another season.

Date #1

It was in my junior year when the gods, perhaps bored out of their omniscient minds from being so godlike perfect all the time, decided to play a practical joke on me, just to see me collapse into a puddle of misery. Out of nowhere, they sent Linda Milks, a senior—*and a cheerleader!*—over to my locker on the last day of the school year.

"Hey—I was thinking—you want to go out on a date with me?"

I assumed she was talking to someone else on the other side of the locker door, so I kept fumbling with my combination.

"Hey, you!" she said, gently slugging me in the shoulder. "You wanna go out with me?"

I was paralyzed with fear and unable to speak. The fear quickly turned into embarrassment as I looked around to see who sent her to play this mean-spirited prank on me. But there was no one around in the hallway. Just Linda, looking up at me with those rich brown eyes, long dark hair and a body (a girl's body!) that was covered by a maroon and gold graduation gown.

"Um, me?"

"Yes, *you!* C'mon, it'll be fun. You like me, don't you?"

"Uh, yeah, sure. Sure, I mean, you're…Linda!"

I was finally able to spit out a two-syllable word: "Lin-da."

"Where's your yearbook? I want to sign it."

I fumbled around my locker for it and gave it to her. She wrote next to her senior photo: *"Your friend is your needs answered. See page 200. Love, Linda."*

She then turned to page 200 in the yearbook and wrote a full-page letter to me about how much I meant to her and how she would always be there for me. She signed it again with "love."

I stood there reading it, not having a clue what to say or do. I finally looked at her, the cheerleader, and she was all gooey-eyed and full of smiles. I wanted to ask her if she was high or had me confused with someone from shop class.

"Thank you. That's very nice. People don't usually write that sort of thing in my yearbook. Are you sure you don't want to scratch any of this out?"

"Hahahaha! Silly! That's why I love you. Well, here's my number"—she was writing on a page she had torn out of her notebook—"give me a call this summer. Let's go hang out and do something."

"OK. I will. Thanks."

"Don't thank me *yet!* And don't forget to call!"

Still not believing this was real, I checked to see if I was still alive: Uncombed hair? Check. Nose with the sinus condition? Check. Roll of fat? Check. Zits on forehead? Check. Yup, I was all there. Still me.

And that's what the cheerleader just asked out?

Linda Milks was a year older than me. She decided to take speech class in her senior year and join the forensics team, an unusual move for a cheerleader. She wasn't intensely interested in the topics covered, but she *was* interested in what I would say in class—especially if I did my Nixon impersonation. That would crack her up, and she would often turn around and flash me a smile that said...*said what?* I had no idea! She was a senior and a cheerleader and she was smiling at *me*. That was enough.

When she would ask me for help on an assignment I willingly gave it to her. But I would do that also for the farm kid in the hand-me-downs or the hoodlum who kept telling me he wanted to see if his fist could maybe help rearrange my face so I'd have "a better chance with the ladies." But Linda said she was taking forensics to gain some "self-confidence," and so I helped her with various ways and methods to give an effective speech. A couple times she stopped by my house to talk, but it wasn't until I read her letter in my yearbook that I realized she was coming by for something more. She really wanted to be friends. I was clueless. I just thought I was getting the opportunity to practice talking to a senior girl, which was a major accomplishment in and of itself. I will admit I did like it when she wore her cheerleader uniform on game days. Made speech class come alive.

After school was out for the summer, I went a full month before I dared to dial her number, and only then after practice-dialing it a dozen times. I finally dialed it for real, and she answered. A deep breath, and then my proposal: we go to a matinee showing of a new film called *Willy Wonka and the Chocolate Factory,* and we then go on a picnic to Richfield Park after the movie.

All innocent, safe, daylight activities. She loved the idea and said to pick her up Saturday at noon.

The most important part of this was that my parents were to have no clue I was going out on a date. If they were to find out, there would be an inquisition I imagined I would not survive.

Who is she?

What? She's older than you?

She's not Catholic?
She's a cheerleader?
Are you sure she doesn't have you confused with another Mike?
We don't know her.
*She lives **where?***
Who are her parents?
How come we've never heard of her?
What kind of grades did she get?
*She's **not** going to college?*
Wait, give me your yearbook. This is her? Oh, no siree, you're
not going anywhere with her!

Something like that, but with more questions.

So the trick was to get the car for the afternoon without any suspicions being raised. I told them I was picking up a couple guys and we were going to go play twenty-seven holes at the Flint Park golf course. This was a lot of golf, especially for me. But I'm sure they were happy to hear that I was getting any kind of exercise, so the keys were handed over and I was off to the Promised Land.

The birth control seat (I mean, the bucket seat) had not yet been mass-produced, so car seats were just one long bench. And when Linda got in the car, she slid over next to me—and I had no idea how I would be able to drive after that. Did I mention she was a cheerleader? Did I tell you about the perfect smile and the angel-white skin and the way her legs crossed like twin beams designed to withstand the worst earthquakes? I didn't think so.

We went to the Dort Mall Cinema, one of the first generation of mall theaters that were designed for "extra comfort," and in this case that meant they had stiff metal-backed seats that reclined so you could be more "relaxed." At least one of us relaxed during *Willy Wonka*. I was anything but. I don't remember much about the movie because I couldn't stop worrying about the picnic lunch I left in my car. I had put a bucket of Kentucky Fried Chicken in the trunk and it was a ninety-degree day. My other worry was, *What was I doing at a children's movie on my first date?* Nevertheless, Linda thought it was sweet and she told me as we left that most boys wouldn't have taken her to a movie like that. I did not take that as a compliment. I wanted to be like most boys.

The second half of the date went better. First, we didn't die of food poisoning. We found a nice place in the park and I broke out the bucket of chicken and some warm lemonade, laid a blanket out on the grass and we sat and talked about Vietnam, Mrs. Corning's art class, and Rod Serling's *Night Gallery*. She told me how I'd been good for her, and I looked at her and tried to figure out what she meant. Then it was time to go (I had to get the car back). We tossed the scraps in the trash barrel, rolled the blanket back up, and got in the car. I drove her home. We sat in the driveway.

"Thanks for the neat time," she said.

"You're welcome. I had a nice time."

"Was this your first date?" she asked sympathetically.

"Uh, what do you mean? No, I've gone out. Lots."

She smiled and leaned over and kissed me on the cheek.

"Let's do this again," she said.

Again?! You mean, go through all this *again?* I was exhausted.

"Sure," I said. "That'll be fun."

She got out, flashed another one of her sweet smiles, and I never saw her again.

Date #2

Sharon Johnson was the vice president of the student council. We often clashed and voted on opposite sides of the issues. She was very much for everyone getting along and finding "common ground." By the time I was a senior, I wanted to organize walkouts, boycotts of the lunchroom, and study-hall revolts. She hated hippies but played folk guitar in the choir and led the school in "Where Have All the Flowers Gone" at the spring talent show. She thought student council should plan school dances and hold theme-oriented "fun days." I thought student council should ask why we had no black teachers. She'd roll her eyes and shake her head at me.

She was perfect dating material.

It had been nearly four months since my one and only date and, being a teenage boy, I was going a bit bonkers. And what better way to push myself right off the cliff than to get fixated on a girl who found me slightly reprehensible?

The local congressman, Don Riegle, a liberal Republican at the time (he later switched parties), had asked to meet with two student reps from each of the county's high schools at his office in Flint. Sharon and I were picked from Davison High. I offered to drive and told her I would pick her up.

It was early on a Saturday morning when I pulled in her driveway. I honked to let her know I was there (getting out of the car and knocking on the door might make me seem too forward; had to play it cool). There was no response, so I honked a second time. At that moment she appeared at her upstairs bedroom window. She was wearing only a bra.

"Hold your horses!" she shouted down at me. "I heard you the first time!"

Simply wishing she had more lines to yell at me so she could stand there a bit longer in her underwear wasn't going to make it happen. She abruptly closed the window. My eyes were frozen on that window and I waited anxiously for the encore.

But when I saw her next, she was coming out the front door, this time fully clothed.

"Let's go," she ordered. "And quit staring at my chest."

"Whaddaya mean—you just showed me your chest!"

That was the best I could do? Act *upset?* Like I was *mad* I got to (sorta) see her breasts? Jesus, I could have thought of something nice to say, I could have offered her a compliment or an indication that she looked nice, I might have even figured out that she came to the window that way because she *liked* me. But that possibility was nowhere to be found in the shallow pool that passed for my total lifelong experience with girls.

We were late for the congressman's meeting. So what? *I got to see Sharon Johnson in a bra!* I was unable to listen to anything the congressman had to say, as I was trying to remember and store those entire four seconds at her window.*

When the time came to send the high school kids on their way, I went up to Mr. Riegle to ask for a favor.

"Congressman," I said, "I was wondering if you would come to our high school and speak about the war?"

---

* This was in the days before instant replay, DVRs, and other devices that kept memories for you. In 1971, you were forced to use brain matter and to keep pleasure stored for long periods of time.

"If it fits with my schedule, sure. Just check with my staff here and we'll see if we can set it up."

I drove Sharon back to her house. She was not happy with my request of the congressman, as he was famous for being only one of two Republicans in Congress who were opposing Nixon's reelection over the issue of the war. Sharon felt that my invitation to Riegle was sure to upset our high school principal.

"What's Mr. Scofield going to say when the congressman calls and says he can speak at the school?" she asked, perturbed. "Do you think he'll be able to tell a congressman no? Of course not!"

"I'm glad you're with me on this," I said with a grin. "You wanna go to a movie sometime?"

Wow. I did it. I said it. And all it took was to see a functioning bra in use.

But wait! *Oh, no — here comes the rejection.*

"Sure. How 'bout next Saturday night?"

"Sure."

"See you in student council Monday."

And on Monday we were right back at it, with her voting with the majority to shoot down my latest proposal to declare "Church Night" unconstitutional (no after-school activities were allowed on Wednesday nights in Davison's public schools, as that was the night the Protestant churches in town held their midweek church services).

When Saturday came around I picked out the movie to take her to, something I had seen back in the summer and could not get enough of: *Billy Jack*. This movie, I believed, would convert her to my worldview. In the movie, an ex–Green Beret is now a Zenlike Native American who takes on the local town

rednecks and conservatives when they try to shut down a hippie "free school." And there were breasts in the movie!

It was a chilly fall evening as I pulled my dad's Impala
into her driveway. This time I got out and went to the door.
Her father answered and greeted me with the justifiable suspicion that was required in those days. As he did a quick
scan into my eyes, let's just say he did not like what he saw.
Sharon appeared wearing a sweater that was modest but low-
cut enough to confirm her father's assessment of what the two
of us were up to.

"When do you plan to have her home?" he asked.

"As soon as the movie is over, Mr. Johnson," I said
doing my best Eddie Haskell impersonation. "Just two
hours, sir."

"OK, don't make it past eleven thirty."

OK. Eleven thirty. Perfect. That should give us a good
twenty minutes of making out, whatever that was.

We got in the Chevy and closed the doors. I put the key
in the ignition and turned it. Nothing. I turned it again. Still
nothing. Dead. I pumped the gas pedal and tried to start it
again. Silence. This car was not going anywhere. Fortunately
it was dark enough to cover how red my face was.

"Wow. I'm so sorry," I said. "It does this from time to
time. Needs a new battery, I think."

"So, what are we going to do?" Sharon said, in a coquett-
ish voice.

"I guess we could ask your dad for a jump."

"Yes, we could do that. I think it's a bad idea."

"So, what do you suggest?"

"We could just sit here and talk."

"Sure," I said. "But won't he see us out here?"

"You can't see anything out here from in there at night. He'll never look out here 'til it gets near eleven thirty. Plus, he thinks we've already left."

Huh. OK. Seemed like a plan. And so we talked.

We talked about teachers we liked and didn't, we talked about having siblings, we talked about the football team and the choir and where each of us were thinking of going to college. We even talked about our battles on student council.

All the while I kept wondering when the "sex" thing would start. I had no idea where to begin so I assumed she would just take the lead—I feel you can assume this when the someone in question comes to the window and greets you in a bra—and so I soldiered on through more conversation about *All in the Family,* Peter, Paul & Mary, the new freeway through Flint, Jarts, Jesus, Uptown Bob's vs. Downtown Bob's, how I got out of gym class in tenth grade, Jim Morrison's recent death, Walt Disney World opening next month, her new bell bottoms, the recent Apollo 15 mission, the Concert for Bangladesh, where was Attica, a new fabric store she discovered in the mall, eighteen-year-olds getting the right to vote—everything but sex. Having exhausted all topics for discussion, I threw caution into the backseat.

"So, we never talked about you at the window last week," I said, as if I was just going on to the next item in the news.

"Oh, you mean these?" she said as she pulled her sweater down a bit to reveal a bit more cleavage.

"Yes, those. Where did you get them?"

This made her laugh, and she slid over on the seat and put her head on my shoulder.

"I just thought you deserved a peek," she said. "Nothing more."

"You mean nothing more then, or nothing more now?"

"I mean, you saw what you saw, now let's enjoy this moment."

I did my best to enjoy it. Her hair smelled like tropical fruit, but I had no idea what tropical fruit *really was* unless bananas counted. I put my fingers through her hair to move it out of her face. She sat up.

"Oh my, look what we've done to the windows!"

What windows? would have been a good question, because I couldn't *see* the windows, or at least I couldn't see *out* of them. Every inch of them was steamed up after two hours of us yapping away and two minutes of me thinking "something" was gonna happen. We could no longer see the house, and certainly no one could see the inside of this car. If this was going to be the moment, then now was the time to act.

"Wow," she went on, "it looks like we've been messing around in here all night!"

"So let's justify the steam!" I suggested clunkily.

"I think I better get inside before my dad sees us."

And with that, she opened up the car door.

"C'mon," she said, "we gotta see if he can get your car started."

I got out and went with her to the door. We walked in and there were her mom and dad and younger sister, all sitting in the living room.

"How was the movie?" her mother inquired.

"Really good," Sharon replied convincingly. "Dad, we pulled back in and Mike's car died in the driveway. Do you think you could look at it?"

Mr. Johnson, like most dads in an auto town, was more

than happy to be asked to display his mechanical prowess. "Sure, let's see what the problem is."

We walked outside and down the driveway. As we approached the Impala, the windows were still half-steamed! I started to prepare my defense.

"Mike, why don't you give it a start?" he said, oblivious to the moisture from his daughter's mouth that had altered the look of my car.

I quickly got in and rolled the windows down in order to help dissipate the translucency of the windshield. I also turned the key in the ignition to the sound of nothing.

"OK, let's give it a jump and see if that'll work."

He went to the garage and drove his car back to mine, got out his jumper cables and connected his battery to the one under my hood.

"Try it again," he shouted.

I gave the key a turn to the right and instantly the motor came on. Finally, something started tonight.

"That's it," he said, looking now through the windshield for the first time, all clear and easy to see through. "Need to get that battery checked out."

I thanked him and said good-bye to Sharon.

"See you Monday," I said, trying to cover the sound of the end of my high school dating career.

"See you Monday," she said.

Twenty Names

"*Moore, your shirttail is out!*"

It was the voice of Mr. Ryan, the assistant principal for discipline at my high school, and he was right on my back. Not figuratively. He was literally *on it*.

"*Turn around!*"

I did as I was told.

"You know the rules. Shirts are to be tucked in."

I tucked it in.

"Bend over."

He was carrying "The Paddle," a shortened version of a cricket bat, but with holes drilled in it to get maximum velocity.

"C'mon, this is not right," I protested. "It's a *shirt!*"

"Bend over. Don't make me tell you again."

I did as I was told. And as I was bending over, I marked the date on my mental calendar as being the last time I would ever do what I was told to do again.

WHACK!

I felt that intensely. The flat board of hard wood smacking

against my rear end, and the two-second delay before the pain set in.

WHACK!

He did it again. Now it really hurt. I could already feel the heat of my skin through my pants, and I wanted to take that paddle and bash him over the head.

WHACK!

Now the greatest pain became the humiliation I was experiencing thanks to the growing crowd and the eyes of everyone in the cafeteria who was standing to get a look at what was happening in the hallway.

"That'll do," the sadist said. "Don't let me see you with your shirt out again."

And with that he walked away. He had no idea how profoundly he had just changed my life—and his. He had, in that one act of corporal punishment, created his own demise. How many times had this man struck a child in his career? A thousand? Ten thousand? Whatever the number, this would be his last.

It's funny, isn't it, how one minute you're just walking down the hall with your shirttail out, you're thinking about girls or a ball game or how you're on your last stick of Beaman's—and then the next hour you make a decision that will affect all the decisions you make for the rest of your life. So random, so unplanned. In fact, it puts the whole idea of making plans for your life to shame, and you realize you really are wasting your time if you're trying to come up with a college major, or how many kids to have, or where you want to be in ten years. One day I'm thinking about law school, and the next week I've committed all my meager teenage resources and energy to stripping an adult of whatever power he thinks he wields with that big paddle.

I straightened upward, red-faced for all to see in the cafeteria. There were plenty of snickers and guffaws, but mostly there was that look people have when they've just seen something they've never seen before. I was known as a *good* student. I was known as someone who had never been given the paddle. No one ever expected to watch me being beaten by the assistant principal. I was not the type of student you would see being told to "bend over." And that was what was so entertaining about this particular beating to the gathering crowd.

It's not like Assistant Principal for Discipline Dennis Ryan hadn't been gunning for me in the past, or that I hadn't done anything to deserve his wrath. I had done plenty. By the time I was halfway through my senior year, I had organized my own miniprotests against just about every edict that Ryan and the principal, Mr. Scofield, had laid down. The latest of these revolts involved convincing nine of the eighteen students in the senior Shakespeare class to walk out and quit the class.

The teacher had just handed back to me my twenty-page paper on *Hamlet* with a giant red "0" on top of it. That was my grade: Nothing. Zip. I stood up.

"You cannot treat me this way," I said to him politely. "And I am officially dropping out of this class." I turned to the students.

"Anybody want to join me?"

Half of them did.

The zero grade would lower my GPA to a 3.3 by the end of the year. I couldn't have cared less.

This was not my first run-in with a teacher. The teacher who ran the student council class also flunked me. I never missed a day of that class. I made more motions and participated in more debates than perhaps anyone else in there. And that's what bothered the teacher who was the student council advisor.

"How can you flunk me?" I confronted him.

"I'm flunking you because you create too much trouble in here," he answered smugly. "I like a nice quiet, peaceful student council. You have made this year too difficult for me."

All of this weighed on my mind on the walk home that day of my public paddling by the assistant principal. How would I exact my revenge? I had to look no further that night than the evening newspaper.

A copy of the local *Flint Journal* lined the box of trash I was cleaning out in our garage. I looked down and between stains of Miracle Whip and Faygo Redpop I noticed a story that reminded me about how the voting age in America had recently been lowered to eighteen. *Hmmm,* I thought, *I'll be eighteen in a few weeks.*

I went back inside the house and, an hour later, I picked up the town weekly, the *Davison Index.* There, on the front page, taunting me, daring me, my future calling me: *Hello, Mike. Read this!* The headline?

SCHOOL BOARD ELECTION JUNE 12, TWO SEATS OPEN.

Huh. I'll be able to vote for school board in a few months. Cool. Wait.

Wait a minute! If I can vote…*can I run?* Can I run for a seat on the Board of Education? Would this not make me one of the *bosses* of the principal and vice principal? Yes? Yes? Whoa.

The next day, I called the county clerk's office, the people in charge of elections.

"Um, yeah," I stammered into the phone, not quite believing I was making this call. "Um, I was wondering that, now that eighteen-year-olds can vote, can we also run for office?"

"No. Not all offices. Which office would you like to run for?"

"School board."

"Hang on, lemme check." Within a minute he was back on the phone.

"Yes. The required age for school board candidates is eighteen."

WOW! I couldn't believe it. But then panic set in. How could I afford such a thing? They must charge you a lot of money to put your name on the ballot.

"How much does it cost to get on the ballot?" I asked the man.

"Cost? Nothing. It's free."

Free? This just kept getting better. Until he added the following:

"Of course you do have to get the required number of signatures on a petition in order to have your name placed on the ballot."

Damn. I knew there was a catch. There were twenty thousand residents in the Davison School District, comprising the town of Davison and the townships of Davison and Richfield. Going all over the school district to collect God knows how many signatures was going to be next to impossible. I mean, I still had lots of algebra homework to do.

"How many names do I need on these petitions?" I asked with resignation.

"Twenty."

"*Twenty??*"

"Twenty."

"Did you say *twenty?*"

"Yes. Twenty. You need twenty signatures on a petition that you can pick up at the board of education offices."

I could not believe that I only needed twenty names on a petition — and then, suddenly, I would be an official candidate! I mean, twenty names was nothing! I knew at least twenty stoners who would sign anything I put in front of them.

I thanked the man, and the next day I went to the superintendent's office to pick up the petition. The secretary asked if I was picking up the petition for one of my parents.

"No," I replied. And instead of adding "Would you like to see the welts on my butt or would you rather I call Child Protective Services?" I simply said, "It's for me."

She picked up the phone and made a call.

"Yes, I have a young man here who says he wants to run for school board. What is the age requirement these days? Uh-huh. I see. Thank you."

She hung up the phone and bit her lip.

"How old are you?" she asked.

"Seventeen," I replied.

"Oh, well, then, you can't run. You have to be eighteen."

"But I'll be eighteen by the day of the election," I blurted out.

"One minute," she said, picking up the phone again.

"Can a seventeen-year-old run if he will be eighteen on election day? Uh-huh. I see. Yes. Thank you."

"Apparently you may run," she said, as she reached into the file cabinet and pulled out the petition. "Make sure that *every* signature is that of a *registered* voter who lives *within the boundaries* of the school district. If you don't have *twenty* valid names, you will *not* be placed on the ballot."

I had the names within the hour. When the twenty signers asked me why I was running, I just said, "To fire the principal and assistant principal." That was my entire platform on Day One, and it seemed to play well, at least to twenty citizens.

"What about college?" my mother asked, perplexed when I told her I had decided to run for school board. "How can you serve on the school board and go to the University of Detroit?"

"I guess if I win, I'll go to U of M in Flint." She liked the sound of that. If I won, I would not be leaving home. My parents were not the type to kick you out at eighteen (though that is when my sisters would leave). They did not like to see us go.

I returned the next day to the school board office and turned in my petition. Word soon spread through town that "a hippie" had qualified to be on the June ballot. I set a goal of knocking on every door in the school district. I handed voters a flyer that I had written up outlining my feelings about education and about the Davison schools specifically. I told people the administrators in the high school had to go. I'm guessing this frightened most parents.

But there were some in town who were delighted with the idea of a young person on the school board. OK, they were all under twenty-five.

And then there was the majority, the ones who noticed I had long hair. The week I began to campaign, the racist governor of Alabama, George C. Wallace, won the Michigan Democratic Presidential primary. Not a good sign for me and my chances. (This was also my very first time voting. I cast my first vote ever as a citizen for Congresswoman Shirley Chisholm for president.)

The Chamber of Commerce types in town were appalled at the thought of me, a kid, winning, as were many of the Protestant pastors, the local rednecks, and the pro-war crowd (which was made up of all of the above).

The problem was, the town pooh-bahs had a really bad strategy to stop me. Six of them went down to the school board office and took out their own petitions to run against me. Six of them against me. Clearly they missed a few days of civics class when they were young. You don't win by running the most candidates – you'll split the vote and your opponent will win with a plurality. It was to my good fortune that they did not know the word *plurality* and I did. I taunted them and challenged more Republicans to go get their own petitions to see if they could beat me!

And that was when I got a taste of my own medicine. In addition to the six older, conservative adults who would oppose me, an eighteen-year-old decided to also run against me—and thus split the already very small youth/liberal vote I was going to get. The other eighteen-year-old candidate was none other than the vice president of the student council, Sharon Johnson—the girl who was one of my only two dates in high school.

"Why are you running?" I asked her, a bit peeved that she was stealing my thunder.

"I don't know, I thought it would be neat. We could both be on the school board!" (Two seats were open on the board, and her idea was that we could both win and serve together.)

Why was she still tormenting me? First student council, then the bra, then the steamed-up windows, and now she's going to split the youth vote and sink any slight chance I might have had to get elected.

A week before the election, I received my first anonymous hate mail. It was addressed to the two eighteen-year-olds running. It read:

```
Sharon Johnson
Michael F. Moore
   What lame-brained fool ever talked you
two brats into running for the school
Board?
   Moore, you talk about your vast
knowledge about all affairs. Where and when
did you acquire this? Why you haven't even
got brains enough to get a haircut.
   You are asking the citizens of Davison
to vote you into the school board,
actually insulting their intelligence by
so doing.
   My advice to you both is this? Have
your good Mother take your diapers off;
get a job or go to school, acquire some
of this wisdom only acquired through
experience and hard knocks and then come
around and run for offices. Why you haven't
even started to live as yet.
```

> Sharon—at least you are a beautiful
> young lady and you deserve a better fate
> than to be elected to a school board which
> is really a thankless job.
>
> One who knows what he is talking about.

Yes, Sharon, you are a beautiful young lady, unlike that long-haired lug. As hate mail goes, this was one of the nicer ones I would ever receive.

On the morning of election day I got up, ate my Cocoa Krispies, and went to school. There were still five days left before graduation, and I had finals to take. The yearbooks were handed out and they contained the results of another election: the senior class had voted me "Class Comic."

When school recessed at 1:30 p.m., I went and voted for me. I had focused my entire campaign on getting every eighteen- to twenty-five-year-old out to vote. There were nearly two hundred eligible voters just in my senior class. I had spent less than a hundred dollars on the campaign. We had spray-painted yard signs with stencils in my parents' basement. There were no ads, only the one-page flyer I handed out going door to door.

There was a big turnout at the polls, and when they closed at 8:00 p.m., the counting of the paper ballots began. Less than two hours later, the results were announced.

"Ladies and gentlemen," the district's assistant superintendent announced, "we have the results. In first place… Michael Moore."

I was shocked. The group of hippie students who had gathered to watch the votes being counted went crazy with delight. A reporter from a local station asked me how I felt about beating seven "adults."

"Well," I said. "I'm an adult, too. And I feel great."

"Well, congratulations," the reporter said, "you're the youngest person ever elected to public office in the State of Michigan."

"Is that true?"

"Yes, it is. You beat the previous record by three years."

Across the gymnasium where the votes had been counted, I could see the disappointed looks on the faces of the realtors, the insurance salesmen, the country club wives. The following day, a reporter from Detroit called to tell me I was the youngest elected official in the entire country (there was no one under the age of eighteen who held public office). Did I have a comment about that?

"Wow."

What else was I gonna say? I was too deep in my own whirlwind about what had just happened to my life. Now I was going to be one of the seven people in charge of the school district, and the boss of both the principal and, most important, the assistant principal, Ryan. I was now in a position to take that fucking bat out of his hand.

The next morning, I went to school as I had for the previous twelve years. Walking down the hall on my way to Mr. Hardy's creative writing class, I saw Assistant Principal Dennis Ryan coming toward me. Funny, there was nothing in his hand.

"Good day, Mr. Moore."

Mr. Moore? That was a first. But hey, after all, how else would you address your new boss? Yet I was still a student under him. Weird. He kept walking and so did I.

It became a week of high fives and black power hand-shakes (I know, I know — this *was* Davison) among the students, many of them relishing what havoc I could wreak. I was given a number of suggestions from my constituents: make the jocks take real classes; put a cigarette machine in the cafeteria; institute the "four-hour school day"; drop the white milk and have only chocolate; find out what's in the "Thursday Surprise" at lunch and kill the person who makes it.

Five nights later on June 17, 1972 (non sequitur alert: at the same time, burglars five hundred miles away were breaking into a place called the Watergate), I lined up inside Davison High School with my nearly four hundred fellow graduates, all of us in our maroon-and-gold caps and gowns. Dress code rules were still in effect, but a number of students chose to secretly wear no pants or skirts. They *did* make sure that the area at the top of the gown had the requisite blouse and shirt and tie, because that could be seen by the authorities. Flashing the nether regions would take place later on the football field at the end of the ceremonies. Water balloons were also well hidden.

Mr. Ryan walked down the line five minutes before the ceremony inspecting each of the students, mostly to make sure that there were no projectile devices in people's hands and to be certain that every boy was wearing a tie.

And it was then that Ryan came upon Billy Spitz. Billy was a kid from a family of simple means. His idea of a tie was what was called a "bolo tie" — two long strings hanging from a knot or a clamp at the neck. For many who came from the South to work in the factories of Flint, putting on a bolo tie was called "dressing up." It was what you wore to a dance or to church. It was a tie.

Not to Ryan.

"Step out of line!" he barked at Billy. "What is this?" he continued, as he pulled the bolo tie out from under Billy's gown.

"It's my tie, sir," Billy responded sheepishly.

"This is not a tie!" Ryan retorted for all to hear. "You're outta here. Go on. *Git!* You're not graduating."

"But, Mr. Ryan—"

"Did you hear me?" Ryan snapped, as he grabbed him and physically pulled him away from the rest of us, showing him the door. It sent a shock wave through the line of graduates. Even in the final *minute* of high school, we had to witness one last act of cruelty.

And not one of us said anything. Not the tough guy in back of Billy, not the Christian girl in front of him. And not me. Even though I was now officially one of the seven in charge of the schools, I remained silent. Maybe I was just too stunned to speak. Maybe I didn't want to cause trouble before we got out to the football field, as I was planning to cause a heap of it out there (I had been chosen by the students to give the class speech). Maybe I was still cowed by Mr. Ryan and it would take more than an election for me to stand up to him. Maybe I was just happy it wasn't me. I really didn't know Billy, and so, like the other four hundred, I minded my own business.

When it was my time to speak on the graduation stage, I got through the only three sentences I had written. I had seven pages from a yellow legal pad rolled up in my hands to make it look like I had prepared a typical graduation speech. In fact, I had something else on my mind that I was going to say.

I had learned that one of our classmates, Gene Ford, was not to receive the gold honor cords of the National Honor Society because, due to a serious disability, he had to be mostly home-schooled. Even though his grades were high, no one made any provisions for counting his home grades, which would have definitely qualified him for the Honor Society.

Less than a minute into my speech, I came to an abrupt halt and told the crowd that the student sitting in the wheelchair in the front row was denied his honor cords because he wasn't "normal" like the rest of us. What if, I suggested, *we* were the abnormal ones? Some of us seniors, I pointed out, had chosen not to wear our honor cords because we did not want to separate ourselves from those who, for whatever reason, didn't have the same grades we had. I went into an extemporaneous rant about the oppressive nature of being in school and not having rights or a say in your own education. I then said I'd like to present my honor cords to Gene.

And so I left the stage and did just that. And the school board members who were present? Well, they just got a coming attractions trailer to the movie they were about to star in with me for the next four years.

The following day the phone rang and my mother said it was Billy Spitz's mom. I took the phone. She was fighting back tears.

"My husband and I and Billy's grandmother were all sitting in the stands waiting for Billy to walk across the stage, waiting for his name to be called. They called the entire class and never called Billy's name. We couldn't see him sitting with the rest of you. We didn't understand. We were confused. And then we got worried. *Where was he?* We got up and looked everywhere for him. We went out to the parking lot and to our car. And that's where we found him."

She began to cry.

"There, in the backseat, was Billy, all curled up in a ball, and crying. He told us what Mr. Ryan had done.

"We can't believe this happened. *He was wearing a tie!* Why did this happen?"

"I don't know, Mrs. Spitz," I said quietly.

"Were you there?" she asked me.

"Yes."

"Did you see Mr. Ryan do this?"

"Yes."

"And you did nothing?"

"I was still a student." And a coward.

"You were also a school board member! Isn't there any-thing you can do about this?"

Of course, there was nothing I could do. They weren't going to hold graduation over to correct this injustice. I had a chance, maybe, to do something about it the night before. But I didn't. I would never forget this small but powerful moment of my silence and looking the other way. I promised her I would not let this rest and that, as I said when I ran for election, I would work toward Mr. Ryan's removal.

Two days later I was told to go to the home of the school board secretary and be sworn in. I rode my bicycle over to her house in my bare feet and was sworn in without my shoes on. She said, "Where are your shoes?"

"I'm not wearing any," I said. She just glared at my feet.

I raised my right hand, and when it came time to say the words about "defending the Constitution from all enemies, foreign and domestic," I added, *"especially domestic."* She looked at me and rolled her eyes. She had taught my mother in high school. "She was maybe the worst teacher I had," my mother told me later. Mom also told me I should have worn some shoes.

The honeymoon period in my first year on the board of education was longer than any of us had expected. Most of the motions I made to improve the schools—including establishing some student rights—were passed. The board listened to what I had to say about how the high school was being run, and how the assistant principal might do better being on the police force (in Chile). I said that the principal was not a forward thinker; he stifled dissent and created a climate where new ideas were not encouraged. In my first year I became a conduit to the board for students, teachers, and parents so that their voices could be heard.

One Monday night about eight months into my term, the superintendent presented "letters of resignation" from the high school principal—and Assistant Principal for Discipline, Dennis Ryan. I was stunned. I couldn't believe that, just ten months after I was beaten with a high-velocity wooden board, the mission I went on by running for the school board had actually been accomplished. It caught me by surprise, as I did not think they were really going to do anything about this problem. True, they were not going to publicly fire them. They let them resign, to save face. Saving face was not yet something I was interested in, as I was not yet old enough to have the necessary compassion and mercy for two men who were just in the wrong job—and had a right to be treated with dignity and respect, even if one of them had not accorded the same to me and Billy Spitz and others. So to twist the knife in deeper, I asked the superintendent at the public meeting if the principal and assistant principal had made this decision on their own or did he, the superintendent, ask for these letters? He nodded his head quietly and said simply, "The latter."

The next day, the students in the high school couldn't believe that one of their own actually got to say "You're fired!" to the principal and assistant principal. We started thinking— what *else* can we do?

That was a dangerous thought.

Milhous, in Three Acts

ACT I: Nixon's the One

Every good Catholic blamed Lyndon Johnson for Kennedy's death. Not that he had anything to do with the actual assassination (though there were those who believed he did). But we all knew he hated Kennedy, and Kennedy didn't care much for him. Kennedy was forced to put Johnson on the ticket in order to get the racist Southern states to vote for him, states that were too dumb to figure out that Johnson shared none of their hatred for black people and would, in fact, ram the most important civil rights legislation since the Civil War down their throats the instant he became president.

What we couldn't accept was that Kennedy was murdered in *Johnson's state,* and if anyone should have been on their toes preventing such a tragedy it should've been Lyndon Baines Johnson. If there was one mental note all Catholics made after November 1963, it was that we would never, ever vacation in Dallas.

Johnson, within nine months of JFK's death, escalated the Vietnam War by telling a lie. On August 4, 1964, he

announced that earlier in the day, the North Vietnamese
attacked a U.S. ship in the Gulf of Tonkin. This did not happen. Johnson then presided over a slaughter of epic propor-
tion, and any other good he might have been remembered
for, like the civil rights laws or his war on poverty, was out
the window.

In March 1968, Johnson gave up and declared he would
not seek reelection. Even though I was only fourteen, I followed all of this and pinned my hopes on either Eugene
McCarthy or Bobby Kennedy to win the Democratic nomination. What was unacceptable to me was the accession of
the vice president, Hubert Horatio Humphrey, to the White
House. He had loyally backed Johnson in the war, and so for
me that was that, done and done, Humphrey was out.

I was up late watching *The Joey Bishop Show* when Joey
was handed a note that made him choke. He announced that
Robert F. Kennedy, who the night before had been shot after
winning the California presidential primary, had just died. I
screamed, and my parents, who were already in bed, came
out in the living room.

"What are you doing up watching TV?" my mother asked.

"Bobby is dead!"

"No!" my mother said, clutching her chest and sitting
down. "Oh, God. Oh, God."

"Just hang it right there on your door," Salt said, instruct-
ing me where to place the "Nixon's the One" poster. "There.
Perfect."

Thomas Salt was a high school senior and in charge of
the Students for Nixon club, and although I was just a fresh-

man, I had already moved up as his number two in charge of everything he didn't want to do. We were students at St. Paul's Seminary in Saginaw, Michigan, and we were certainly in the minority when it came to supporting the scoundrel Richard Milhous Nixon. We lived in a haven of Democrats (obviously, they were all Catholics, and Nixon was the evil one who'd been defeated by our only Catholic president). The entire seminary was blindly supporting Humphrey—but not Salt and not me, and not a few brave others. We weren't supporting warmongers, period, regardless of what their party affiliation was.

Well, I'm not so sure about the *we* of that statement, as the four others were the sons of well-to-do Republicans whose fathers were either corporate attorneys or executives at Dow Chemical or one of the car companies. They probably liked Nixon because that was how they were wired. Me, I had joined in with them because I refused to support Humphrey on purely moral grounds—and while it may seem strange to use the word *moral* while backing Richard Nixon, the way I saw it, I just didn't have a choice.

Oh, sorry—there *was* a choice. There was George Wallace running as an independent Klandidate for president (he would go on to win five Southern states). My congressman from Flint, Don Riegle, said that Nixon told him he had a "secret plan to end the war." He promised that Vietnam would be over within six months of his election. (And it was. Six months after his *second* election, in 1972.)

But for now, Nixon was the "peace candidate," and that was all I needed to hear. He was also in favor of lowering the voting age to eighteen years old. He said he would create an environmental protection agency (the EPA). He said he would make it illegal to treat girls in schools any different than boys (Title IX). He was also a shady, shifty character, and your gut knew he couldn't be trusted any further than you could throw his dog, Checkers. But he said he would end the war.

In addition to our campaigning on the high school campus, we spent Saturday afternoons knocking on doors in Saginaw, a blue-collar town that didn't have much use for Republicans. We soldiered on nonetheless, and we did our best for the man everyone called Tricky Dick.

I was a freshman, so I needed to get special permission to campaign off campus for Nixon. This was granted, so long as I agreed to do some extra chores at the home of the diocese's auxiliary bishop (and the seminary's former rector), James Hickey.

It was early October 1968, and my job was to help drain and clean the bishop's outdoor pool. Bishop Hickey remained close to the goings-on at the seminary he helped to found a decade ago, and in turn that meant he had heard about our efforts for Richard Nixon.

"I hear you're interested in politics," he said to me, as I mopped up the pool's interior.

"Yes, Bishop. My family has always paid attention to government and stuff."

"I see. But why Nixon?"

I was nervous enough because I hadn't the slightest idea how to clean a pool. I was afraid I might give the wrong answer — and it would be "good-bye priesthood."

"The war is wrong. Killing people is wrong. He will end the war."

"Will he, now?" the Bishop said, looking at me squarely over the top of his wire-rim spectacles.

"Uh, that's what he says. Six months and no war."

"You know this man has a—how shall we say it?—a history of not telling the truth."

I was now in huge trouble. The next thing I expected to hear was that I was committing a mortal sin by helping Richard Nixon.

"I remember when he first ran for the Senate in California," the Bishop continued. "Made up a bunch of things about his lady opponent that weren't true. Awful things. People didn't find out until later. But it was too late. He was already a senator then."

I had no idea what he was talking about. The October temperature was dropping, and the water from the hose that would splash on me was cold and unpleasant. I did not want to listen to this sermon. Besides—what's a bishop doing with his own swimming pool?

"I didn't know that," I said respectfully. "I wasn't for him in 1960," I added, hoping that would give me some dispensation.

"How old were you in 1960?"

"First grade. I even memorized President Kennedy's inaugural address."

"Can you still recite it?

Of course I could. I'd been giving the speech to the nuns for years for extra credit.

"Well, let me hear a little of it."

And so there I stood, mop and squeegee in hand, and gave him my favorite part:

"The world is very different now. For man holds in his mortal hands the power to abolish all forms of human poverty and all forms of human life. And yet the same revolutionary beliefs for which our forebears fought are still at issue around the globe—the belief that the rights of man come not from the generosity of the state, but from the hand of God."

He enjoyed that. So I thought I'd continue with another one, this time with the Kennedy accent:

"To those peoples in the huts and villages across the globe struggling to break the bonds of mass misery, we pledge our best efforts to help them help themselves, for whatever period is required—not because the Communists may be doing it, not because we seek their votes, but because it is right. If a free society cannot help the many who are poor, it cannot save the few who are rich."

"Very impressive!" he offered, an approving smile on his face. "These are important words. Never forget them."

He paused.

"And, of course, I'm not telling you how to vote, but if you would, please do me a favor and reflect on those words you just recited to me."

The war, of course, didn't end six months after Nixon took office. It got bigger. We invaded another country (Cambodia), antiwar groups and journalists were spied on, and to celebrate Christmas of 1972 we dropped more bombs on North Vietnam than we dropped during any campaign of the war. In all, we would end up killing over three million southeast Asians, and over fifty-eight thousand of our troops would never come back alive. The bishop knew this, and I later would realize he had me over not to clean a pool but to clean my head. The following spring Bishop Hickey was sent to Rome and then later became the bishop of Cleveland, and finally, the cardinal of the archdiocese of Washington, D.C. Two women missionaries he dispatched to El Salvador were brutally murdered along with two other religious women by the American-backed government there. He became outspoken while in D.C., opposing the U.S. wars in Nicaragua and El Salvador.

A year later, after leaving the seminary, I made a pact with myself never to reveal to anyone that I had campaigned for Richard Milhous Nixon.

ACT II: Horses on the Ellipse

"You're not taking your sister to Washington," my father said, sitting at the dinner table. "No, you are not," my mother chimed in.

I was eighteen and an adult and could do what I wanted, but my sister Anne was seventeen and still in high school. I had announced that I was going with friends on a trip to Washington, D.C, to participate in a massive antiwar demonstration on the day Nixon was to be inaugurated for his second term. The car was to contain myself; our church's youth leaders, Gary Wood and Phyllis Valdez, and their friend Peter Case; my buddy Jeff Gibbs; and my sister Anne.

The fight at the dinner table for Anne to go became more intense. All subjects were now open to debate: the war, the long hair, the guitar Mass, John Sinclair (who grew up down the street), the Weathermen gathering in Flint, the peace signs we painted on the walls in the basement, the effect all this was having on our younger sister, Veronica, etc., etc.

In the end, Anne said she was going and there would be no further discussion. Silence. End of dinner.

We got to my cousin Pat's house outside D.C. before midnight. We crashed there, and when we awoke, we made our plans for the day. There was a teach-in, and Leonard Bernstein was going to conduct a "Concert as a Plea for Peace" at the National Cathedral, with Senators Edward Kennedy and Eugene McCarthy speaking.

When we got to the cathedral the following evening, we were shocked at the size of the crowd trying to get in. The line stretched for what seemed like a mile. There was no way we were going to get inside — until Peter said he had an idea.

"Just keep your eye on me," he said, "and one by one come up and join me."

Peter broke out a bag of peanuts and went up toward the front of the line, found someone who looked like he had a friendly face, and offered him some of his nuts. A jovial conversation ensued, making it seem like Peter knew the guy who was "obviously" holding a place for him. Now five more of us had to make this look casual enough to walk up and appear as if we belonged there. And one by one we did. This apparently was too much for one guy in line who was watching the whole ruse unfold. He left his place in the line and walked up to us.

"I'm wondering how your conscience is handling this right now," he said in a voice that sounded remarkably similar to my conscience. "Do you think it's right to make cuts like this and deny people who've been here before you a chance to go inside?"

None of us said anything. No one made eye contact with him. It's as if he wasn't there. But we were.

"Amazing," he remarked, shaking his head. "Nothing to say for yourselves? And at a church, no less."

None of us felt very good about ourselves. What we had done was wrong. We'd also driven six hundred miles and didn't really give a shit. Or at least tried to pretend we didn't. Everyone around us heard the scolding and all eyes were on us. We couldn't wait to get inside the church and be taken off the cross.

The concert was unlike anything I had ever attended. Bernstein conducted members of the National Symphony and other orchestras in Haydn's "Mass in Time of War." It was a haunting, beautiful work of classical music, and I noticed the sadness on the faces of many around me. There were readings and poems, and it deeply moved the twenty-five hundred who were present (another twenty-five thousand listened on loudspeakers outside on the lawn of the cathedral).

On Inauguration Day we got there early so we could try to get a glimpse of Nixon's limo before he went to Capitol Hill. Security was very tight, but we got close enough to see the armored car and jeer at it and hold our signs so he could see them. As he passed, he waved, and we waved back, though not with the entire hand. I was a long way from the seminary.

The rally on the Ellipse by the Washington Monument was not as large as previous antiwar rallies, but it was still populated by upwards of seventy-five thousand people. It was the largest crowd I had ever been in, and it was intense and angry. People were fed up with Nixon and his murderous ways. We stood on top of the hill at the base of the Washington Monument, looking out across the demonstration and to the White House, hoping Nixon was back and looking out the window.

After about two hours, some of the demonstrators decided it was time for more aggressive action. The Washington Monument is encircled by fifty United States flags. A group of students thought the flags might look better if they were flown upside down. And that's what they did. The National Parks police were outnumbered and called for reinforcements. Within minutes, in rode the cavalry. Dozens of cops on horseback ascended the hill to the monument. As we were not participating in this sidebar demo, we weren't worried about anything happening to us. Wrong assumption. The horsemen started attacking anyone in sight with their clubs. We took off, like most of the crowd, running down the hill. The police decided to pursue us. I did not know it was humanly possible to outrun a horse, but somehow we shot down that hill like bullets. I could hear one horse right behind me, and at that moment I figured I could do something instantly that the horse couldn't do.

Stop.

As I stopped dead in my tracks, the horse just kept going. There were plenty of other protesters to chase. I yelled at the others in our group to follow me, and we moved out to the right side of the crowd where there were no police. Out of breath, we all agreed that was too close a call and decided that we had done enough to make our voices heard. We flipped off the White House one last time ("Did you see him in the window?" "Yes, I think I saw him!"), and headed back to Michigan.

ACT III: Bad Axe

I had worked for him, I had protested him. And now I wanted closure. I wanted to say good-bye.

It was clear that Nixon wasn't long for the White House. By the late spring of 1974, after the break-in of the Watergate offices of the Democratic Party, after the Senate Watergate hearings and John Dean's revelations, after Alexander Butterfield admitted Nixon taped every conversation in the Oval Office, after the White House authorized the break-in of Daniel Ellsberg's psychiatrist's office, after Nixon lost at the Supreme Court and the Pentagon Papers were published, and after he tried to cover it all up, President Richard Milhous Nixon was hanging on by a thread when he decided to pay a visit to three small towns northeast of Flint, Michigan.

He had been hiding in the White House, drinking, talking to old paintings on the wall, afraid to go out and be with the public, the majority of whom now wanted him to either leave the presidency of his own volition or be the first president to be tossed out. He wanted neither. He was a fighter. He never gave up, even when all his chips were down, many times before. He was Dick Nixon of Yorba Linda, California, and he wasn't going anywhere but where destiny intended him to be.

Forced to have to say during a press conference, "I'm not a crook" (the mantra of crooks everywhere), Nixon was looking for a way to bypass the press—"the enemy," "the

Jews"—and reach out directly to the people, his "silent majority," whom he knew loved him.

That opportunity came when he appointed Republican congressman James Harvey to the federal bench in January of '74. This created the need for a special election to fill his seat, and Nixon decided that the solidly Republican "thumb" area of Michigan was the perfect place to go for the pick-me-up that he needed.

It was also where I decided I would finally meet the man and ask him to leave. It was April 10, 1974, and my friend Jeff, my sister Veronica, and I got in the car and drove over to Bad Axe, Michigan, the small town where Nixon would make what would turn out to be the last campaign appearance of his presidency.

Bad Axe was the county seat of Huron County, Michigan. It had a courthouse and a movie theater and was surrounded by miles and miles of farmland. (It was on one of these farms south of Bad Axe where Timothy McVeigh and Terry Nichols stayed with Nichols's brother before the Oklahoma City bombing.)

The area was part of a peninsula surrounded on three sides by Lake Huron, and it was full of some of the most conservative people in the state of Michigan. How conservative? The nearest liberal probably lived across the lake in Canada.

Bad Axe had never had a presidential visit. So the whole town showed up in full red, white, and blue regalia to greet the nation's First Felon. A parade for Nixon was planned, and we were prepared to join the welcoming party.

Fortunately, when we arrived in Bad Axe, we were not the only ones who thought Nixon had to go. There were at least three hundred other protesters among the few thousand happy Bad Axers who were anxiously awaiting Nixon's arrival.

I found a good spot right on the curb of the town's main street. I brought a sign that said in big, bold letters: NIXON'S A CROOK. Jeff and Veronica had signs that said IMPEACHMENT NOW and WAR CRIMINAL. Basic, straightforward stuff. No ambiguity or subtlety. Short enough for him to read as he passed us by.

The locals standing around us tried to block our signs. But with three hundred fellow travelers there with us, it was impossible to make us go away. People shouted at us: "Outsiders go home!" and "Hippies burn in Hell!" Simple. No ambiguity. But no violence.

After about an hour, the parade/motorcade began to make its way down Huron Avenue. There were fire trucks and police cars and a marching band and cheerleaders and Boy Scouts and Future Farmers of America. On the tops of convertibles sat the mayor and the Republican candidate for Congress, James "No One Has Ever Heard of Me" Sparling, waving to the cheering crowd. If this was what Nixon was hoping for—an emotional outpouring of support—he was about to get it in Bad Axe.

Finally, his presidential limo came into view. He was standing up and sticking out of its sun roof, bobbing and waving like a forlorn jack-in-the-box. He flashed his famous Nixon smile, thrusting out his hands with the "V for Victory" sign he made with his index and middle fingers. We weren't more than ten feet from him, and I held up my sign at eye level so he could clearly see it.

And he did. The car was not going more than five miles per hour. As it crept past me I looked directly into his eyes—

and he into mine. It seemed in that instant everything went into slow motion. He looked at me, standing there in my bibbed overalls and long hair. I looked at him. The pancake makeup on him was so overdone, so thick and caked, that his face was like a slab of petrified orange, and his attempts to smile were somehow being impeded by the plaster that had been put on his mug. He looked ill. Seriously ill. I did not expect to see this. For reasons that I will have to explain later at St. Peter's Gate, I felt an instant sadness for him. He was like a corpse who had been wheeled out to whip up the people and get them to vote for a man he didn't even know. Though the small-town crowd was spirited and happy to see him, he really wasn't happy to see them. You know when you go to a play or a movie and you can *see* the acting, *see* the actor performing his lines, going through the motions, and at that moment the performance has lost you and it is over and it can't be recovered? That was Nixon in Bad Axe. The man who had been a congressman, senator, vice president, and now president, the man who had met with world leaders and at one time considered dropping The Bomb on North Vietnam, the man who clawed and climbed his way to the top more than once—now here he was in a place he'd never seen, reduced to sitting on the pop-top of a Pontiac in a staged parade of hopeful photo ops, a nice piece for the evening news, but there was no fooling anyone: This was not Nixon in China. This was Nixon in Bad Axe. Crushing, and irrevocably humiliating. It was all that he had left.

As his eyes glanced down at my Nixon's a Crook sign he did his best to look away and pretend to be happy, but there was just the next sign after me and the one after that and the 297 after that. When I saw his sad reaction to my

sign, I instinctively lowered it, ashamed that I was now kicking a man when he was down—a pretty ruthless, despicable
man, but nonetheless, a man shamed and alone. A man on
his way back to Orange County or to prison. He may have
been surrounded by thousands there in Bad Axe, but the only
axe that mattered now was the one that was just weeks away
from being lowered on his head. The Republican governor
of Michigan, William Milliken, declined to join him in the
parade. Milhous was a pariah, he knew it, and, really, what
was the point at this juncture?

I'll tell you what it was. He said he would end the war—
he told us he would end the war!—and instead he sent another twenty thousand American boys to their deaths. He
rained so many bombs down on the civilians of Vietnam and
Laos and Cambodia that to this day no one can give an exact
body count. (Is it 2 million? 3 million? 4 million? At this
level, you're talking Holocaust numbers, and if you paid your
taxes, then you supported this and you are culpable and you
know it and you just want to puke.) He had committed war
crimes so heinous that we still live with the legacy of his actions to this day. We lost our moral compass with him and
we've never gotten it back. We no longer know when we're
the good guys and when we're the terrorists. History has
already written our demise, and History will say it began
with Vietnam and Nixon. Before Vietnam there was so much
hope. Since Nixon we have known only the Permanent War.

For some reason, not knowing then what would come of
our country, I lifted my sign back up. I wanted none of it and
none of him.

We walked down to where he was going to give his
speech, but the police made sure we got nowhere near him.

He got on the loudspeaker and bragged about his subsidies to the local farmers. He asked the crowd if their doctor "should work for his patients or for the government?" And then he addressed the young people who were there.

"I have brought you a lasting peace," he told them. "Yours will be the first generation in this century who will not know war. And to you young boys here, you will be the first group of eighteen-year-olds not drafted in over twenty-five years!"

The crowd cheered. Nixon, the peace president. We booed as loud as we could. It was more like a howl. Nixon would not make another campaign appearance before resigning from the presidency a few months later. We were there for his last one.

If only we could have said the same about that being America's last war.

Crisis
Intervention

———◡———

HE WALKED STRAIGHT in through the front doors, wielding a shotgun.

I had been told by the teachers at my crisis intervention training that this day would eventually come. They called it the "audience suicide."

"This is it, motherfuckers!" he yelled out after entering the Hotline Center where I worked. *"This is good-bye and fuck every last one of you!"*

"Hold on," I said quietly as I emerged from the room that contained the crisis phone lines. "Hold on. Talk to me."

There are a number of situations in life that the average citizen tries to avoid: (1) Oncoming Semi Truck in Your Lane; (2) Floating in the Niagara River 200 Feet from the Falls; (3) Crazy Distraught Man with Double-Barreled Shotgun Yelling in Your Hallway.

Unfortunately for me, I was the only one there, pulling the graveyard shift. Shit, did I just call it that?

"C'mon," I continued, trying to hide the shakiness in my voice. "It's gonna be OK. We're here for you."

With the word *you,* his scattershot eye movements came to a halt and locked on me. And then he started to sob, but without tears.

"C'mon, brother, it's OK. Let it out."

And with that the sobbing stopped.

"Are you who I talked to on the phone?" he asked.

"I don't think so," I replied. "You might have been talking to Craig. His shift just ended and he's not here. But I'll talk to you. Let's say we put down the gun first, OK?"

And with that he put his finger on the trigger.

My lungs slammed shut and my heart felt like it went with them. I had a half second to make up my mind about what to do. Do I run? Do I rush him? Do I beg him to let me live? Do I try to stay calm and appear strong so as to steady him? Do I say my last prayer?

"Wait!" I said forcefully, without shouting. "*That* is *not* an option."

He stopped and looked at me like a dog that didn't want to obey his master's order, but for some reason his brain knew only that he must.

"*What do you mean it's not an option?*" he screamed back at me.

"Because," I said firmly with the sternest look I could muster through my own holy-shit terror and fear. "Because. I. Said. So."

A thought from my training clicked in my head: They call it an audience suicide because the suicide needs an audience. He kills me, there's no audience. I knew he wasn't going to kill me. He was going to kill himself. And let me live with the image of that for the rest of my life. I was the stand-in for the abusive parent, the cheating wife, the disloyal friend, the bastard of a boss, the voice in his head. I was to be punished the way "they" had punished him his whole life—or, maybe, just this past week.

With his finger on the trigger, he placed the shotgun barrel under his chin and prepared to pull.

"I am *not* impressed," I blurted out. "*Do you hear me?* And right now, you are pissing me off because you have no idea how much I *care* about you, and right now I'm all you got, and goddammit, if you took a second to put that gun down and talk to me you'd know you've got a friend here—*me*—right here, and *fuck it,* I'm worth at least a couple goddamn minutes of your time!"

I had no idea what I just said. What I did know was that it sounded all wrong. Nothing like what was in the "empathy training" the county workers gave us when I came up with the idea to open this place. I was nineteen then, and I didn't see any adult organization doing much good when it came to truly helping young people. A teenager would run away and get caught, and instead of anyone listening to them to find out *why* they ran away—like, maybe they had a *reason* to run away—they were just sent back home, often for another beating or molestation. The experience I had with a friend who needed an abortion but couldn't get one because it was illegal in Michigan, plus a classmate who had overdosed and another kid from my old Boy Scout troop who had hung himself was enough for me to start this hotline center. My rules: It would be run by young people for young people. You need a place to crash, you got it. You need a pregnancy test, we do it for you. You high on drugs? Drop by and let it wear off while sitting with us. We will never call the cops, and your parents will never know.

The ethos of this was shocking to many of the adults in the area, although some, like the VFW and the Rotarians, wrote us checks because they saw the good work we were doing, even if it was a bit unorthodox. But the results were that the runaways didn't keep running, young girls weren't forced to have babies they couldn't care for at sixteen, we handed out free birth control, and our phone lines were open from 3:00 p.m. to midnight ('til 2:00 a.m. on weekends), seven days a week.

It was now 1975 and I was twenty-one. This was my first confrontational encounter with a loaded gun. My only goal was to keep both shells in the barrels of that gun. The very next sound I heard was not a shotgun blast.

"Don't yell at me!" he shouted back.

Whew. He had chosen to engage me instead of the trigger.

"I'm sorry, I didn't mean to yell," I said, my own voice now quivering. "It's just that I've had a rough day and it just can't fucking end like this with you killing yourself."

Making it all about *me* really threw him off.

"Hey, man," he said, lowering the gun from his head. "You OK?"

OK. So now I had confused a distraught crazy guy. This could go any of a number of ways. I decided to try to pull it together.

"I'm sorry," I said. "Not very professional of me."

"I just can't go on," he said, calming down a bit. "Nothing in my life has worked out. And I don't want you stopping me. I just want you to let me leave this world and…"

"Hey, you're the one with the gun." (I really didn't need to remind him.) "You have the right and the power to leave

this world anytime you want. All I'm asking for is a few minutes of your time. Can you please give me that?"

The muscles in his body relaxed a bit more, and he
seemed to forget he still had a ready-to-fire gun in his hands.

"Yeah, I can do that."

"How 'bout you let me hang on to the gun while we talk.
When we're done, I'll give it back to you. Still loaded. You
can make your decision then."

There was a long pause and a longer stare at me and he
considered my offer.

"C'mon. Gimme the gun," I said with a faint smile. "The
last fucking thing you and I need right now is a gun!"

As I said that, I laughed a nervous laugh, and a faint grin
briefly grazed across his face. I had moved closer to him
by now and was holding out my hand. He reached out and
gave me the gun. I gently switched the safety on with my
shaky hand and then cracked open the shotgun and removed
the shells.

"Safekeeping," I assured him. "Let's go in here and talk."

And for the next two hours I heard the story of his life.
As I was the only one there, I could hear the phones ringing
in the other room and automatically going to the answering
machine. He told me about flunking out of a trade school and
then losing a series of jobs due to his drinking. His wife had
left him and returned twice, but now she had started seeing
another guy in the same apartment complex. He had no kids
but wanted some, and his parents thought of him as pretty
much a loser. I could see how far down the rabbit hole he
was, and I began to wonder if there was a point of no return
beyond which one could not climb their way back up out of

their pit of despair. He grew tired after a while and asked me if we had any booze in the place. I told him that wasn't allowed, unless it was for special occasions like some guy wanting to blow his brains out. He got a good laugh off that and then decided to turn the tables on me.

"So, what's your problems? Everybody's got problems. What's yours?"

I did not want to depress him further. I told him it's the same as every guy: chicks.

"You got that right, man. They got our number. And then they don't let up."

"Yeah," I said, "but they got their good points."

"Heh-heh, you got that right, mister!" he said in that special code spoken only between guys.

"We just gotta keep at it and find the right one," I continued. "She's out there. Yours is out there. Mine is out there. Too many fucking women on this planet for there not to be the right one out there for us. Just gotta keep on keepin' on."

"Yup, keep on truckin'!"

We were just about out of mid-seventies catchphrases when all of a sudden it dawned on him that the phones had been ringing nonstop.

"Man, you the only one here?"

"Yeah."

"Oh, shit, man, I'm keepin' ya from your job. You better get back to it." He paused and thought for a moment. "Unless you need me to stick around and give ya some help on the phones."

"Nah, that's OK. I'm about ready to close down for the night after I do my paperwork. You OK now?"

"I think so. You gonna gimme my gun back?"

"Yup. That was the deal. Your life is in your hands. I'll just ask you to consider not ending it anytime this week. Maybe try an AA meeting. Hang out with your sober friends. Can you do that?"

"Sure. I can give it a try."

I handed him his shotgun.

"How 'bout dem shells?"

"Nah, I think I'll keep those. A memento of this night. Cool?"

"Cool," he said with a nod of his head.

As he left in his truck I could hear his radio blasting out "Fly by Night" by the band Rush. As I watched him go down Coldwater Road to the intersection of M-15, I noticed that he dutifully obeyed all traffic signals and speed limits, small indications given by those who at least, for now, on this balmy summer night, might want to live.

A Public
Education

I'M NOT QUITE SURE when the honeymoon ended.

But my days as a novelty of being the youngest elected official were about to come to an end. And it was God who would do me in.

It was a regular monthly meeting of the Davison School Board, pretty much like any other monthly meeting. Recognition of visitors. Done. A request for maternity leave. Approved. A motion to pay some bills. Passed. Then I made a motion that our public schools be opened on Wednesday nights for extracurricular activities, just as they are on every other weeknight. As this was "church night" (the night the Protestant churches held midweek services), the public schools were always closed. I suggested to the school board that this was illegal. I brought a lawyer from the ACLU to the meeting to make the case. I might as well have flown him in from Moscow. They looked at the ACLU man like an interloper who had no business here. The entire issue was tabled and referred to "further study."

At the following meeting, the committee set up to

investigate whether or not to keep the ban on Wednesday night school activities presented its findings: the ban should be dropped. Amen.

The superintendent also mentioned that denying access to our schools by students who don't go to church night may be in violation of the Constitution. And that we would probably not prevail in court.

I had not threatened any legal action, but I guess that was what they assumed when they saw the lawyer from the ACLU sitting in the front row. I made the motion again, one of the two other Catholics on the board seconded it, and the board voted unanimously to do the right thing. But it was a reluctant vote, and the other board members did not like being put in the position of voting against the wishes of the born-again Christians in town.

The Free Methodist and Baptist churches in Davison were now keeping an eye on me. They were not going to forget what I had done to challenge their influence and power in town. And just saying a few prayers for my soul would not be all that they would do.

Prudence would have dictated that I perhaps ease up, maybe back off a bit, try to get back into their good graces so that I could still have some effectiveness on the board. And for a while that was what I did. But I was nearing the age of twenty, life was moving by so fast, and I was getting older. "Wisdom" had not yet set in.

"Mr. President," I said, "I'd like to make a motion that we endorse the directive from Lansing that we publicly reaffirm that our schools have a nondiscrimination policy and that we believe integrated schools provide the best education."

And then — why not? — a twist of the knife:

"And that we invite people from all races to come and make their home in Davison."

A long, long pause.

"This is ridiculous," board president Russell Alger finally said, exasperated. "We do not discriminate in Davison, and there is no need for this. Next order of business."

"You didn't ask if there was a second for my motion."

"Why are you doing this? Anyone can move to Davison and go to our schools," the dentist on the board said.

"Then why, out of six thousand students, are there only about fifteen who are black?"

"Fine," he said, "I'll second the motion."

A roll call was then taken and they all voted against it.

"Are there other motions?" President Alger barked.

"Yes," I said, not down yet for the count. "I'd like to move that we name Central Elementary School 'Martin Luther King Jr. Elementary School.' I think this will send a positive message to the students and to the rest of Genesee County that Davison is indeed the place that you just described."

"Michael," said board member Patrick McAvinchey, the only one who was still friendly to me. "You don't have to keep proving your point. Everyone gets it. Let's move on."

There was no second for that motion. The local paper covered my idea in a way that inflamed the local residents. I decided I needed to have a record of what I actually said at these meetings.

I walked into the next meeting and set my little Sears Silvertone tape recorder down on the table.

Mrs. Ude, the board secretary, asked me what that was for.

"It's so I can record our public meeting. Just for my use." I then hit the record button.

She looked over to President Alger with a *Stop him, PLEASE!* look of horror. Alger got up, reached over, and turned my recorder off, the way a parent would turn off the TV when you refused to go to bed. I put my finger out and hit Record again. This time the dentist on the board, Dr. McArthur, reached across the table and turned it off.

"You're not taping these meetings," he said. "Don't make us take this from you."

I have seen gangs on the street and, granted, they can look threatening at times. To have a gang of elected officials — adults who are at least thirty years older than you — threatening you like this, well, that took a minute to process.

"Listen," I said, "you should not see this as anything other than what it is — a chance for me to have a record of what is said here, especially what *I* say. This is a public meeting. This should not be a problem."

"Mr. President," board member Mr. Greiner said, "I'd like to make a motion to disallow any recording devices of any kind to be used during our meetings."

"Second," said Dr. McArthur.

"All in favor?" the president asked.

The vote was 6 to 1. I was ordered to turn it off or they would end the meeting.

I told them to have their sergeant in arms turn it off. As they didn't have a "sergeant in arms," the dentist turned it off.

The next day, the reporter from the *Flint Journal* who was present at the meeting wrote a story about what had happened. It caused quite a stir among the journalists in the area — and of course with those ACLU types. At the next meeting, they, and a few citizens, showed up and placed their tape recorders on the school board table.

I noticed they were letting people record without having to ask permission. I asked them if they were going to enforce their policy.

"We are not going to allow any recordings of these meetings," President Alger bellowed. "Turn them all off now and take them off our table."

"You do realize that Michigan has passed an Open Meetings Law," the reporter from the *Journal* piped in.

"You're out of order. Remove your device."

Nobody moved. The board members all looked at me: *YOU did this to us! YOU ARE FINISHED!*

The meeting was abruptly adjourned. Angry voices filled the room.

The next day I called the county prosecutor, Robert Leonard, to see if he could help me. For a D.A., Leonard was a pretty liberal guy. He had established the first Consumer Protection office in the state. One day, while speaking at an antiwar demonstration, he stood on the stage and pointed out to the crowd the FBI undercover agent standing among them.

"There he is, spying on you for exercising your constitutional rights!" Leonard shouted into the microphone. This did not endear him to the FBI.

Prosecutor Leonard was more than happy to help me. He had his deputy prosecutor inform the board that they were breaking the law by not allowing the public or the press to tape the meetings. For such a clean-cut law-and-order group of elected officials to be dressed down by law enforcement in such a public way was a humiliation that went beyond anything I'm sure they had ever experienced. It would be safe to say that this group had never even seen a parking ticket in their lives. If they could have sent me to my room and grounded me for a year they would have done it right then and there.

I also filed a lawsuit against the board. They couldn't believe what was hitting them. At the next meeting they backed down and quietly withdrew their rule to prohibit recording devices.

Upon passage of the motion, I hit Record. They wanted to hit me.

All but one board member would now keep their swivel chairs turned away from me. They avoided eye contact or any conversation with me. I was the snitch, and they had reached their boiling point.

The next few meetings went by with little or no fanfare, and business was decided quickly and smoothly, without much discussion. It was quiet. Too quiet. Something didn't seem right.

About this time, one of the board members referred to something one of the others had said at the "previous meeting." But I was at the previous meeting—and thanks to the wonders of magnetic cassette tape, there was nothing of the like said at that last meeting. After the meeting, I approached the one friendly board member who was still talking to me. I asked him what this issue was that they discussed.

He sighed. "We've been holding meetings and not telling you," he said apologetically. "It's not right and I'm not going to any more of them. I've told them we should stop."

I was floored. Secret board of education meetings were being held behind my back? He said they had met at the president's house so that no one would know.

I went home, my head in a fog. There was no Internet in those days, so I had no way to look up "How to Make a Citizen's Arrest." The next day I drove down to the county prosecutor's office and told him what happened. He blew his top.

"Those fucking bastards! I've had it with them. I'm throwing 'em all in jail!"

I considered asking him if he could say that one more time, just for my own pleasure.

"Kenny," he said shouting over to his assistant prosecutor, "call the radio and TV stations. We're bringing criminal charges against the members of the Davison Board of Education!"

And he meant it. And he did. It was only a misdemeanor, but still, he told the media that he was issuing warrants for their arrests. In case they preferred jail time to working with me, he also filed suit to make sure they would comply with state law requiring open meetings. Prosecutor Leonard had had it after the numerous violations of church/state separation, banning tape recorders at public meetings, and now this.

"They're recidivists!" the prosecutor told the local radio station. "They keep breaking the law—and I don't know any other way to get their attention."

The news shook the little Republican town—and the lawbreaking school board president immediately met with the prosecutor and signed an agreement to never ever do it again.

"You brought this on yourself," an unrepentant Mrs. Ude told me before the next meeting. "It was your behavior that forced us to meet without you. What makes you think that we would want you at our meetings?"

"They aren't *your* meetings," I said to her. "These meetings belong to the citizens of this district! And they elected me to represent them. And when you hold secret meetings and don't inform me, you take away those people's right to be there."

"Oh, you!" was all she could say, and walked away.

A few months later, I noticed the school district was handing out contracts for services and construction without taking competitive bids.

"It's illegal not to do it," I said, using their favorite "I" word. "State law requires us to have competitive bidding that's fair for all concerned and will get the best price for the school district." I sat and wondered why was I having to give people who claimed they loved capitalism and free enterprise a lesson in the competitive marketplace being a good idea for all. But they ignored me, saying it was impractical and unnecessary.

A few days later I set up an appointment with the state attorney general's office and drove down to Lansing to meet with an assistant attorney general about this illegal practice.

The assistant attorney general looked at the records I brought him and he agreed: the Davison Board of Education was breaking the law.

"Why don't *you* tell them?" I suggested. "I think they're tired of hearing that from me."

"I intend to do just that."

Word spread through town that now the top law enforcement men in Michigan were investigating the Davison school board. And sure enough, at the next meeting, it was announced that a competitive bidding process was being instituted. We were also told, bitterly, that "being forced to take the lowest bid will not guarantee the best work, and this may end up costing us more in the long run."

~

So, what does one do when he is looking to bring the level of animosity down? He writes a one-act play in his spare time and enters it in the school district's annual community talent show to be held at the high school. And what would that play be about? Oh, say, a little avant-garde number about Jesus's crucifixion. At the last minute on Calvary, Jesus, high up on a cross wrapped in aluminum foil, decides he doesn't want to die crucified like this.

"This is where you people want me?" Jesus shouted to the audience on the talent show's opening night. "Just nailed to a cross? So you don't have to listen to me anymore about caring for the poor or the sick or the downtrodden? So you can stick little replicas of me on your walls at home, while I'm hanging on this cross, suffering? Well, I say NO!"

And with that, Jesus yanked the nails straight out of his hands and flew down off the cross.

I had a bunch of my friends planted in the audience and, with that as their cue, they randomly stood up and started yelling at Jesus.

"Get back up on that cross where you belong!"

"We don't want you alive, we like you dead!"

"Back on the cross! Back on the cross!"

Then they all started to charge the stage. One man pulled out a "gun" and "shot" Jesus. The now-dead-again Son of God was dragged back to his cross and left there. The actors then exited the stage cheerfully.

The election to recall and remove me from the school board was set for the first Friday in December. There would be only one question on the ballot: Should Michael Moore be tarred and feathered and run out of town on a rail? Actually, I believe the official wording was: "Should Michael Moore be removed from the office of trustee of the Davison Board of Education?"

That was it. Just one question on the entire ballot—and the whole town was to show up and vote on just that question. Not exactly a confidence booster, to be sure.

To my credit, it was not easy for the recall committee—consisting of businessmen and friends of the school board members—to gather the necessary signatures in the required amount of time to put the question on the ballot. In fact, when the deadline arrived, they were hundreds of signatures short. So the school board gave the group an extra ten days. When the ten days were up, they were still short by quite a bit. So the board granted another (illegal) ten-day extension. And when those ten days were up, guess what? Still not enough names of people wanting to remove me! So, unbelievably, the board gave them a *third* ten-day extension.

I went and got myself an attorney. By the end of the third ten-day extension, they finally had the signatures they needed. Or did they? As I combed through the names on the petitions, I came across at least a half-dozen people who had died, and a number of people who had signed their names twice. And then there was Jesse the barber. He signed it *three* times! He sure did want me gone.

I sued in the county court to overturn this entire circus.
The judge, who shaved his head bald each morning to convey
a Kojak-like appearance, issued the following ruling:

> It appears that both the recall committee and the board
> of education have committed a number of irregulari-
> ties and possible violations of the law. But it does seem
> to me that the people of Davison want their day at the
> polls regarding you, Mr. Moore. So, I'm going to go
> ahead and let the election take place. If the election
> goes against you, Mr. Moore, then you can come back
> here to this court to seek relief.

My head was spinning. The judge had just pointed out
numerous instances of the law being broken—but he was
still going to let the election take place. I was doomed.

Scheduling the election on a Friday during the Christmas season was a genius move by the school board. Have
you ever gone to vote on a Friday? Exactly. So who would
even know when this particular Friday rolled around that it
was "election day"? The haters who wanted me out of there,
that's who.

Each side got to write something on the official ballot.
The recallers had a hundred words where they outlined my
"crimes." And I had a hundred words to answer their charges.
I decided it wasn't worth wasting my time. I wrote, simply,
"The question that is placed before you on this ballot is a
moral question that must be decided between you and your
conscience. I sincerely trust that you will make the best decision possible for you and your children. Love, Mike." In

addition to being the youngest elected official, I might have been the first person to inscribe the word *love* on an election ballot.

On recall day I was back in the same gym where I had won the seat two and a half years earlier. When I arrived at 7:00 a.m., the citizens recall committee was already in action. The school board clerk allowed them to sit at the table where the voters sign in and check off who had shown up and who hadn't. Every half hour or so, they would hand off the names and go call those who hadn't come in to vote yet. It was quite the operation to watch, and once again I had been outsmarted (and outspent). In the weeks leading up to the election I did what I had done before to win. I wrote up a "Letter to the people of Davison" and went and knocked on every door in the district.

The line snaked the length of the gym to the back by the doors, out through the hallway, and to the front of the school. By the time the polls closed thirteen hours later, it was clear this was a huge turnout.

In the middle of the gym they set up four long lunch-room tables to form a square on which they dumped out the paper ballots. The count began with the "YES" ballots placed on one table and the "NO" ballots stacked on the other. For the next hour and a half, who had the highest pile went back and forth. Higher and higher, neck and neck they climbed. And then something happened. The pile of "NO" ballots kept growing: 100 higher. 200 higher! 300 HIGHER! The final ballot was placed atop the pile favoring me and the clerk declared that the recall had failed and I had won.

On the bleachers on the south side of the gym, where a hundred or so student supporters had taken perch, there was a scream from someone, and then more screams followed. A spontaneous party broke out and there was jumping and dancing all across the gymnasium floor. Me, I was just relieved. The TV cameras were there to record the event and I went live with the anchorman at 11:00 p.m. I thanked the people of Davison, declared the local Republican Party dead, and promised to remain who I was. I also apologized to my parents for putting them through this. It had been especially hard on my mother. The recall committee was made up of the people she had lived with in Davison her whole life. The head of the committee — my dad was his coach in junior high football. The copies of the recall petitions I was able to obtain in court revealed the names of many we thought were family friends. The guy my dad ushered with in church signed it. My mom's friend from high school signed it. The girl I sat next to in band — her, too. They were all there. And to this day, if you ask my dad (now ninety) if "so-and-so" had signed the petition, he would be able to tell you in an instant.

They call it "Irish Alzheimer's": you forget everything — except holding the grudge.

I served out the rest of my term, always voting the way I wanted, but worn down from the whole experience. I was asked to speak to the students at the high school, and I used the opportunity to read an expletive-filled poem I wrote about the genocide of the Native Americans. That resulted in me being banned from the high school for life (I have, to this day, never returned).

I lost my bid for reelection and retired from public office at the age of twenty-two — to pursue a more quiet life. I kept in mind that it took the consent of only twenty people

to start me on this road. I realized that this was the big secret
of democracy — that change can occur by starting off with
just a few people doing something. You don't need a whole
movement or even a whole school district. It can start with
just twenty people. Even twenty stoners. It was a good, but
dangerous, lesson to learn at such an early age. The intimidating thing about democracy is that it seems so impossible,
so unmanageable, so out of reach to the average person. By
twenty-two, I knew that to be a myth. And I was grateful to
Davison for teaching me what a great country this is.

But I never got my hair cut at Jesse's Barber Shop again.

Raid

⌣

I BECAME A NEWSPAPERMAN at the age of nine. St. John the Evangelist Catholic Grade School did not have a student newspaper, so I thought I would start one. I did not ask the nuns for permission. Why would I? I only wanted to cover our sports teams — mostly. I also wanted to write about what happened during science class last Friday. Mrs. LaCombe had wheeled the school's one TV set in on a movable cart and turned it on so we could watch a science lesson on NET (National Educational Television), a special channel devoted for use in the classrooms across America (it would later become PBS).

I loved these special days when we got to watch TV in school. It seemed like we were getting away with something. And I loved the science shows, especially when they would blow something up in a test tube.

As we were watching the lesson, the picture on the screen was abruptly interrupted and all of a sudden Chet Huntley, the anchorman on NBC News, broke in with a bulletin.

"We have just learned that President Kennedy has been shot in Dallas…"

Mrs. LaCombe let out a gasp and left to get the Mother Superior. She came in and watched the report with us. When they said he was still alive and had been taken to the hospital we were all instructed—and the other classrooms were alerted—to head directly over to the church, get on our knees, and pray, pray, pray that he would live.

Proving once again that either God has a great mysterious plan that none of us can alter, or he does indeed occasionally take a day off, Kennedy succumbed. We were all sent home early. When my dad got home from the factory, my mother went outside to greet him. It was raining. We ate fish silently that night.

Two days later, as I was sitting on the living room floor watching the live broadcast of the Dallas police transferring the alleged assassin, Lee Oswald, I saw Jack Ruby put a gun in Oswald's abdomen and fire a shot. My mother was vacuuming.

I screamed at her, "Turn the vacuum off! They've shot Oswald!"

She couldn't hear me so she kept vacuuming. I reached over and pulled the vacuum's plug out of the wall.

"They shot Oswald! I just saw it."

Not all nine-year-olds get to watch a real person being killed, live on TV. Over the weekend I decided I wanted to write about that. I asked my dad if I could start a newspaper.

"How exactly would you do that?" he asked me. We were a GM factory family. We didn't start newspapers.

"I was thinking I could write it up on a piece of paper. You said you have a new machine where you work that will print pages of paper. So if I wrote something on a couple pieces of paper, could you make thirty pages of that?"

He thought about that for a minute.

"Well, it's called a mimeograph. And it's in the foreman's office. I'd have to type it up for you and get permission. Let me see."

The following Monday Dad came home and said he could make twenty-five copies of my two-page paper. Excited by the prospect, I sat down with my pencil and wrote up Page One: my thoughts on why we no longer had a seventh-and-eighth-grade football team, what our upcoming basketball season would look like, and my favorite baseball stats from the backs of my Topps bubblegum baseball cards.

Page Two was about how I felt about Kennedy's death and what it was like to watch Oswald get shot.

The next day my dad made the twenty-five copies of the *St. John Eagle* at AC Spark Plug and brought them home from work. He had personally typed, printed, and stapled each copy together himself. It was like an early Christmas present, and I could see it made him happy to see me so happy to have in my hands my very first newspaper.

The following morning I took the *St. John Eagle* into my fourth-grade classroom and handed them out to the classmates I thought would read it. Mrs. LaCombe saw this and asked for a copy. A big smile came across her face.

"Why, look at you!" she said. "This looks quite good."

Would that the Mother Superior felt the same way. For when Mrs. LaCombe showed her my paper, she requested my presence in her office.

"Can you tell me what this is?" she asked bluntly.

"It's our new student paper — the *St. John Eagle!*" I said proudly, not expecting any blowback.

"We don't have a student newspaper, Michael," she said.

"And we don't need one. This is not authorized and we cannot approve it. So you will have to collect the copies you've passed out and hand them over to me."

I was crushed. It made no sense to me. What did I do wrong? But I dared not object, so I offered up a "Yes, Mother," and went back to my classroom to gather the contraband.

The following year, still wanting to publish a newspaper, I started a new one called the *Hill St. News,* this one intended not for school but for our neighborhood. Again, my dad made the copies for me at work on GM's dime, and this periodical lasted a whole three issues before a neighborhood parent called my mom, furious that I had listed her house for sale in my Want Ads section.

"But they have a FOR SALE sign in their yard," I pleaded. "I was just trying to help."

Of course I had no idea what houses cost, so I went ahead and listed theirs for $1,200 — which, to a ten-year-old, is a *helluva lot of money!* No matter; the *Hill St. News* was shut down.

Two more times I would attempt to start a school paper at St. John's – in sixth grade and eighth grade. And each time the plug was pulled. I got the message and retired from the newspaper business for the next nine years.

When you live in a company town like Flint, nearly all the media is bought and paid for and controlled by that company or its lackeys (aka the local elected officials). In the case of our one and only daily paper, the *Flint Journal,* it provided for a particularly pathetic situation. The *Journal* was so in love with General Motors, it never would turn a critical eye on its operations. It was a cheerleading newspaper: *the company could do no wrong!*

The working people of the Flint area hated this rag, but it was our only daily so you read it. Everyone called it the "Flint Urinal." Editorially, the paper had historically been on the wrong side of every major social and political issue of the twentieth century,— "the wrong side" meaning: whatever side the union workers were on, the Urinal took the opposite position. In the early years it attacked the socialist mayor whom the people of Flint had elected. It attacked the formation of the UAW and the Great Sitdown Strike of 1936–37 that forced General Motors into its first contract with the union. It endorsed the Republican candidate for president while the workers voted for the Democrat. It supported the Vietnam War. And it would become an unapologetic booster of boondoggle downtown developments that would leave the city devastated.

By 1976, my friends and I had complained enough to each other about the state of the newspaper in Flint that we decided to start one ourselves. At first, we called it *Free to Be,* but that sounded too hippie, so we changed it to the *Flint Voice* in honor of the great alternative weekly we received in the mail each week from New York, the *Village Voice.* There were seven of us, between the ages of nineteen and twenty-five, who founded the *Voice,* but only three of us had any journalism experience: Doug Cunningham, who had an underground paper in high school, the *Mt. Morris Voice;* Alan Hirvela, who helped run an alternative paper on the campus of Central Michigan University; and me, with my history of four failed grade-school newspapers. Only Al had a college education.

Our first issues came flying out of the gate pointed directly at the established order in Flint. There were stories of Flint's hangin' judge, who gave blacks longer sentences than whites, county commissioners fleecing the treasury, Buick rigging the test cars they sent to the EPA in order to show better gas mileage, and some other issues that rang familiar to me: *another* school board in Flint holding secret meetings, students in Flint being paddled 8,264 times in one school year, and a poll showing the majority of Catholics no longer believing in hell. There were also stories that seemed ahead of their time: an op-ed from a local Palestinian entitled "Where Is *My* Promised Land," a story on how processed sugar was poison (with an accompanying recipe for a "natural food" snack), and a warning that GM, then employing eighty thousand people in Flint, had a master plan to leave the city bone dry. That last story established me firmly as the local crazy guy.

The paper quickly became a must-read for those who paid attention to the politics of Flint. The *Flint Voice* was a true muckraking paper that didn't care who it pissed off. We did not do cover stories on the "Ten Best Ice Cream Places in Town" or "Twenty Day Trips You'll Want to Take." Our journalism was hard-hitting and relentless. We did sting operations on establishments that would not hire black employees. We chronicled how General Motors was taking tax abatement money and using it to build factories in Mexico. One night, we caught them literally dismantling an entire GM assembly line, loading it on a train, and sending it off to be shipped to a place called China. Many could not believe a story like that—"What on earth would China do with an automobile assembly line?! Michael Moore is nuts!" I suffered much derision for exposing such goings-on.

We also offered a place where brilliant Michigan writers could find an outlet. Many, such as Ben Hamper, Alex Kotlowitz, James Hynes, and the cartoonist Lloyd Dangle would go on to become best-selling authors and syndicated journalists. We never missed an opportunity to go after the *Flint Journal* and, in 1985, I wrote an investigative piece on this miserable daily paper for the *Columbia Journalism Review*.

Other than the plan by General Motors to destroy Flint (a story that only we would cover in the late '70s and early '80s), nothing consumed our attention more than the mayor of Flint, James P. Rutherford. He was also the ex–police chief of Flint. He left behind a number of disgruntled officers who were more than happy to slip us documents and evidence of his controversial activities. One of our first front-page stories on him was entitled, "Did Mayor Rutherford Receive $30,000 'Gift' from Convicted Gambler?" We scooped the *Journal* time after time (not that that was hard), but one day they got tired of us beating them to the story, so one of their columnists simply lifted our investigative piece and ran it as if they had done the legwork themselves. When things like this happened, we had ways of dealing with it. As we were not educated and did not run in the circles of polite society, we didn't tolerate the actions of thieves very well, especially if the thief was the *Flint Journal*. The day after their plagiarism, we paid a visit to their newsroom. We brought with us a pie to give to the editor. No, we were not pie throwers,

we were more like re-gifters. The pie tin was filled entirely
with dog shit. On top of the pile of steaming poo was a big
copyright insignia made from Reddi-wip.

The editor wasn't in, so we hung around for a while waiting for him to come back. Someone must have tipped him
off 'cause he never showed up, so we eventually got bored
waiting and just placed it on his desk and left. The next day
they ran a correction/acknowledgment that the story that
they had published was originally ours.

We did not let up on the mayor and his dealings with
developers, General Motors, the Chamber of Commerce, or
the Charles Stewart Mott Foundation. In September 1979 we
ran a front-page story outlining how public employees had
contributed to his reelection campaign and done door-to-
door canvassing for him on city time.

The mayor was furious and threatened to sue us for libel.
He didn't. We kept at it. He was not happy.

The city ombudsman took our findings and did his own
investigation of the mayor. The city charter required him to
present his findings to the mayor four days before he could
release it to the public. Our sources got a copy of the confidential report—which found 100 percent of our accusa-
tions against the mayor to be correct—and we published a
story in the *Flint Voice* saying the ombudsman had backed
up our story.

The mayor accused the ombudsman of violating the city
charter and asked the police department to investigate how
we at the *Voice* got ahold of the report. We refused to cooperate and continued publishing stories about them as we
entered the new year of 1980.

In May 1978, the United States Supreme Court had ruled

that it was OK for police to raid a newsroom and take materials from that newsroom, with certain restrictions. *Zurcher v. Stanford Daily* involved a student newspaper, the *Stanford Daily,* and the photographs it had taken at a student demonstration where nine police officers were injured while the students occupied the campus hospital. The police wanted to see all the photos the *Daily* had taken in order to help them identify the students involved in the fracas. The students sued, claiming their constitutional rights were violated. The Supreme Court disagreed and said the police had the right to conduct such a search, just as long as they weren't going on a fishing expedition.

The court's ruling was hailed by both law enforcement and haters of the media everywhere. Journalists were appalled by it and warned that there would be abuses. They pointed out that sources would be afraid to trust newspapers if they knew that the cops could just waltz in and scoop up file cabinets full of confidential information.

Two years passed and there had been no further police raids of newsrooms anywhere across America.

Until the morning of May 15, 1980.

At 9:05 a.m., the Flint police, having obtained a search warrant from Judge Michael Dionise, raided the newspaper offices where the *Flint Voice* was printed and seized all materials relating to the November 1979 issue that contained the critical report of the mayor's alleged lawbreaking— including the very printing plates used on the presses to print the *Voice.*

The *Flint Voice* was printed at the *Lapeer County Press* (a weekly paper in the county that was settled, in part, by my family in the 1830s). This was not the first visit by the Flint police to our printer. They had called back in November asking to be given anything the *County Press* had on us. The publisher, citing the First Amendment, refused. Six months later, the police showed up in person. The publisher asked if they had a search warrant. No, said the cops. Then you can't come in, said the publisher.

A few days later they were back with the warrant in hand and took everything *Flint Voice*–related. They told the publisher not to disclose that they were there. The publisher complied.

Five days later, on May 20, my phone rang at the *Voice* office.

"Mr. Moore, this is the Flint police department," the voice on the phone said.

The officer who called did not tell me—and I did not know—that five days prior they had raided my printer's offices. He did tell me that they knew "exactly" the time and day that I received the ombudsman's report—and that it appeared a crime may have been committed. He asked if the ombudsman was the leaker. I told him that was none of his business. He suggested that I tell him the truth, as he was going to find out sooner or later—and things would just be easier if I cooperated.

I thanked him for his time and hung up. Four hours later, I got a call from the *Lapeer County Press* who felt "obligated" to tell me that the search had taken place there and all things regarding the *Flint Voice* were removed by the Flint police. This sent a chill down me. Were the police already on their way over here to do the same thing at our editorial offices?

I called the Flint police department back. I told them I had just heard about the raid. Were they planning to do the same thing here?

Oh, no, we're not going to raid you! The officer on the other end of the line said that would probably cause too much grief for him — and for me. Why for me?

I told the officer that if he were to come out here I would have the TV stations on their way within minutes.

"Listen," he said bluntly, "if we wanted to search you, do you think we'd tell you? You wouldn't even know, just as you didn't know about our search of your printing office in Lapeer."

I called a source of mine in the Flint police department and asked him to find out what he knew. He called me back within the hour.

"Oh yeah, they're planning to search your place. They already have the affidavit for the judge drawn up."

I immediately called the local news stations and the Associated Press. "I need your help," I said to each of them. "The cops are going to raid our newspaper. They've already conducted one raid at the newspaper office where the *Voice* is printed. Can you come out here soon?"

To their credit, they were at our office on the corner of Lapeer and Genesee roads within minutes. Everyone but the *Flint Journal*.

Stories were filed. The police denied they were planning a search and seizure at our office. But they couldn't explain why they seized all of our materials from the newspaper that was our printer. Was the raid meant to intimidate us? I spent the night removing all of our files and documents from our building and storing them safely where the police couldn't find them.

Within twenty-four hours CBS had flown a crew in from Chicago, and the *New York Times* was covering it. This was, after all, the first newspaper search since the Supreme Court decision allowing them. More reporters arrived from Detroit and Chicago. The ACLU called, as did the Reporters Committee for Freedom of the Press. Its director, Jack Landau, offered whatever legal assistance we needed. "You're the first," he said, "but you won't be the last. We need to nip it right here."

We filed suit in circuit court to get an injunction to prohibit the police from raiding our offices. The judge granted a temporary order and got the police to promise not to take any action until he could hear the case.

Newspapers across the state, from Detroit to Battle Creek, ran editorials chastising the Flint police for their actions and encouraging the judge to take a stand for the First and Fourth Amendments. Media around the country covered the case, and the spotlight on Flint was not a pleasant one. I did not get much sleep and was worried about what else the police might be up to. I encouraged everyone at the paper to not bring anything to the office that made them suspiciously happy and over-hungry.

Two weeks later, we were back in court. After hearing the arguments, the judge ruled in our favor, telling the police that if they later decided they had grounds for a raid, they had to go through him first. A cheer went up from our supporters in the courtroom. It was a rare victory against this mayor and his police force.

The incident revived a dormant bill in Congress (introduced right after the Supreme Court's *Stanford* decision) to prevent police searches of newsrooms. Within a week of the judge's verdict in Flint, the United States Senate Judiciary Committee called for hearings on the legislation. Jack Landau, the man from the Reporters Committee, rang me back and asked if I could come to Washington, D.C.

"We think the timing is perfect after what happened to you in Flint to get this bill passed. Could you come down to D.C. and help us?"

"I was once asked this question, when I was seventeen, to come down to D.C. and testify," I told him, which sounded too weird to explain, so I didn't. "I just don't think I'm good for that sort of thing. Plus, the Republicans are coming here in a few weeks for the Republican National Convention. I need to be on top of that. Reagan's going to ask Jerry Ford to be his vice president." (Just hours before the convention vote, the former president from Michigan started insisting that Reagan also promise to bring back Henry Kissinger. Reagan then changed his mind at the last minute and went with the surprise pick of George Bush. The future of America's descent unfolded from that one decision. I don't have time to get into what happened over the next thirty years. There are other books in libraries where you can read about it.)

On June 20, 1980, the Senate committee voted in favor of the Privacy Protection Act, otherwise known as the "Newsroom Shield Law," a bill that would prohibit police from ever entering a newsroom unless an actual crime like a robbery or a murder was taking place on the premises. But then the bill was stalled and was not scheduled for a vote of the full

Congress. First Amendment groups wondered if it would ever be passed.

One month later, the local police in Boise, Idaho, raided the newsroom of the CBS affiliate in Boise and seized videotapes of a protest so they could find out the identities of those who had participated. The TV station sued and got their own injunction against the Idaho cops. The media around the country covered the story, and politicians in D.C. demanded again that action be taken on the proposed bill. I wrote letters to members of Congress and I did interviews.

And then one day I answered the phone.

"Hello," the voice with the British (or Irish?) accent said. "I'm looking for Michael Moore."

"This is Michael Moore," I said.

"This is John Lennon."

As I was known by now as a skilled prankster, I was also repeatedly the victim of others' pranks who were seeking revenge.

"OK, Gary, really funny," I said. And then I hung up.

Twenty minutes later, the phone rang again. It was the Flint City ombudsman, Joe Dupcza.

"You just hung up on John Lennon!" he said sternly. "Why the fuck did you do that?"

"C'mon, Joe," I said, "are you in on this, too?"

"I'm not in on anything," he said, getting pissed. "Lennon called me a couple hours ago. I didn't believe it at first, either. So I don't blame you. We're all a little jumpy after this shit."

"Uh—yeah," I said. "Thanks for stating the obvious. But how do you know for sure that this was John Lennon?"

"I took his number and told him I'd call him back. Then I ran it."

"Ran it" is police-speak for taking a phone number or license plate number and running it through a central law enforcement computer to check it out. Joe Dupcza was a Flint
cop before he was the ombudsman. John Lennon's phone
number was no doubt well known at the FBI and in their
computer. The agency had spent the better part of a decade
building a file on him and trying to have him deported.

"I ran it—*and it checked out!* I mean, holy shit—*it was
the real fucking John Lennon!*"

I felt instantly sick that I had hung up the phone on a
Beatle. *Jesus,* I thought, *I'm so discombobulated by what's been
going on, I don't trust anyone now. Not good.*

"We talked for some time," Dupcza continued. "He read
about our case in the paper and has followed it and thought
it was awful and wanted to know what he could do to help.
Then he asked me for your number."

Dupcza gave me Lennon's number so I could call him
back in New York, but as soon as I hung up, the phone rang
again. This time I could identify the accent. Liverpool.

"Hi, this is John Lennon again," he said, trying to reas-
sure me.

"I know, I know!" I said apologetically. "I just spoke to the
ombudsman. I am soooooo sorry. Please forgive me. It's just
been a little hairy here."

"No, no, I understand," he said, still trying to calm me. "I
know a little bit about police surveillance making your life
a bloody hell."

I laughed. "Yes. You do."

"Well," he continued, "I've been following what you've
been going through, and with this possible law in Congress,
and I was really just calling to see if there was any way I

could help. Maybe I could do a benefit or something for your legal fund or for your paper."

"*Really?* Um, wow, I don't know what to say."

"Well, you don't have to say anything right now. I'm a little busy working on a new album, so I won't have time 'til the new year."

"Wow, *that's great news!*" I interrupted, my voice going up half an octave to fainting-schoolgirl level. "A new album!"

"Well, I've been sorta quiet for a while, being a dad and all. But I'm ready to get at it again, and now that I'm legally a resident of your fine country I plan to be more involved and [going into the accent of an American] *exercise my constitutional rights.* And so if there's something you need, I can give you my number and you can give me a call if you want."

Listening to this amazing offer, from the voice of the man who had meant so much to so many of us, I just didn't know what to say. So I tried.

"Can you get Shea Stadium again?"

He laughed. "God, bloody no! Once there was enough! Hey, I did do that concert in Ann Arbor…"

"For John Sinclair. I was there. 'Ten for Two!' He went to my high school."

"You don't say. Small world. Well, I have to get going…"

"John, I, uh, um—thank you so much! It's been a crazy few months here. I will definitely call. Thank you so much. This will mean a lot to everyone here."

"Keep your spirits up, mate," he concluded. "I'll be around."

On September 29, the Senate passed the Privacy Protection Act of 1980 by a voice vote. Two days later the House passed it 357–2. On October 13, 1980, the president signed it into law. That's how things worked back then, both parties unanimously coming to the defense of their citizens' privacy and First Amendment rights. And to support the need for a press to function without threat or intimidation.

And all that needed to happen to kick-start Public Act 96-440 into becoming the law of the land was for two cops to raid the printing office of a small underground paper in an out-of-the-way place called Flint, Michigan. Check. And then do it again in Boise. Mate.

I never got to make that return call to John Lennon. Eight weeks later he was gone. And the month after that, Ronald Reagan and George H. W. Bush took the reins of the country for the next twelve years. A Dark Age had begun. Few noticed at first.

Bitburg

GARY BOREN DIDN'T really have an issue with the Germans, at least not with the live ones. In the 1970s, while in high school, he had been an exchange student in Bremen, West Germany, living for a year with a German family. So Gary was familiar with the younger, post-war generation of Germans, and he knew that they were not at all like their parents.

It was May Day, 1985. My conversation with Gary went something like this:

GARY: "Bitburg."

ME: "Pittsburgh?"

GARY: "Bitburg."

ME: "Why do you want to go to Pittsburgh?"

GARY: "I don't ever want to go to Pittsburgh. I wanna go to **BIT**burg."

ME: "Oh."

Gary grew up in Flint. I did not know him when I was younger, but now as an adult he was, among other things, the pro bono attorney for my newspaper (and for me personally whenever I needed to get out of a traffic ticket or a landlord dispute).

"Mike, can you believe this business with Reagan going to Bitburg?" he asked, hoping I would share his same incredulousness, which I did.

"I want to go there and let him know how I feel. You wanna come?"

In the spring of 1985, the seven leading economies of the world (which would later be known as the G-7, then the G-8, then the G-20, and so on) decided to hold an economic summit in Bonn, West Germany. President Ronald Reagan would attend, representing the United States.

Somewhere along the way, someone in his administration thought it would be a good idea while Reagan was in the Fatherland to go and lay an official wreath on the graves of some Nazi soldiers. When various Jewish and human rights groups objected, he dug his heels in and refused to cancel the ceremony—and in fact, just to prove his stubbornness and his point, he upped the ante and said he would now lay the wreath on the graves of not just any run-of-the-mill Nazis, but on the burial plots of the psychopaths known as the Nazi SS. Nice.

The ceremony would take place in the small town of Bitburg near the Luxembourg border. And Gary wanted to go to Bitburg.

Gary was not a political activist. He was not prone to act on impulse. He was the kind of guy whose pattern of daily activities—eating, exercising, sleeping—is the kind you can set your watch to. So the anger in his voice and his eagerness to act politically—and publicly—was a pleasant jolt to my afternoon.

Gary was unique in another respect. His father *and* his mother were survivors of both the Auschwitz and Bergen-Belsen concentration camps. Over one million died in Auschwitz, and 50,000 in Bergen-Belsen. His parents survived both. They were from a small city in Poland called Kielce. In 1940, Kielce had a population of 200,000, with about 20,000 Jewish citizens. The Germans and the Poles established the Jewish ghetto in 1941, but by August 1942 the ghetto was liquidated and most of its inhabitants were sent to the Treblinka concentration camp. Only a couple thousand was kept behind to work as forced laborers (i.e., slaves). Gary's parents, Bella and Benny, were among the slaves. Each of them was married to their respective spouses, but neither of those spouses survived the war.

In 1944, they were sent to Auschwitz where they survived the "selection" process (they were deemed fit enough to do the slave labor). In 1945, when the Russians were days away from Auschwitz, the Germans took those they still needed for the slave work and marched them in the dead of winter to a rail station in Gliwice, Poland, a twenty-mile distance. Many died. Those who lived, including Gary's parents, were loaded into cattle cars to Bergen-Belsen, where the British liberated them on April 15, 1945.

While in a refugee camp in Munich the following year they met and got married. One of them had an uncle who had emigrated to Flint, Michigan, twenty years earlier to work in the General Motors factories. Because of that connection they were able to come to the United States and to Flint, where they were welcomed and where they thrived.

The ordeal of Bella and Benny Boren took a toll not just on them, but, in years to come, also on their children, Gary and his three brothers. Nearly everyone else in his family in Europe — grandparents, aunts, uncles, cousins — were killed in the Holocaust.

The trip to Bitburg, he told me, would be his personal statement against those who did this to his parents — and perhaps, more important, his one-man act of defiance against his own president who was either insensitive or stupid or cruel. Each was inexcusable.

And what exactly was my purpose in going?

"You'll know how to sneak us in to the cemetery," Gary said matter-of-factly. Gary then ticked off my résumé of major break-ins: getting on the floor of the 1984 Democratic convention in San Francisco with no press credentials; traveling through Nicaragua to the Honduran border without proper papers or visas; sneaking backstage past security at concerts to meet Joan Baez or Pete Seeger.

"When's Reagan going there?" I asked.

"This Sunday."

"This Sunday?"

"Yes. C'mon. I'll take care of the plane tickets."

I didn't need any convincing. I was up for the adventure and I was up for anything that would stick it to the Gipper. If Bonzo was going to Bitburg, so was I.

Forty-eight hours later, we were on a plane from Detroit to Hamburg, West Germany. We arrived in Bonn, the West German capital, late Friday afternoon.

Our first step upon deplaning was to go and convince the German authorities to give us the necessary press credentials we would need to follow Reagan into Bitburg. This was not going to be easy, considering the cutoff date to apply for said credentials was a month ago, and the Bonn Economic Summit was already half over.

There were thousands of press people in Bonn, all there to cover a major non-event conducted by the leaders of France, Germany, Italy, Great Britain, the United States, Canada, and Japan. At the end of the summit, the leaders posed for pictures and issued a joint statement saying they were going to stay the course (they didn't say which course was getting the "stay" treatment). They also said that they all opposed inflation. OK.

But the big news of the economic summit—other than the revelation that Reagan was staying in a castle owned by a guy whose godfather was Adolf Hitler—was Reagan's first act when he got off the plane in Bonn. Unlike the rest of us who rush to file missing baggage claims, Reagan issued an Executive Order banning all trade with Nicaragua. The other world leaders were perplexed by this move—it had nothing to do with their economic summit—and they quickly tried to put as much distance between themselves and Reagan as possible. Not one of the leaders—not even his fellow righties, Margaret Thatcher of the U.K. or Brian Mulroney of Canada—endorsed Reagan's embargo of what he called a "communist regime."

We went to the summit's press office and were told by the White House press officer that we should speak to "Herr Peters at the U.S. Press Center near the Bundestag" about press credentials.

"I'm sorry, but I believe you're a little late," Peters told us when we finally found him. "There are no more press credentials to be issued."

We insisted that we were assured of credentials and that
he was supposed to take care of us.

"I'm afraid all you can do at this point," he said, "is to
take it up with Frau Schmidt."

Oh, great. The old "Frau Schmidt" handoff.

We found Frau Schmidt. She was packing up to go home
when we got to her desk.

"I'm sorry, you're not on the list," she said as she leafed
through a file of index cards.

"But we must be on the list," I replied. "I spoke to the
White House last week and we were guaranteed press credentials: 'Just check with Frau Schmidt when you get to
Bonn,' I was told. So now we've flown all the way here, at
great expense to our newspaper, and because of some *foul-up,*
there are no credentials here for us!"

The possibility that there may have been a "foul-up," a
mistake made through carelessness, perhaps laziness, was a
revolting thought to an older German, and highly insulting.
She walked away—and within ten minutes she returned,
handing us our official PRESIDENT REAGAN STATE VISIT press
passes with complimentary lanyard embroidered with the
colors of the flag of the Federal Republic of Germany.

We didn't have much use for the passes in Bonn, except
they got us our first real meal in thirty hours. The German
government had opened up their parliament building to feed
the press with all the free food and drinks they could con-
sume. The spread of food was easily two blocks long.

"You know what they say," Gary remarked with a smile as
he wolfed down his fifth caviar pâté. "A well-fed press always
tells the truth."

We took off for Bitburg in the morning. Located about one hundred miles south of Bonn, Bitburg was a town of 24,000 inhabitants — 12,000 Germans and 12,000 American servicemen and -women and their dependents from the nearby air force base. Leveled by the United States in an air attack on Christmas Eve, 1944 (Bitburg was a staging area and supply depot for the Nazi troops in the Battle of the Bulge), it was now a quaint little city nestled in the hills of the Rhineland.

We weren't off the bus five minutes when we were approached by the local Welcome Wagon that had been set up for the visiting press. No running from office to office begging for press credentials here in Bitburg — these people had the red carpet rolled out for anyone with a camera, notepad, or sharpened pencil. Bernd Quirin, a financial officer with the city and head of the local German Army Reserves, recognized us as Americans and offered to give us a personal tour of Bitburg, including the cemetery.

We took him up on it, and he chauffeured us around in his Audi for the next two hours. We heard the whole history of Bitburg, how his father was wounded on the Russian front, how much he and all the Bitburgers loved America and Ronald Reagan. The 12,000 U.S. soldiers never caused a problem in town, and there was no dissension over Reagan's visit to those SS graves — after all, he explained, those SS were "just kids forced into the Nazi army."

Bernd then took us to the cemetery. Of course he had no idea he was participating in a reconnaissance mission, aiding and abetting a Jew and a journalist who planned on raising a ruckus the next day. We felt bad that after our arrests he'd probably be hauled in for questioning as to why he was "the driver" for these anarchists.

At first glance, what one notices about the Bitburg cemetery is how small it is. If you had visions of Arlington or Normandy in your head, they were quickly dashed by this half-acre plot of flat grave markers with six cement crosses and a chapel that more resembled a crematorium.

This was The Day Before, and the local Germans were busy laying flowers on all the graves and tidying up for the president's visit. The press was there, too, photographing the SS graves from every angle imaginable and interviewing Bitburgers about their connection to the SS.

One elderly German woman was going around and taking flowers off non-Nazi graves and placing them in abundance on the SS graves. She was mumbling something nasty in German as she went about her one-woman "up yours" crusade as the cameras rolled. Her presence was making the Bitburg city officials a bit nervous. "Why are you filming her?" the deputy mayor of Bitburg asked the ABC-TV crew.

"Just try to stay out of our way if you can" was the response of an ABC field producer as the crew shoved the deputy mayor aside.

Humiliated by this treatment, he turned to me and said, "You Americans. You don't listen. You print what you want to fit your ideas of what is and what isn't." He then pulled out two covers of *Newsweek* magazine. One was the U.S. edition, the other the international. Both had the same cover of an SS grave, but the U.S. edition had two West German flags stuck into the Nazi grave.

"*Newsweek* doctored this photo," he said, "so as to imply that we Germans today honor the Nazis. Have you read *The*

Lost Honor of Katherina Blum? This is what you Americans want—to strip us of our dignity and our honor."

We awoke Sunday morning for the big day and began to implement our plan. Underneath his sweater, Gary wrapped around his torso a forty-square-foot banner our friends Jack and Laurie had painted for us back in Ann Arbor. It read:

> We Came from Michigan, USA, to Remind You:
> They Murdered My Family

With both real and fake press passes around our necks and camera bags in hand, we set off on our two-mile walk to the cemetery.

What we discovered was that overnight Bitburg had turned into a police state, with 17,000 German army soldiers, security officials, and cops from every walk of life having surrounded the town and set up a series of checkpoints, making it almost impossible to get to the cemetery. One thing the Germans were making certain of: no one would get within a mile of the Bitburg cemetery without having proved that they were Walter Cronkite or David Brinkley. And there on the road leading up to the cemetery, about a half mile away, the German police nabbed us.

"This is as far as you go," the officers barked at us in German. Gary, who is fluent in German, told him that we were assured that we would be allowed in the cemetery.

"You'll have to discuss that with the police chief," he said and then motioned us to start walking back into town.

We returned to town and went to the city hall, where we found the police chief besieged by other reporters who apparently had met the same fate as ours. Sizing up the situation, it appeared that the reporters from the Knight-Ridder group were having the most luck with the chief, so we moseyed over to them and hung close as if we were part of their team. Finally, the chief got on the phone and told the command post on the cemetery road to let this group of reporters through. So off we tagged along, looking like we were their photographers.

Once back at the checkpoint, the barking cop let us pass. Our joy at this coup soon subsided as we were told this was only the first of *seven* checkpoints we would have to get through.

The next two police checkpoints were fairly easy with lots of *Guten Morgens* and *Howdy-doodies*. The fourth stop required a search, but not of our bodies, so Gary's banner went unnoticed.

The fifth group of police—now looking less like police and more like a well-muscled group of blond army rangers with a strange homoerotic vibe—were a bit more testy because our credentials were not the *official* White House ones which were for the select group of thirty news people in the preapproved pool who were allowed to be in the actual cemetery just feet from the president. But because Gary spoke perfect German—and I spoke perfect bullshit—we somehow were able to talk our way through this, the penultimate checkpoint.

The cemetery was now in sight. We were amazed we had made it this far and decided that a bold move would now be required to make it past the final gate that would bring us into the Promised Land. Out of nowhere a truck carrying the TV equipment for CBS News pulled up. The guys driving it started to unload their metal boxes and crates. I sauntered up to them and asked them if they needed any help.

"Sure," said one of the crew gruffly. "Grab a couple of those."

And this, dear readers, became one of the few times in my life that looking like a roadie was turned into a plus. I picked up the box, Gary walked in tight behind me, and before you could say *"Deutschland über alles,"* we were inside the Bitburg cemetery, free to roam around as we pleased!

The Bonn bureau chiefs for *Newsweek* and the Associated Press, both of whom we had met in Bonn (where we confided in them what our real plans were) spotted us and ran over to greet us.

"How the hell did you guys do this?" asked Ken Jones of AP, a big grin on his face.

"I mean, all they've (the Germans) talked about for two months," added Andrew Nagorski of *Newsweek,* "is how they've worked out the most sophisticated security arrangements for this trip—and then you come into town, crack it, and just walk right in." We smiled the smile of those who have swallowed the canary. They promised not to blow our cover.

About an hour before Reagan was to arrive, the Secret Service appeared in two black vans to "mag the cemetery," meaning they were going to do one final sweep of the place for bombs—and re-check everyone's credentials.

We were all herded back to the outside of the cemetery so the police could "sweep it." All that work—and now we were no longer in the cemetery! They put us in a field beside the cemetery and promised we'd all be let back in once the sweep was completed. When the cemetery was deemed secure, they set up an airport-style metal detector and lined us all up to go through it. Ten, fifteen minutes passed and the Secret Service couldn't get the metal detector machine to work. (This led one of the German police to remark, in English, "Stupid Americans—they can put a man on the moon, but they can't get a simple thing like this to work!")

The Feds finally gave up on the contraption and got out their handheld metal detectors and began wanding everyone in line, one by one. They were also doing full-body hand searches—the kind that would discover a humongous banner tucked inside Gary. It looked like the adventure was over.

We were about twentieth in line and things were moving pretty slowly. Then, as the person in front of Gary stepped up to be searched, the Secret Service chief came over and said, "We're running out of time. Skip the body searches and just use the detectors." Whew. Gary and I walked through without a hitch.

But now we had to get back into the cemetery, and to get back in we would have to prove we were part of the press pool again. Damn. We didn't have those blue White House press cards, and we noticed them hauling a few people away who didn't have them, either. They were being sent back over to the field and out of sight of the cemetery. This was not acceptable for Gary and me. We decided that instead of being sent to the time-out field, our best bet was to circle back just outside the cemetery gate but still be right in the middle of all the action. We placed ourselves beside the path that Reagan's limo would have to go down in order to enter the cemetery gate. The location was perfect. There was no way Reagan was going to miss us. We didn't need to be with the pool anyway, as they continued to be led around by their noses to the officially approved spots. None of these reporters would be within earshot of Reagan in order to ask any questions. Plus, where we were now, we were with the pack of real journalists who were not under any obligation to follow the rules.

It was just minutes away from Reagan's arrival, so we took our place on the path and prepared to take out the banner. We were in an area that was filled with German police, the international press, and a few families who had the misfortune of living in the neighborhood.

Word spread that the motorcade was on its way. Gary and I—mostly I—were getting increasingly nervous. Suddenly, I began to freeze. *What the hell were we doing?* I knew that the instant we reached inside our coats to whip something out, we were going to be pounced on, or worse. This was nuts, I decided. The face of every German cop and grunt looked like they meant business. And we were about to become their business—their bloody business.

In my panic, I spotted ABC news correspondent Pierre Salinger (former press secretary to President Kennedy), and instantly came up with an idea that might protect us from being pummeled. I went over to talk to Salinger.

"Mr. Salinger," I said nervously. "My friend and I are here and we're not part of the press. We're here to perform an action when Reagan arrives—a nonviolent action. His parents are Holocaust survivors."

"How did you get in here?" he asked, bemused.

"We had some credentials and we're from Flint," I said, thinking that sounded dumb.

"OK, well, I won't blow your secret," he promised.

"Could you do something else for us?" I asked. "We're really scared that they are going to hurt us. When we pull out our sign, will you make sure your camera is right there on us so that they will see that this image is going out live on TV. I have a feeling the last thing the Germans want today is footage of themselves beating a Jew in the Bitburg cemetery."

He laughed heartily at that. "No, they don't want that," he said, still chuckling. "I like this. I like this. OK, you have my word—we'll have the camera right there on you to protect you."

"Thank you," I said. "Thank you."

Down the street we could begin to hear a rolling cheer from the crowd. The motorcade was in sight. This was it. Gary put his hand quietly under his coat. He was trying to time it just right so that he would have time to get it out and hand me one end while he took the other—and have that occur just as Reagan got to us. Do it too soon and the cops would have us out of there before the limo ever hit the gate. Do it too late and we've missed our opportunity. At what he believed to be the precise moment—this man of Flint who was as anally organized and on time more than anyone I knew— yanked out the bedsheet, flipped one end over to me, and quickly unfurled it before anyone noticed what was going on. Now with Reagan just ten feet away, we thrust the banner toward the limo, inches away from the windows where we could plainly see the expressions of the faces of Ronald and Nancy Reagan. The smiling president read the banner and his face turned instantly to what could best be described as confusion. Nancy was not confused and stared right at us with disgust.

The police surrounded us immediately — as did the cameraman from ABC News. The police saw the camera and made the snap decision not to beat the living crap out of us. We had humiliated them with this security breach — and God knows they wanted to mete out our punishment right then and there. But this was the New Germany, and cooler heads prevailed. As the Reagans were now through the gate and getting out of the car, we remained in our spot. The authorities asked us to put away the bedsheet and, not wanting to press our luck, we complied.

The wreath-laying ceremony at the graves lasted an entirety of eight minutes. Before we knew it, here came the Reagans again! So, disobeying orders not to, we pulled out the bedsheet, one last chance for the president to think about what he just did. "THEY MURDERED MY FAMILY."

With the Reagan limo speeding out of the cemetery and into the history books, the real craziness began. The locals, who had been cut out of the shortened presidential ceremony, now were allowed to march into the Bitburg cemetery and conduct their own wreath-laying action. They kicked it off with some rogue old German shouting randomly, "Jews, go home!" (He was quickly silenced as, well, there were no Jews left in Bitburg who had a home to go to.) It became obvious he was referring to Gary and me, upset at us for unfurling our banner. He had nothing to worry about. We had no interest in staying in Bitburg.

With the roadblocks now removed, a steady stream of Bitburgers were jamming the road to get into the cemetery.

By the hundreds they came to make a point—by laying wreaths and flowers on the graves of the dead Nazis.

The highlight of this "People's Wreath Laying" came when the representative of the American Veterans of Foreign Wars, Gerard Murphy, and his German counterpart from the Nazi veterans group laid a joint wreath on the SS graves and declared World War II over—again.

"We need to forget about the war and the Holocaust," Murphy said in his speech at the cemetery. "It does no good to remember the past. The present situation demands that we join together to fight our common enemy—communism." The crowd cheered. We left.

Heading out of town, we hitched a ride with a German woman who was headed to Hanover and in the direction we needed to go to fly home. She stopped at the Bitburg gas station to fill up before we hit the road.

"You know," I said, "this gas station used to be the Jewish synagogue here before the War. A man in town told us it was burned on Kristallnacht (the night in 1938 when Nazis across Germany destroyed Jewish businesses, homes, and temples). Some people wanted to put a plaque on it."

She said she knew nothing of this, and we had a quiet ride north—except for her wanting to know more about our extermination of the American Indians. Oh yeah, baby, ev'rybody got their holocaust.

As we got near Hanover, Gary suggested we stop at the Bergen-Belsen concentration camp, which his parents were liberated from in 1945. The lady said she didn't know where that was—or *what* it was. We thanked her and got out in town and took a taxi out to the site.

We arrived at Bergen-Belsen as the sun was setting over the many weed-covered mounds that were the mass graves. Hill after hill concealed the fifty thousand bodies that were piled underneath. No gravestones, no Stars of David, no names of anyone. Just dirt piled high and grass growing on top. No one else was there besides us.

Gary said he wanted to be alone for a while.

I went and sat on a bench and wrote this story.

A Blessing

MY PRIEST HAD A CONFESSION he wanted to make to me.

"I have serious blood on my hands, Michael," Father Zabelka said softly. "I want you to know."

We were sitting on the porch of my newspaper office, Father George Zabelka and I. He was the former pastor of Sacred Heart Church in Flint (the church in which I would later be married). Father Zabelka was now retired but still working, doing a whole host of projects in the Flint area, including helping out as a volunteer at the *Flint Voice*.

Living in downtown Flint, I had stopped going to Mass about six years prior, and so "Father George" was the closest thing I had to a priest, as I still very much believed in the central tenets of the Faith: to love one another, to love your enemy, to do unto others as you would want them to do unto you. I agreed that one had a personal responsibility to assist the poor, the infirm, the imprisoned and the looked-down-upon. But I wasn't much in favor of many of the church's edicts when it came to certain issues, usually the ones that hurt people (gays), made others second-class

339

citizens (women), and used the fires of hell to scare people about sex.

I enjoyed my weekly or monthly meetings with Father Zabelka, and I would even attend services he would conduct at churches in Genesee County. He became my de facto pastor.

But now he wanted to tell me something. I had only known him at this point a few short months, and so the talk of "blood on my hands" was a bit shocking, and I was instantly uncomfortable.

He pulled out an old photograph and pointed to it. In the center of the photo was a plane, and in front of the plane was a group of airmen. And in the middle of the airmen was a chaplain, a priest.

"That's me," he said, pointing at the much younger version of himself. "That's me."

He looked at me as if I were supposed to know something, or say something. I looked at him, confused and trying to understand what it was I was supposed to understand. It then struck me that he, like my dad, carried with him all the scars of that war. Just from being there, this good priest must have still felt that he was part of a lot of the death and dying. I understood.

"So you were in World War II," I said sympathetically. "So was my dad. So much death and destruction. It must have been horrible to witness it. Where were you stationed?"

He continued to look at me as if I weren't getting it.

"What does it say on the plane?" he asked.

I looked closely to see what the writing on the nose of the plane said.

Oh.

"Enola Gay."

"Right," Father Zabelka said. "I was the chaplain for the 509th on Tinian Island. I was their priest."

And then he added: "On August 6, 1945, I blessed the bomb they dropped on Hiroshima."

I took a deep breath, staring at the photo, then looking away, and then looking at him. His dark eyes seemed even darker now.

"I was the chaplain of the *Enola Gay*. I said Mass for them on August 5, 1945, and the next morning I blessed them as they left for their mission to slaughter two hundred thou sand people. With my blessing. With the blessing of Jesus Christ and the Church. I did that."

I didn't know what to say.

He continued:

"And three days later, I blessed the crew and the plane that dropped the bomb on Nagasaki. Nagasaki was a Catholic city, the only majority Christian city in Japan. The pilot of the plane was a Catholic. And we obliterated the lives of forty thousand fellow Catholics, seventy-three thousand people in all."

There was now a mist in his eyes as he told me of this horror.

"There were three orders of nuns in Japan, all based in Nagasaki. Every last single one of them was vaporized. Not a single nun from any of the three orders was alive. And I blessed that."

I didn't know what to say. I reached out and put my hand on his shoulder.

"George, you didn't drop the bomb. You didn't plan the destruction of these cities. You were there to do your job, to minister to the needs of these young men."

"No," he insisted, "it's not that easy. I was part of it. I said nothing. I wanted us to *win*. I was part of the effort. Everyone had a role to play. My role was to condone it in the name of Christ."

He explained that far from being repulsed when he heard the news about Hiroshima later that day, he felt what most Americans felt—relief. That maybe this would end the war.

"I didn't quit over this," he said emphatically. "I remained as a chaplain, even after the war, in the Reserves, and the National Guard. For twenty-two years. When I retired, I was a lieutenant colonel. Few chaplains achieve that rank."

He then recounted how, a month after the two bombings, he joined the American forces as they entered Japan after the Japanese surrendered. He ended up in Nagasaki and saw firsthand the people who survived and the suffering they were going through. He found the headquarters, in rubble, of one of the orders of nuns. At the cathedral, he dug out the censer, the top half of it fully intact. He participated in the relief effort. It made his conscience "feel better."

"But did you know on the morning of August sixth that the *Enola Gay* was going to drop that bomb? Did you even know what that bomb was?"

"No, we didn't," Zabelka said. "All we knew was that it was 'special.' We said it was 'tricked up.' Nobody had any idea that it had the capability to do what it did. The crew had special instructions, they knew not to look, and to get out of there as fast as possible."

"Then if you didn't know, you're not responsible."

"Not true!" he said firmly. "Not true! It is the responsibility of every human to know their actions and the consequences of their actions and to ask questions and to question things when they are wrong."

"But George, this was war. No one is allowed to ask any questions."

"And it's exactly that kind of attitude that continues to get us into more wars—no one asking any questions, especially in the military. Blind obedience—we didn't let the Germans get away with that excuse, did we?"

"But George, the difference was, we were the good guys, we were the ones who were attacked."

"All true. And history is written by the victors. A good case can be made that the Japanese had already decided to surrender. We wanted to drop those bombs. We wanted to send a message to the Russians."

He looked straight at me.

"You can say I didn't know anything before Hiroshima, about what that bomb would do. But what about three days later? I knew then. I knew what would happen to the next city, which turned out to be Nagasaki. And yet I blessed...I blessed the bomb. I blessed the crew. I blessed the slaughter of seventy-three thousand people. God have mercy on me."

George told me how in the mid-to-late sixties he had his "St. Paul moment" where he was "knocked off his horse" and he realized that the men in power were up to no good and that it will always be the poor who suffer. He decided to dedicate his life to total pacifism and became an outspoken critic of the Vietnam War in his Sunday sermons. He got involved in the civil rights movement in Flint. He was the very definition of a radical priest. He supported SDS, and when the Weathermen had their infamous War Council meeting in Flint in 1969, he opened up the doors of his church to the participants (who were all certainly not pacifists) so they'd have a place to sleep. He became known as the priest who wouldn't back down, wouldn't give in on matters of war and race and class. I had heard of Father Zabelka during all those years. I just never knew why he was the way he was. Now I did. And no matter how much he worked for peace, he could never *not be* the priest who "blessed the bomb."

"I will have much to answer for when I meet St. Peter at those gates," he said. "I am hopeful he will be merciful to me."

I was grateful he told me his story and I wrote about it in my paper. He continued to help at the *Voice,* doing whatever menial tasks needed to be done, like dropping stacks of the paper off at locations in the north end of Flint.

Four years later, Father Zabelka decided it was time to perform further penance — and spread his gospel of peace. He began a walk across America to the Holy Land — a literal walk from Seattle to New York, then a plane ride over the ocean (he hadn't perfected the walking-on-water bit), and then continuing on to Bethlehem. A total of eight thousand miles. And he did it in just over two years. At stops along the way he would tell the story of his transformation from pro-war atom bomb chaplain to hardcore pacifist.

When he returned, he stopped by the *Voice* one day, saying he wanted to see me.

"Michael, I've been thinking for some time and wondering why you left the seminary, why you didn't go on to be a priest."

"Well," I said, "a number of reasons. I was only fourteen when I went. By fifteen, the hormones kicked in. Plus, I didn't—and don't—care for the institution and its hierarchy. And what the institution says it stands for has little to do these days with the teachings of Jesus Christ.

"Oh, and they also told me not to come back."

Zabelka may have been a "radical priest," but he was still a priest and still very faithful to the Catholic Church.

"I've been reading some of your comments about the Church and the Pope in the *Voice,* and I'm just worried about you. And your soul."

I laughed. "George, you don't have to worry about me or my soul. I'm doing just fine."

"But it seems that you've left the Church."

"Let's just say I'm a recovering Catholic."

That did not go over well.

"Would you do me a favor and pray with me right now?"

"Are you serious?"

"Yes. I just want to make sure you are going to be OK."

"I'm going to be OK. And I pray when I need to."

"Just say the Lord's Prayer with me right now." He began: "'*Our Father, who art in heaven, hallowed be thy name…*'"

"George—stop. This isn't necessary."

"…'*Thy Kingdom come, Thy will be done, on Earth…*'"

"*George! Stop!* This is creeping me out!"

"Don't say that about the Lord's Prayer, Michael," he said, interrupting the Lord's Prayer. "I think you need this."

"I don't need it. I don't want it. And I don't know what's gotten into you."

He became silent. He looked at me. He said nothing. I didn't know what to say. The silence was excruciating.

"It's important you carry on," he said when he finally spoke. "It's important to do what you do. But you can't do it without the Church. You need the Church and the Church needs you. You need to go back to Mass. You need to find a place within the Church where you can find peace."

I realized he was talking about himself. I realized that he still blamed himself for what happened on Tinian Island, and that were it not for the Church, for his faith, who knows what would have become of him. For every whipping he'd given himself over Hiroshima and Nagasaki, he had the Catholic Church there to give him a chance to redeem himself. He was still a priest. He could still do good with that, and maybe in his mind, if he did enough good, he would be forgiven on Judgment Day. I looked at this old man and understood the demons he still carried with him. I wasn't offended that he thought I needed some sort of "saving." It was an easy thing to forgive him for.

I spoke.

"'Give us this day our daily bread and forgive us our tres-passes, as we forgive those who trespass against us, and lead us not into temptation but deliver us from evil, forever and ever. Amen.'"

He smiled. "There. That wasn't so hard, was it?"

"No, George," I said kindly, "it wasn't."

"Good! Now, what do you want me to do for next week's paper?"

Abu 2 U 2

~~~~~~~

ABU NIDAL HAD A CHRISTMAS PRESENT for me. He was going to kill me.

It wasn't like he wanted to kill *me* specifically. It was more like we drew names. Or perhaps he was just planning a sick game of Secret Santa.

But he and I, for better or worse, had an unplanned rendezvous one morning during Christmas Week, 1985, at the Vienna International Airport.

And I lived to tell you about it.

Abu Nidal was the most feared terrorist in the world in the mid-'80s, the Osama bin Laden of his time. He was even feared by Yasser Arafat and the PLO. Having broken away from Arafat a decade earlier, Nidal formed the Fatah Revolutionary Council, or as he preferred to call it, "The Abu Nidal Organization." Nidal believed Arafat to be too soft on Israel. He was opposed to any concessions whatsoever and believed that striking military targets was a waste of time—he thought all efforts should be aimed at civilians. He just wanted to kill Jews—and any Palestinians who wanted to sit down and negotiate with Jews. He was like that.

What led Nidal to this career path seemed evident in his childhood. His real name was Sabri al-Banna, and his father, Khalil al-Banna, was one of the richest men in Palestine, owning thousands of acres of fruit groves and exporting that fruit to Europe. It was said that 10 percent of the citrus fruit that went from Palestine to Europe came from the al-Banna family trees.

The British partitioning (such a polite word!) of Palestine and the subsequent creation of the Israeli state — and the various wars that followed — left the al-Bannas with next to nothing. As Sabri was the twelfth child of one of Khalil's many wives, there wasn't much left for him. In fact, when his father died, his mother was kicked out of the family, and Sabri was ostracized and pretty much left to fend for himself. This led to a series of abusive situations which made him a very angry boy — who then became a very angry young man who wanted a fruit tree or two returned to him.

He chose the name Abu Nidal ("father of the struggle") and grew impatient with the PLO. One of his first jobs when he formed his own splinter group was to start bumping off the PLO leadership. He hated them more than he hated the Israelis, but he did leave time for killing the Israelis, too. Over a span of twenty years he coordinated terrorist actions in over twenty countries that killed at least nine hundred people. He was good at what he did.

In October 1985, just two months before I would cross paths with Nidal, his rival splinter group, the Palestine Liberation Front, run by the equally-feared Abu Abbas, hijacked a cruise ship, the *Achille Lauro,* off the coast of Egypt and killed an elderly American by the name of Leon Klinghoffer. They put a bullet in his head while he sat in his wheelchair, and then wheeled Leon in his chair straight off the ship and into the Mediterranean.

This act stunned most of the world, and it was fair to say that Palestinians, Muslims, and Arabs were developing a PR problem.

I lived in the part of the United States — southeastern Michigan — that had (and still has) more Arab-Americans and people of Arab descent per capita than any other part of the non-Arab world. I grew up with Palestinians, Lebanese, Syrians, Iraqis, Egyptians. But mostly Palestinians, whom we called Arabs, but thought of as white people, the way you used to think of Hispanics as white people (sure, they were brown, but they were Catholics, so they got half a point).

The Arabs in Flint owned the grocery stores, the movie theater, the department store, the real estate agency, and a lot of gas stations. Saying that the people of Flint liked the Arabs would be like saying they liked themselves. A man who was born in Palestine was more likely to have delivered you in the hospital than blow you up on a plane. *Much* more. We simply did not have this view of them as "terrorists," and so when *Arab* or *Palestinian* became a dirty word, it didn't become one for most of us. Ask anyone in Flint who grocery-shopped at Hamady's, bought their school clothes at Yankee's, ate at the American diner or danced at the Mighty Mighty Mikatam, and they will not know what you are talking about when you point out to them that the proprietors of these establishments had their lands invaded or snatched from them by the Israelis on the other side of the world.

This was not the sentiment throughout much of the rest of America. *Arab* had become pretty much synonymous with "evil," and between OPEC jacking up the price of oil and causing "oil shortages," the two recent wars with Israel, and the murder of the Israeli athletes at the Munich Olympics, Americans had pretty much seen enough to make up their minds that the last person you wanted to see in your neighborhood or on the flight to Fargo was an Arab guy.

An Arab-American foundation decided that they'd seen enough, too, and opened up an information and education office in Washington, D.C. They tried to put out press releases to counter the terrorism stories in the media with news about what Arab-Americans were doing to make America great. They sent speakers to talk to students on campuses. And they sponsored journalism fellowships to take groups of writers and reporters to the Arab world and show them firsthand how most Arabs lived and behaved.

In the summer of 1985, I applied for one of those fellowships. Issues regarding Arabs were a concern for the readers of my newspaper, the *Flint Voice* (which was now the *Michigan Voice*), many of whom were Arab-Americans in Flint and Detroit. I had never been to that part of the world, and the foundation promised full access to whatever we wanted to see in the countries we would visit—including interviews with those countries' leaders. In November, I learned that I had been selected for one of the fellowships and that the trip would begin the day after Christmas.

I flew from Flint to New York's JFK Airport on the evening of December 26 in order to connect to the Royal Jordanian Airlines flight that would be taking our group to the Middle East. We were all told to meet at check-in, and there I was introduced to the people from D.C. who would be conducting the two-week tour, as well as to the other journalists in the group, about a dozen folks who came mostly

from the world of alternative weeklies or left-leaning magazines. There was no one from the mainstream media and
no one whose media outlet reached more than a few thousand people. I guess the Arab image burnishing had to start
somewhere.

We loaded ourselves on the overnight Royal Jordanian
flight from New York to Amman, Jordan. The flight was
scheduled to stop in Vienna, where we would change planes
to another Royal Jordanian flight that would then take us on
to Amman.

I slept most of the way across the Atlantic on the jumbo
jet that was filled with mostly Arab passengers. I studied up
and read articles I had copied about the countries we would
visit: Jordan, Kuwait, the United Arab Emirates, and Saudi
Arabia (later dropped from the itinerary). We would also
visit the Israeli-occupied territories of the West Bank and
Gaza Strip.

As we came across the coast of Europe the sun was up,
and within an hour or two we began our descent into Vienna.
The pilot informed us that we were about twenty minutes
behind schedule.

We landed safely and began taxiing to the gate. As we
arrived near the gate I could see an El Al jet parked next to
our gate. I unbuckled my seat belt and began to gather my
belongings for deplaning when, all of a sudden, the pilot hit
the brakes. The force of it was so hard, my head hit the seat
in front of me.

We were no more than thirty to forty feet from the gate.
I looked out my window, and within seconds there were
military vehicles surrounding our plane *and* the El Al plane.
There were a few jeeps with soldiers and riot police and a

larger vehicle that I didn't recognize, but I did understand that that was a huge gun attached to it. This was not the Von Trapp family greeting us in Austria with a rendition of "Edelweiss." This just looked, at first, downright weird, then Hollywood-like, then eerily frightening.

"Folks," a voice on the intercom said. "We're going to be here a little while, so sit back and we'll keep you posted."

That is what they did not do. There was silence from the cockpit. An hour's worth. Nobody said anything—though the collective mind-fuck going on in this Royal Jordanian jet was fierce and full of imagination:

- Had we been hijacked? Were there hijackers in the cockpit?
- Was there a bomb on board?
- Were there terrorists who had been identified as passengers on this plane?
- Had the El Al plane been hijacked? Was there a bomb on board their plane?
- Was there an incident inside the airport, perhaps at the El Al gate next to us?
- Was this a drill? And why were we the guinea pigs?

I did not understand why we weren't being told anything, and the flight attendants were beginning to feel the same way. I chose a simple method of discovering the truth. I got up out of my seat and went up to the cockpit and knocked on the door. A flight attendant told me to sit down. The cockpit door opened. It was the co-pilot. Cross "hijacking" off the list.

"I'm sorry to bother you," I said politely, "but people are

getting frightened by all this activity and no one knows what is going on."

"We're just about to announce it. There's been gunfire and grenades launched just inside here, and they think a number of people are dead. They are holding us here. That's all we know. And I need you to go back to your seat."

I was speechless. It really wasn't the answer I was expecting. I was probably hoping that the movable ramp, the jetway, had had a malfunction or something. Of course, this would not explain the presence of the Austrian military.

"Why haven't you said anything?" I asked.

"Like I said, we were just getting ready to. Please take your seat."

I felt a bit nauseous as I walked back down the aisle. One of the people traveling with me asked me if I was OK.

"No," I replied. "We're not OK."

At that moment, the pilot went on the intercom.

"I'm afraid we have some bad news, and I want everyone to remain at ease as we are all fine," he began. "There has been an incident in the terminal that has caused them to shut the airport down. It appears to be a terrorist attack directed at the passengers on the El Al flight next to us. The attack seems to be over and we are not in danger. We just ask that you remain in your seats and we will give you information as we receive it. Thank you."

So you're sitting on a plane full of Arabs and Muslims and you get a friendly announcement like that. And you're not just sitting on any plane, you're sitting on the *Jordanian* plane, next to the intended target, the *Israeli* plane. What's the mood on your plane? Everyone continues leafing through their complimentary in-flight magazine, *Better Homes and*

Jordan? Flight attendants apologize for the inconvenience and announce that the headphones for the in-flight movie will be free? Complimentary apple juice and honey-roasted peanuts? Bulletproof vests for first class and duck-and-cover for the rest of us?

No. The plane turned into a panic zone. Not a boisterous one, but a fearful, quiet one where the passengers settle into a feeling of near suffocation. They know that they are all — *all* — instant suspects. Those of us who aren't Arab avoid eye contact and sit still in our seats. Being on an Arab-filled flight on an Arab airliner helped one recall that these things usually end badly — and they usually end right here, on the airport tarmac, right where we were sitting. The Munich athletes and their captors were killed on the tarmac. So was an American soldier on a hijacked plane, brutally beaten to death and dumped out the door of the jet and onto the tarmac. Raid on Entebbe? The Israelis came in with guns blazing at the Uganda airport. And then there was the Air France jet. They just went ahead and blew that sucker up. On the tarmac.

Another hour goes by, and there is a knock from the outdoors on the main cabin door. Airport officials have wheeled up a metal staircase to the forward cabin door of the plane. The door opens and on come men in uniform carrying guns. They are not from catering.

"Ladies and gentlemen, may we have your attention. The Austrian officials have boarded the plane and they would like to see everyone's passport, so if you would be so kind as to cooperate with them we would greatly appreciate it. This should not take long."

Due to the color of my skin and the lack of any decorative scarf on me, I was pretty much a safe bet and was probably not who they were looking for. *But who <u>are</u> they looking for? I thought the attack was "over." They ARE looking for someone on this plane!*

None of this felt good, and it didn't matter that I wasn't an Arab. I looked over at our group leaders with eyes that asked, *What the fuck?!* Thanks for taking me on this trip to improve the image of Arabs! We're off to a smashing start! Can't wait to see the next stop on the trip! Scenic ride to a crowded West Jerusalem bus stop at rush hour and a "hey-did-anybody-leave-their-bag-here-BOOM!"

I lived in Flint. I lived near Detroit. By 1985, the murder rates in both cities vied with each other to lead the nation. I was not unaccustomed to danger or random acts of see-ya-in-the-hereafter. But this was not that. I had found myself inside a terrorist incident where I am told that people inside this building have died.

They do not tell us the whole truth: that a total of forty-two people have been hit with bullets and grenade shrapnel. Worse yet, they have not told us that, at the same exact moment the attack took place a few paces from us here in Vienna, *another* group from the same terrorist organization has opened fire inside *Rome's* International Airport. Sixteen people lay dead there, along with ninety-nine others who had been shot or wounded.

Because these attacks were timed to go off together, the police believed the attacks of the morning weren't over and that there were possibly more to come. Were there terrorists on our Jordanian Airlines plane who had planned to get off when we were supposed to change flights and join the attack, perhaps right here at the gate next to the El Al plane? *But they couldn't because we were twenty fucking minutes late?!* Had we been on time, we would have been right inside the terminal where the killing took place. Never had I been happier for my flight being late (and never since then have I complained when a flight is late).

The police weren't taking any chances. They wanted to see who was on board our jet. And they were prepared to take action.

The "Passport, please" process went quite smoothly. Everyone was on their best behavior, and it was so quiet that even the babies knew to not cry or babble about anything. After about forty-five minutes, without incident, the authorities left the plane. Then it was back to waiting in the black hole of no information.

At some point, perhaps four hours into the ordeal, the pilot came back on the intercom.

"OK," he said with a sigh. "Here is what we are going to do. The Austrians do not want anyone on this plane to get off and enter Austria. As most of you on this flight were going to transfer anyway to another plane going to Amman, we are just going to refuel this plane and take everyone to Amman. For the few of you who were connecting to another flight in the Middle East, we will rebook you in Amman and fly you there. If you are an Austrian citizen, you may get up now and come forward and we will release you from the plane. The rest of you, sit back and get ready to depart Vienna in twenty minutes."

Here we were, just feet from our gate, but the Austrians weren't going to take any chances. Better to just get the whole lot of them outta here as quick as possible and dump them off out there in their own pathetic desert. The fuel trucks appeared, hooked up their hoses of Arab oil, and filled up our wings for our flight to Jordan.

Twenty minutes later, as promised, they moved away the army vehicles and let us go in reverse. We taxied to the runaway and took off. Less than three hours later we were in Amman. The group leaders did their best to put the whole day in context, and there was no one among us who needed any drilling on the wrong-headedness of smearing all Arabs with this paintbrush. We were fine, we were safe, and we still didn't know the whole story of what had happened. Our driver took us into Amman, and it was a beautiful sight coming in from the hills above the city. I thought, this is perhaps what Rome once looked like before it was modernized. It was dark by the time we got to the hotel and checked in. I went to my room and lay down on the bed, turning on the television. We were in Amman's finest hotel (wanting to make a good impression!), so they carried the channel known as the "Cable News Network." As I lay on the bed, I watched in horror. Everything I, we, hadn't been told about the entire day's events in Rome and Vienna, I was now learning for the first time—with color footage and color commentary. The forty-two bodies strewn across the terminal floor in Vienna, the 115 in Rome. The work of Abu Nidal. Abu had chosen this day, this moment, for a mass murder. I was merely supposed to be an extra in his snuff film, acted out on the world stage he had commandeered. He didn't know me or anyone else on that plane or in that terminal. We were each just one of the faceless, nameless dozens who were to be hit by his machine gun fire or by a grenade or both, and then, should luck have it, bleed to death in front of the duty-free shop. Of course, we weren't nameless, faceless, *and* landless, because when you're landless, there's no duty-free shops in the refugee camps, no Jamba Juice stand next door made with the oranges that were once yours. You were left to a life where you would bleed to death (though in a much slower way), just like you wanted me to, because you had been written off by the Israelis and by the world as meaningless, insignificant, a nuisance that should just go away. I hated the whole of it and I hated this world that I didn't sign up to live in. *All are punish'd.*

The newscaster told the story of what happened in Vienna and Rome with a beginning, a middle, and an end — and, even though I had been right there, it was like I wasn't. Someone who *truly wasn't there* — this anchorman in *Atlanta, Georgia* — knew more than I did! And at that moment I became part of that select group of people from the late twentieth century who were present at an act of terrorism. I sat up on the bed and felt the way most said they had felt on the grassy knoll in Dallas on that day some two decades earlier. You knew something bad had happened, you *think* you saw something horrific, but it *couldn't be that,* just *couldn't be that!* And it was all over so quick your brain could not take the images fast enough from the corneas and process them into a reasonable explanation of what just occurred. As there was no play-by-play in Dealey Plaza or at the Vienna Airport, there was no one there to be your narrator, your guide — your calm, soothing voice that could make sense of it all for you. And to comfort you. But you can't be comforted. Because you did not watch this on a twenty-five-inch screen in a bar in Boulder; *you were there*. And you are not your own narrator because it's not a "story" to *you*—it's a real goddamned moment of "Am I going to survive?" And what the *fuck* is going on here? The TV explained it all to me. On the plane earlier I was relatively calm—confused, yes; worried, definitely. But I kept it together, as did everyone else on the plane. We knew people had died. But we also needed to go to the bathroom.

Now, for the first time that day, eyes affixed to CNN, I began to shake, and then cry. Hard. The story on the TV box was more real than the real I had been so close to. I thought about those twenty minutes of the plane being late to that gate. I picked up the phone and called my wife back in America. She had been calling everywhere trying to find me. I was quiet. And then I began to cry again.

Hot Tanned Nazi

⌒

YES, SHE WAS HOT. Yes, she was tanned. She had long blonde hair and a sweet smile. What was she doing here?

I walked over to ask her that very question, but at that moment her Nazi boyfriend stepped in (no, I don't mean her boyfriend was *acting* like a "Nazi," I mean he was a *real* Nazi in a black storm trooper uniform). He took her by the arm and walked her over to his Ford Econoline van, slid open the door, and loaded her into the back so they could, I presume, make tender Nazi love on a sunny April afternoon.

A few weeks earlier I had received a call from James Ridgeway, the political columnist for the *Village Voice* in New York City. He wanted to make a documentary on the rise of the extremist right wing in the Midwest in the wake of the Reagan recession. The economy was in the toilet for any place that did manufacturing, and Flint, Michigan, was especially hard hit. The various far right movements saw these out-of-work autoworkers as potential recruits for their

363

Aryan supremacist movement. They had a simple answer as to why Flint was beginning to come apart: "It's the niggers and the Jews!" That didn't play well with most people, but it did draw enough of those who were at the end of their rope to consider the teachings and preachings of these men.

Robert Miles was the former head of the Michigan Ku Klux Klan. He was born in the Washington Heights section of Manhattan, and if you looked at him you'd never guess he was one of the most notorious Grand Wizards of the Klan. He was soft-spoken, intelligent, literate, and had this disarming New York accent that made him sound more like a priest in a Bing Crosby movie than an avowed racist who spent seven years in prison for setting fire to ten school buses in Pontiac, Michigan, his contribution to trying to halt that district's integration plan.

Miles believed in violence and the separation of the races. He wanted the U.S. government to declare an "all-white" area where white people could go and live in peace: Montana, Idaho, Wyoming, Oregon, and the state of Washington. He would give the Hispanics Arizona and New Mexico, and the blacks could have the states of the Deep South.

In order to pull off this revolution, he needed to gather together the disparate groups that made up the white supremacist movement and get them to agree to work together. So he put out a call for a convention of racists to take place on an April weekend in the spring of 1986 on his farm south of Flint. Everyone twisted and white, regardless of their differences, was invited: the various Klan groups, the Aryan Nations, the American Nazis, Christian Identity, the white power conclaves—you name it, if it was racist and nuts, it was going to be there.

Ridgeway had called me to see if I might be able to convince Grand Dragon Miles to let him and his crew into the gathering to film it. He was certain the answer would be no, but he wanted to see if I could give it a shot and try to convince them.

I hosted a weekly radio show on the rock station in Flint called *Radio Free Flint*. I had had Mr. Miles on my show a couple of times. I was exactly the type of vermin that he and his people wanted to rid the earth of, but he couldn't have been nicer or more polite when he visited the radio station.

So I thought I could convince him to do this. I understood that when someone's mind has taken a psychotic turn it's hard to reverse that. Clearly, in his case, prison didn't do the job. He had his beliefs set in cement: he saw white people as the chosen people, and everyone else was here to serve us. Not a bad setup if you're the white guy, eh?

I called Bob and asked him if I could come out to his farm to ask him a favor. He was delighted to hear from me and invited me out to have lunch on a Friday afternoon. His wife, a gregarious and good-hearted woman, made a pot of Irish stew and homemade biscuits and some fresh-brewed ice tea. He sat and talked to me about his early years in New York City. As a teenager he joined a youth group whose main activity was to go down on weekends to Union Square and beat the crap out of socialists and communists. He went to George Washington High School, where Henry Kissinger was a year ahead of him.

After the attack on Pearl Harbor, Miles joined the Navy and fought for the duration of the war. When he got out, he and his wife moved to Michigan, where he became an insurance man. He would eventually rise to become the head of the Michigan Association of Insurance Executives. In those days, insurance men went door to door to convince people why they needed life insurance and a homeowner's policy. It was hard work, as this new demographic known as "the middle class" were unfamiliar with the concept of giving someone their hard-earned money for something they might never use. To succeed in the insurance business back then, you had to be a smooth talker but also be able to possess the voice of reason—and of fear. You had to make a family fear all the possible what-ifs: what if my house burns down, what if my child gets sick, what if I die before my time and leave my family penniless. It wasn't long before nearly everyone had someone whom they referred to as their own personal "insurance man."

Bob Miles must have been great at it, and once he crossed over to the dark side of the Klan, he was the perfect recruiter for the Aryan Nations—your friendly insurance man selling you a simple policy to protect yourself from the crazy "mud people" who are coming to burn down your house, steal your daughters, and take your life. His pitch was gentle and it sounded reasonable. He had a skill set the average redneck didn't possess, and he used it to build the Michigan Klan into one of the most potent racist groups in the country.

But on this Friday afternoon, as another pot of tea was brewing, Miles said he was more than happy to let my "Hollywood" friends come to his farm and film him and his convocation.

"I know you don't believe in what we're doing," he said, as he wiped the bottom of the stew dish with his white powdered biscuit, "but I think if you get to know us you will see that we don't have horns or a tail. All we ask is that you honestly show what you see here and let the people in the theater decide for themselves."

I told him that James Ridgeway was bringing two co-directors with him: a woman, Anne Bohlen, who had received an Oscar nomination for a short film about the Flint Sit-Down Strike, and Kevin Rafferty, who had made a number of documentaries. I told him that they do not editorialize in their movies, that they don't use a narrator, that they just like to be flies on the wall and let the cameras roll. He liked all of that and gave his blessing for his gathering of hate groups to be featured in a movie.

Ridgeway, Bohlen, and Rafferty flew in the day before the convention so they could meet me and map out a plan. It was the first time I had ever been around a film crew or anything like this. I was all ears.

"OK," said Kevin Rafferty, who was clearly the leader of the pack. "Mike, they trust you, so you stick by us. No need to say anything; we'll direct the questions. Jim's done all the research. Just hang nearby if we need you."

"Sure," I said, excited about being part of a film crew, whatever that meant. "Whatever you need."

"I'll be on the main camera, Robert will be second camera [Robert Stone, the acclaimed documentary director of *Radio Bikini*], and Anne [Bohlen] will do sound with Charlie and Mo [two film students]. We're a pretty big crew, so we want to try to blend in and not get in their way."

"Blending in" was not possible. When we arrived at Miles's farm, greeting us were a few hundred solid American citizens bedecked in Nazi uniforms, spiffy sportswear emblazoned

with various versions of the swastika, KKK outerwear, Aryan
Nations buttons and badges, sashes that proclaimed white
power and Christian superiority, and a whole lotta guys
and gals who looked like they did not follow the cautionary
guidelines from the National Institutes of Health regarding
the downside of breeding within one's family.

They viewed us with appropriate suspicion, yet nearly all
were willing to be filmed. All, except Miles's two co-gurus:
Robert Butler, the head of the Aryan Nations in Hayden
Lake, Idaho, and William Pierce, head of the National Al-
liance (the descendants of the American Nazi Party) and
author of *The Turner Diaries,* a novel about America being
overthrown by Jews, which leads to a race war in which all
Jews and nonwhites are exterminated.*

Pierce and Butler were clearly smart enough to know we
were up to no good, and they did not share Bob Miles's attitude that they had nothing to hide. Miles was treated like
the elder statesman of the event and, because this was his
farm, all others deferred to his decisions, even if somewhat
reluctantly. We were allowed to stay.

We began to spend time with some of the attendees.
They were not shy with us.

"Who are you?" one man angrily asked, as he got right up
into our collective face. "Where are you from? You working
with the Feds?"

"We're from New York," Anne responded while doing her
best to hide her nervousness.

---

* Less than a decade later this book would become an inspiration for a young man
and his Ryder truck full of fertilizer in Oklahoma City.

"Figures—a bunch of Jews!" he grumbled. "I'm a violent anti-Sematic! I hate 'em all," he said as he started to walk away.

"None of us are Jews," Kevin said, trying to relax the man so he would keep talking. I picked up on his cue.

"I'm not from New York," I offered. "I'm from right here."

As I was not well-known at this time—and, truthfully, I looked a lot like most of them—the man turned around, sized me up, and continued on, speaking only to me.

"You don't look like a race traitor. You are white and this is your country. It's been taken from us by a bunch of race traitors. I will not rest until they are all removed."

I kept the best straight race-traitor face that I could. There were six of us and two hundred of them. We had cameras, they had guns. Lots of them, I presumed. It was like we were the ducks in a shooting gallery, but instead of bopping up and down from thirty feet away, here we were walking among the most vile, hateful, and scary people you could conjure up in the U.S.A. I thought, *This is really stupid to be on this farm in the middle of nowhere.*

I was not alone in this thinking. Kevin and Jim suggested we head back to the van and regroup. When we got outside of earshot of the supremacists, Jim expressed the collective sentiment of the group.

"I don't want to be on camera," he said to Kevin. "I don't think any of us should be on camera. It's too dangerous."

"The last thing I want," added Anne, "is for them to know who I am or where I live when this film comes out."

"I think that's smart," said Kevin, concurring with the sanity being expressed. Then he turned to the least sane one of the group.

"How 'bout you, Mike? You doing OK? I like how you interacted with that guy. You feel like doing more of that?"

Kevin, the director, was now casting—and he was casting me as the sacrificial lamb! I had no clue why you would have to worry about people hating you once they see you in a movie mocking the shit out of them.

"Sure, I'll do whatever you need. I don't mind interviewing these guys."

"You mind being on camera?" Kevin asked, double-checking.

"Well, I can't stand to see a picture of myself, that's for sure!" I answered honestly. "But I'll go on camera and mix it up with them if that's what you want. I'm not really afraid of these whatever-they-are. I live around them. Lots of angry white people."

I told them the story of the Klan burning a cross in my grandparents' yard because she was a Catholic and he was Protestant.

"Happy to do what you want me to do," I said.

"You should think about this before agreeing," Anne said. "When this movie is out, they may not like it. You have to live here."

I reminded them that, due to the worsening economy, I had decided to close my newspaper down. I had taken a job in San Francisco, so I wasn't going to be back in Flint.

"It'll be OK," I reassured them. "I think Flint and I have seen the last of each other."

"Fine," Kevin said, "just trust your instincts and we'll be able to capture what you do with them. Let's just all get out of here alive."

And so began my foray into the movies. At least for this weekend. It seemed like it would be fun, and I quickly found my groove with my fellow white Christians.

"We are here to defeat the ZOG!" one man explained to me. I quickly rifled through my memory, thinking he was referring to the god in the movie *Zardoz*.

"What is ZOG?" I asked.

"The Zionist Occupied Government!" he responded. "That is what we have now—a government occupied by Jews and race traitors."

Inside his barn, Miles had set up a stage and podium and chairs for different plenary sessions. These were certainly the funniest of the weekend's events as each speaker tried to out-kook the previous speaker. One man stood up and said that his white power group accepts no members from any- where south of Milan, Italy.

"We will not take anybody in our clan below Milano," he said, showing off his mastery of both European geogra- phy and the Italian language. "If they're down below there, they're not our people. Won't take anybody below the border between France and Spain. No way.

"We're more Nazi than the Nazis," he concluded.

The next speaker stood up and talked about the time he paraded his Aryan group down a main street in North Carolina.

"I yell out, 'We thought y'all had some niggers down here. Where are they at?' And we got about two more blocks and I seen where they was at. They were about eight deep on each side of the street and we marched right in the middle of them. But we didn't have any trouble because they didn't attack anybody. They just jumped up and down on the street. If you've ever seen monkeys when they get excited, how they jump up and down, that's what it looked like."

A friend of Miles's went on the stage with his slide presentation pointing out on a screen how whites would take over the Pacific Northwest, and other races would be given other parts of the U.S.A. after the revolution. This angered a man in the audience.

"I'd have to say it's the most stupid and ridiculous proposal I've ever heard in my life," he shouted from his seat. "If we're the Aryan warriors that have conquered the world, why in the hell should we back into some corner of the country? I don't care how pretty it is."

This rattled the man on the stage, but he went ahead and asked his wife to hand out the maps to the audience. Clearly things had taken a turn as the place was now in agreement with the man who was opposed to "moving off in some corner."

"I live here in Michigan," another man chimed in. "I ain't movin' nowhere."

Things calmed down as William Pierce took the stage. He was the closest thing to a rock god here.

Pierce spoke like an intellectual, and far from turning off this wildly uneducated crowd, he wowed them with his vocabulary and his passion. It must have felt good to have someone this smart (and not Jewish!) on your side. He had a physics degree from Rice University, a master's from Cal Tech, and a doctorate from the University of Colorado. In the 1950s he was cleared to work at the Los Alamos laboratories. He then went on to become an associate professor at Oregon State.

Pierce spoke eloquently of the need to have their movement use scholarly works and even "racially oriented comic books" to reach new people. There was also a new technology that could help.

"Most American homes will have these VCRs that allow them to play videotapes," former KKK leader Don Black chimed in. "What we will have is our own private network of video programming."

For two days the speakers droned on, and just when you thought you'd heard everything, a new speaker would present his theory about how "race mixing is now occurring just by working and breathing too close to the colored," the scientific evidence that a black sperm fertilizing a white egg is no longer the only way to get "nigger blood" in your body.

"Studies have shown that you can pick up nigger cells just by being in their proximity."

"You don't see a turkey mating with a chicken, do you?" one old man asked me during a break outdoors. "Or a dog with a cat? Animals mate with their own. We're the same way. It's unnatural any other way."

At that moment an aroused German shepherd mounted another dog. I appreciated the timing of such an act, and I noticed that Kevin was right on it with his camera. In fact, I noticed that Kevin would film with one eye in his lens and the other eye open, looking for what else may be going on outside the peripheral vision of his camera.

But the copulating dogs quickly went from being a source of amusement to a huge problem.

"Hey!" said one man, "Is that a female, the light-colored one?" He realized that, in fact, both dogs were male. He was now in the presence of gay humping dogs. He was witnessing his first homosexual act, and I felt a sense of pride being able to share its viewing with him.

The other men nearby did not think any of this was funny. To even imply that the *dogs* of Nazis were queer was too much for them to handle.

"Stop filming that!" one of them said. Kevin quickly apologized and pulled the camera away from his face—but was still shooting everything. It took real balls, I thought, to keep that camera on.

We moved over to another area, and I began engaging with more of the participants. I asked some of the young adults what they were doing for work. One worked in a record store, one was in the auto industry, another was unemployed. Their leader spoke wistfully of a time when they would make their move.

"And when is this going to happen?" I asked.

"As soon as the nigger decides to make his move and this economy that the Jews have built up falls apart. In about twenty-five years."

Standing next to him was his girlfriend. She, too, was dressed in the same black Nazi uniform as the others, but she gave it a bit of flair with a powder-blue scarf and a shiny pendant. She wore her shirt without a tie, and she had unbuttoned a button or two (or three). She had long, curly-permed blonde hair and a hat with no swastika on it. She spoke in a high, soft, sexy voice, her eyes highlighted with indigo eyeliner, and she had an even tan from head to toe. I waited for half the day to make my move.

"Hey," I said to her after lunch, "can I talk to you for a second?"

"Sure," she said, in a sultry way.

I lowered the volume of my voice. "What the heck are you doing here?"

She smiled.

"You don't look like the typical Nazi. You know, the ones we're used to seeing in the movies," I said, surprised at the flirtatious sound coming from someone who, at thirty-two, hadn't yet figured out how to flirt. "You could be in a Coppertone commercial!"

She giggled. "Ohhhh," she said in an aww-shucks tone that was a cross between Marilyn Monroe and *The Dukes of Hazzard*. "I'm just against Jewish people. And blacks."

She batted her eyes. "You know — white power." Another big smile. Yeah, white power. Hot.

On the final day of the hate expo, I sat inside the living room of the farmhouse with a number of the "pastors" of the Christian Identity movement. They each operated "churches" within their communities and preached a gospel of white superiority, not because they believed they were better than black people, but because God *said* they were better than black people.

"I have more contempt for the so-called small-c Christian leaders than I do for the colored," said Allen Poe, the pastor from Grand Rapids, Michigan. "The [Billy] Grahams, the Falwells" — and then under his breath he derisively muttered, "*Schwartz!*" (This was his way of indicating that he didn't believe "Jerry Falwell" was his real name and that he must be a Jew.) "If we really wanted to take this country by force, we should stack those people up and silence them."

"Not you or me but somebody else," came a voice from across the room, conscious of the cameras being on.

"We are into computers now," the reverend from Grand Rapids continued. "And we are making lists. Lists of those white people who are not with us, lists of those who are not on the side of their own race. We are sharing these lists of race traitors with each other. So that when the day comes for the revolution, we will know who we have to deal with."

At one point he looked me right in the eye.

"When they do squash us, where are we gunna look for you? Under the same steamroller?"

Did he just threaten me? I looked over at Kevin. I didn't know the proper documentary protocol for handling a moment like this. Kevin looked at me with his free eye and smiled.

"You will never see the day that you want to see come to be in this country," I said coolly. "You are not going to be able to do *jack shit* about any of this."

Wow. I couldn't believe I just said that. Everyone in the room felt I had crossed the line — our side, their side, even the gay dog over in the corner. My words turned Rev. Poe's face purple and he exploded, looking as if he were about to pounce on me. His eyes were on fire.

"Mr. Man, we're not going to lose!" he shouted back. "I don't care if there's ten of us left. We're going to win!"

Then he pointed to the ceiling. "He says so."

I readied myself for a possible attack. Poe looked at the camera and then realized that striking me would not make him the hero of this movie. After all, who was I — just some lowly production assistant on a little documentary who got wrangled into asking some questions. But I had heard enough of "Nigger this" and "Nigger that" all weekend long, and should he attempt anything with me, my principles of non-violence were going to have to go stretch their legs and come back in a half hour. He sat back in his chair.

It was clearly getting time for us to pack up and go.

We went to say good-bye to Grand Dragon Miles out in his barn. Once inside, Kevin had something he wanted to get off his mind.

"Why did you let us come here?" he asked Miles. "You can probably guess we don't share the same beliefs. So why did you do it?"

"We invited you here so that we could use you just the same way you were using us," Miles said quietly. "But what you don't know is *how* we were using you. We have used you to get our message out to a wider audience. True, for every hundred people you show this film to, ninety-nine may hate us—but one will *love* us. And that's how we will build our movement. One here, one there, one at a time. You just make sure you show this to as many hundreds or thousands of people as possible. We're just looking for that one soul in each and every audience. And you will have made that happen for us."

It was a sobering and bitter pill to swallow as we heard Bob Miles say these words. We knew what he was saying was true. So what would be our responsibility in all this? Is it better never to film people or events like the Aryan Nations, to just ignore them? Or is it better to expose them outright, hoping that will become our best defense against them?

We stopped at the gas station on our way out of town. There was a sign in the window that read: MOVIES ON HOME VIDEO HERE!

"Wow," I said. "Look at that. You can rent a movie at a gas station. Is that what it's coming to? Movies are now sold like a bag of Doritos or a Hostess cupcake?"

"I think that's the future over there," Anne said, pointing to a large satellite dish in someone's backyard. "And I'm sure our Aryan friends will find a way to make good use of it."

"This was a good shoot," Kevin remarked. "Thanks for setting it up for us," he said to me. "You were a real natural with these folks. You should think about doing more of this."

"Hanging out with hot Nazis?" I asked.

"Yes, that," he replied with a grin.

I went inside and got them all some coffee and other snacks.

Parnassus

In 1986, I was witness to a murder plot. I was there, in the room, when those in charge hatched their plan to kill the American Middle Class. It took place in a penthouse of an exclusive Acapulco resort, in a private gathering organized by top officials in the Reagan administration. I snuck in and I saw it, I heard it all, and I got out alive so I could tell a story that, unfortunately, no one at the time wanted to hear or believe. *"The death of the middle class? Planned by our own government?* HA HA HA HA HA HA!!"

But, forgive me—I think I'm a bit ahead of myself.

Let me begin again:

I used to think all liberals and lefties were the same: good hearts, good politics. It took a real wake-up call in the capital of liberalism, San Francisco, for me to realize that there were various forms of "liberals," and the one I had never encountered back in Flint was the Wealthy Liberal Who Loved Humanity But Hated People. He's the liberal whose conscience is eased by the generosity of his checkbook—just as long as you, the recipient of his largesse, look the other way and not consider how he came to have that money in the first place.

But I'm ahead of myself again....

For the nearly ten years I edited and published the *Flint Voice* (which, in 1983, became the *Michigan Voice*), I never earned more than $15,000 a year. On two different occasions, the *Voice* was so broke I had to lay myself off. It was not unusual for me to be late on paying the $200 a month for my rent. There weren't a lot of businesses interested in advertising in a muckraking paper that was constantly raking the muck out of the very businesses being asked to advertise.

Case in point: the local Howard Johnson's Motor Lodge. They had a policy of not hiring blacks and refusing to rent out rooms at night to anyone who was African-American. How did I know this? A clerk who worked there told me. One thing I learned as a journalist is that there is at least one disgruntled person in every workplace in America—and at least double that number with a conscience. Hard as they try, they simply can't turn their heads away from an injustice when they see one taking place.

Such was the case with Carole Jurkiewicz, the head desk clerk at the Howard Johnson's Motor Inn on Miller Road in Flint. One day she walked into my office and brought with her a number of applications filled out by people looking for a job at Howard Johnson's. Many of them had a star marked in pen at the top.

"These are the white people who apply," Jurkiewicz said. "I was told by management to star the application of anyone who was white. I would then see the manager rip up any app from someone who was black." Out of 130 employees, only seven were African-American (in this now majority-black city)—and four of them were related to each other.

Jurkiewicz was told by her manager on various occasions that: "Black people don't mind being called niggers…They drive big cars…They're lazy…They usually make trouble… They talk back, have no respect…They all look alike."

This was the 1980s, and this story simply seemed too rotten to be true. This was not the South of the 1950s. This was Michigan, a state that bordered Canada. And this was Howard Johnson's, a respected national chain of restaurants and hotels, not Billy Bob's Grits and Grinders. I asked Carole if she would sign a sworn affidavit attesting to these facts, and both she and another employee did so.

To further verify it, I decided to see what would happen if a black friend of mine went over to Howard Johnson's to apply for a job. Lamont went in, filled out an application, and left. Then Dan, a white guy, went in a half hour later to also apply for a job.

The next day, Carole brought me copies of both apps, and sure enough, the white applicant had a big red star plastered on top of his form. Lamont's, though, had none.

It was then time for part two of the sting. George Moss, an African-American teacher at Flint's Beecher High School, walked into Howard Johnson's the following evening, and asked for a room. Outside, on the lawn, I lay facedown on the grass so no one inside could see me. I crept closer to the window where I had, with my long-lens 35mm camera, a clear view of the front desk. And, sure enough, as I snapped through a roll of film, George was turned away after being told that there were "no vacancies."

Ten minutes later I motioned for Mark, a white guy, to head in to try and get a room. "No problem," the man behind the counter said, and signed him up for a single with a double bed — all of this, of course, captured by my camera.

I put it all in the *Flint Voice,* and it wasn't long before the civil rights commission brought the hammer down on Howard Johnson's (they were ordered to pay a $30,000 fine to one of the black women who had applied for a job and been denied). There would now be one less business that would discriminate in Flint — and one less business to advertise in the *Flint Voice.*

Doing stories like this every month for ten years had the uncanny knack of depleting advertising revenue, and I began to see why the larger media is loathe to tell the public the truth about *anything* that may cost them cash. Before long the *Voice* was the pariah of not only the business community in Flint but also of its political establishment (which was owned by the business community) and the local media (also dependent on the same advertising revenue).

By the end of 1985, with unemployment in Flint well above 20 percent, there were fewer and fewer ways available to fund the *Voice.* Our main benefactor had been the wonderful folksinger Harry Chapin. Years earlier, I had snuck backstage at a concert of his in Grand Rapids. A security guard grabbed me as I approached Harry's dressing-room door.

"Where the hell do you think you're going?" he barked at me.

"Oh, I'm just stopping by to see Harry," I said matter-of-factly.

"The hell you are," he said, as he started to drag me away by my collar. The commotion was loud enough to cause Harry to open his door.

"What's going on out here?" Harry asked.

"This guy says he was coming to see you," the bouncer said.

"Well—let him come see me!"

The guard reluctantly let me go and I walked into Harry's room.

"So, you wanted to see me?" Harry asked, smiling.

"Uh, yeah, I'm so sorry about causing a ruckus. I just wanted to ask you a favor."

"Shoot."

"Well, a bunch of us in Flint want to start an alternative paper and we were wondering if maybe you could help us by coming to Flint and doing a benefit."

As I said the words, I could not believe how presumptuous and ridiculous they sounded. "Hey, rock star—you've got nothing better to do—come to Flint and perform for us!" Jesus.

"Tell me about your paper," he said. And so I did. I told him about how the local daily was in the pocket of General Motors and that we wanted to present the news that wasn't being covered.

"Sounds like a worthy effort," Harry said. "Here's my manager's number. Give him a call and I'll see what I can do."

Dumbfounded, I left the backstage area on cloud seven (for some reason, my eternal pessimism about myself always

kept me from getting any higher). I returned to Flint to tell
the staff what happened. Within months, Harry Chapin was
in front of a sold-out audience in Flint, and we now had the
money to fund our paper.

And for the next five years, until a tragic accident on the
Long Island Expressway took his life in July 1981, Harry
Chapin came to Flint each year, doing a total of eleven benefit concerts for the *Flint Voice*. Those proceeds kept us afloat,
and after Harry's death, his brothers, Tom and Steve, and
his band would continue the tradition of playing the annual
concert in Flint.

But by 1985, it was not enough to sustain the paper, and
the struggle to continue its publication was worsening.

It was at this time I received a phone call from a man in
San Francisco. He was Adam Hochschild, the multimillion-
aire liberal who ran the foundation that owned *Mother Jones*
magazine, the largest circulation publication on the left. He
said he had been following the *Flint Voice* and liked what he
saw, and he wondered if I would be interested in doing what
I was doing in Flint, but on a national scale.

The offer sounded too good — and it was. I closed up my
beloved *Voice,* sold everything I had, and moved to Parnas-
sus Avenue in the Upper Haight district of San Francisco. It
wasn't long, though, before I realized what a huge mistake I
had made. I wanted to turn *Mother Jones* into a magazine for
the working class (the namesake of the magazine, after all,
Mary "Mother" Jones, was a radical union organizer from
the nineteenth century). Hochschild (whose family fortune
and inheritance came in part from the mines of the then-
apartheid South Africa) wanted a more erudite and "sublime"
periodical of commentary and reporting that would rival the

New Yorker or the *Atlantic*. In fact, his second choice for
his new editor had been Hendrik Hertzberg, an instinct he
should have gone with. (Hertzberg later became executive
editor of the *New Yorker*.)

I was a true fish out of water in San Francisco. I didn't
understand the way things were done at this magazine, and
my efforts to make changes were met with much resistance.
They wanted neo-nudnik Paul Berman covering the Sandinistas in Nicaragua. I had wanted Alexander Cockburn.
They wanted to do an investigative piece on herbal teas; I
wanted to give a monthly column to an autoworker on the
assembly line in Flint. They were Mars and I was Bluto.
On the day after Labor Day, after just four months on the
job, Hochschild fired me. He said we weren't "a good fit."
He was right. I sued him for breach of contract and fraud
and won $60,000.

There was now no newspaper for me to return to in Flint,
and all attempts to seek employment with other lefty/liberal
publications on both coasts were met with the embrace one
gives a leper. No one on the left wanted to upset *Mother
Jones*. No one wanted this guy from Flint. Other than the
people who worked at Ralph Nader's office in D.C., there was
no one who would offer me work.

And that, my friends, was supposed to have been the last
you were to have heard from me. My fifteen minutes on the
national stage were over.

After a month of lying in bed and bemoaning my fate,
I got up one day and went to a bookstore. There, while
mindlessly roaming through the racks of magazines, I ran
across a notice in a business publication that caught my eye.
It said:

"EXPO MAQUILA '86"

PRESENTED BY

UNITED STATES DEPT. OF COMMERCE

AND

THE AMERICAN CHAMBER OF COMMERCE IN MEXICO

DISCOVER HOW TO USE MEXICO TO BETTER YOUR BUSINESS

'MOVING PRODUCTION HERE SAVES JOBS AT HOME!'

BY INVITATION ONLY   CONTACT USDOC

Huh. I wondered what this was about. I contacted the Department of Commerce to find out.

"This is a three-day conference in Acapulco to assist American businesses and help them grow," the woman's voice from the Department of Commerce on the phone said. "It is only open to business owners and executives, not to the general public or the press."

"I see. I own a small auto parts company in Michigan," I said, making it up before I knew what I was doing. "How can I get more information?"

She said she would send me a packet.

I didn't know what I would do with the packet but it sounded interesting. I had been talking to the people in Ralph Nader's office about coming to Washington to do some work for them. They had two dozen public interest projects going, including a magazine called the *Multinational Monitor* that did pretty much what its name implied. I told them about this crazy conference happening in Mexico, that it had to be some sort of joke, because why would our own Commerce Department be helping to eliminate jobs here in the U.S. and move them to Mexico?

"The Reagan administration," said John Richard, Nader's

chief of staff. "They've been on a mission to do this since they took office."

"Yes, I know—but this seems to really cross a line, doesn't it?"

I had covered this issue back in Michigan: how GM was using tax breaks to move jobs offshore, but back then I couldn't get anybody to listen.

"We'll send you to Acapulco if you want to sneak in there and tell us what they're planning to do," Richard said. "Then maybe write something up for *Multinational Monitor.*"

Wow. An international mission, me in disguise, the intrigue! A paid job! My wife took me to a used clothing store and got me fitted in the appropriate resort apparel. I bought a couple golf shirts, some linen slacks, a Hawaiian shirt, and a cheap yellow seersucker suit. That was one whole week's unemployment check. She gave me a corporate-looking haircut and some of her hair gel. I purchased a little American flag lapel pin. I put on some man jewelry I bought on a street corner in the Tenderloin. I did not look like me.

I signed up as the CEO of my small manufacturing company ("less than 50 employees") and headed to Mexico to learn how I could throw them all out of work.

I'd be lying if I didn't admit how nervous and scared I was when I deplaned in Acapulco in my seersucker suit. I did not want to be discovered. People go missing in Mexico. Bodies aren't found.

I walked onto the penthouse floor of the Excelaris Resort, high above the beautiful golden beaches of Acapulco. The sign over the door read: WORK MAKES EVERYTHING POSSIBLE (for you German speakers, that's *Albrecht Acht Alles Möglich!*).

I overheard two men talking about how the Commerce Department had to be "not so public" in its support of this weekend as apparently some Democratic union-sympathizers in Congress found a clause in some "ridiculous law" stating that it was illegal — *illegal!* — for U.S. tax dollars to go toward anything that promotes jobs being moved overseas. So Commerce was here, just not officially, leaving it to the Chamber of Commerce and the Mexican firm of Montenegro, Saatchi & Saatchi to be in charge of running the show.

The room was filled with bankers, executives, entrepreneurs, and consultants — all of whom were primed to help those of us who had come to Acapulco to learn how to close up shop in the U.S. and move our operations south of the border. I did my best to blend in, and on the first day no one suspected otherwise when they saw me. I forgot that just being a nicely dressed white male was what the majority of these guys simply call "showing up."

By late 1986, many American companies had quietly begun making their move to Mexico. Not so much, though, that anyone had taken any real notice. General Motors had only 13,000 Mexican workers (a drop in the bucket to GM's American workforce, which numbered over a half million); General Electric had 8,000 employees in Mexico. American corporations had set up factories in the dozen or so border cities — on the Mexican side of the border. Some of these American facilities were barely five hundred feet outside of the United States. It was just like being at home — except you paid your workers forty cents an hour, made them work ten hours a day, and made sure they had no rights. Seventy percent of the Mexican workers in these plants were women, often under twenty-one and sometimes as young as thirteen or fourteen. U.S. corporations did not want to hire male heads-of-households, as they were more likely to unionize or demand a bathroom break. The young women were more pliable. The only real problem with them was that they, like young women everywhere, were prone to getting pregnant. They were also malnourished and hungry. So GM and the others did something nice: they handed out free birth control to stem the high turnover rate, and they provided a free breakfast (because fainting on the assembly line caused things like windshields to miss the front of the car).

Al Cisneros, of the Texas Economic Development Commission, spoke glowingly of General Motors' plans to become "Mexico's number one employer."

"They are going to have a total of twenty-nine factories in Mexico," he told me. "They are opening twelve in the coming year alone!"

He told me that the chairman of General Motors, a man by the name of Roger Smith, had recently said that "moving to Mexico is a matter of survival."

I thought about this for a moment and wondered, what planet was this guy Smith on? *"Survival?"* In the previous year, 1985, General Motors had posted a profit just shy of four billion dollars. In the year before that, they broke their all-time record with a profit of $4.5 billion. They were the number one corporation in the world. And yet they were constantly talking about how they were "struggling" to survive. It was all a con game to somehow convince the public that if they didn't move some of their production to Mexico, they might go under—and then the economy would collapse with them. It was a Big Lie, but at least the Reagan administration bought it and was here selling it. They were selling it because Reagan, the former union leader, wanted to crush unions. He won the presidency by getting a lot of white union workers to vote for him. Appealing to their fears—of Iranian hostage takers, of black people, of the government—he rode a wave that would eventually drown the very people who put him into office.

Of course, I could say none of this to Mr. Cisneros—partly because I did not know the future then, and mostly because I would definitely blow my cover. I worried that even the look on my face was such that every word of that last paragraph was written all over me.

"Absolutely," I responded. "GM has to remain competitive. If it doesn't cut costs, it…it…" I struggled to find the end of that sentence. I should have practiced my lines better. "Well, all hell's gonna break loose."

"Indeed," Mr. Cisneros agreed (to what, I'm not sure).

Cisneros had another concern: Communism. He was worried that if corporate America did not get down to Mexico and establish a capitalist foothold, Mexico could easily go the way of Castro or the Sandinistas.

"Free enterprise is the only thing that's going to save Mexico from a Communist revolution," he said. "If we don't help Mexico develop, we're going to have another Nicaragua at our doorstep."

Ha! Of course. How else could the Reaganites rationalize and sell the exporting of American jobs to Mexico? Because we have to save Mexico from the commies! By raising the standard of living of every Mexican by having them work for us, they will not want socialism because they will be enjoying the middle class life.

"I expect in less than fifteen years, these Mexican border towns are going to look like American suburbs," Cisneros added.*

Paul D. Taylor, Reagan's deputy assistant Secretary of State for Inter-American Affairs, earlier that year had stated that if we began to build American factories in Mexico, it could help stem the Red Tide on our southern border. U.S. factories could help Mexico "reorient" its economy from its socialist tendencies to the capitalist nirvana of its northern neighbor.

"We are making history here," one of the speakers announced. "Those of you here tonight will be remembered as the pioneers, the heroes, who helped move America from a manufacturing-based economy to a service economy, a high-tech economy. And you will be able to say that you were here when it all started!" He stopped short of comparing this historical moment to the Wannsee Conference, or the gathering of the family heads by Don Corleone. But the headiness of the moment — the importance of who they were and what they were up to — was not lost on anyone in that room in Acapulco.

I discovered that there were executives from at least ten or so Michigan companies at the conference, including top people from Iroquois Die and Manufacturing, Deco Grand, and Dynacast. I thought it wise to avoid them as they would know I was not running an auto parts company in Flint. But I couldn't help myself. I wanted to know why these turncoats

* That, um, never happened. With their massive amounts of drug-related violence, they did start to resemble America's inner cities.

were planning to sack fellow Michiganders. I wanted to look in their eyes, I wanted to know if they went to Ohio State.

I took off my name tag and sat down at a table where some of them were gathered. Arthur Goodsel was the president of Huron Plastics. He had ten plants around Michigan and the United States. He told me that the move to Mexico he was considering was not voluntary.

"The automakers are moving here, there's no doubt about that," he said with the tone of resignation. "They won't admit that too publicly, but this is where they're coming. And they're telling suppliers like me if you want to do business with us, you'd better move here, too, to be close to us. If not, then bye-bye. So what am I supposed to do?"

That was the story I kept hearing from the smaller businesses. They were being coerced and extorted into making this move. From the looks on their faces I could see the invisible gun being held to their heads. They did not look like they were down here on vacation.

"Yeah, me too," I said. "Don't you think when people in Michigan find this out they're gonna tar and feather us on our way outta town?"

"Oh, I don't even know how I'm gonna break the news to my employees," a man named "Bill" said sadly. "Some of these guys have been with me for twenty years. They have families. But, I guess they'll find other jobs. There's lots of work in Michigan to go around."

"You got that right," I added.

Forgoing the parasailing and the jet skis, I attended all the lectures and presentations. They were mesmerizing. Up on the screen they laid it all out, how this or that American governmental agency would help grease the skids for "your move to Mexico"! Little time was spent on trying to justify it ("Think of all the shipping and trucking jobs this will create in the U.S.!"). One speaker after another told the assembled about the fields of gold that awaited them south of the border. And if they did not get in on this gold rush, well, they were just going to be left behind like the buggy whip manufacturers were at the beginning of the twentieth century when they pooh-poohed the new "horseless carriage."

One nice feature in the presentations was the racism. And the generous plantation mentality that was expressed. Speaker after speaker kept using the generic name "Pancho" whenever they referred to the hypothetical Mexican worker they were so excited about exploiting.

"Pancho will do this for you! Pancho will do that for you!"

"Pancho won't be joining any unions."

"Pancho is an obedient worker."

Pancho, of course, was not present at the gathering, other than those Panchos serving us our filet mignons and flaming fried ice cream.

By the third day, I had, remarkably, not been caught. It was slightly disappointing on some level that I looked that believable in the role of CEO. But I knew my auto parts well enough to talk the talk, and I knew all the appropriate slags to make on the unions and the greedy factory workers. One guy did say he had never heard of my company, and he kept pressing me for more info until I finally told him that "my company has just invented a breakthrough device— and I'm prohibited by Chrysler from saying any more." Then he stopped. I could see that it made him happy to think of himself saying in six months that he knew the guy when this invention was top secret!

The closing-night dinner was held outdoors, where a whole pig was roasted on a spit for us. The keynote speaker was Republican congressman Jim Kolbe from Arizona. Kolbe was a big backer of the move of American business to Mexico because, as he pointed out, "70 percent of the wages these Mexicans get, they come across the border and spend them in El Paso and Yuma—so it's a win-win for us!"

Everybody was now wearing the WORK MAKES EVERYTHING POSSIBLE stickers on their outerwear. And Kolbe's main point?

"These American factories in Mexico do not take away jobs from the U.S.," he said with a straight face. "They *save* jobs!"

Kolbe said that "a free country has to allow U.S. business to operate freely." And besides, he added, if we didn't make it easy for corporate America to operate in Mexico, "then these cars and other items are going to be made in Asia." The crowd snickered. Ha! Americans buying Asian cars! Please! And pass me some more of that pig.

When Kolbe finished, the Mexican official who was the evening's emcee made a "motion" to "nominate Congressman Kolbe for president of the United States!"* The audience responded with wild applause. Yup, that's how we roll in the United States—a bunch of corporate executives sitting in a room and just nominating the president! The Japanese banker

---

* In 2010, Barack Obama appointed Jim Kolbe to his Advisory Committee for Trade Policy and Negotiations. The reader can draw his or her own conclusions.

sitting at my table, who had earlier taken slight umbrage at the "Asian" remark, took it all in with detached amusement.

"What you see here," he said to me, "is just the beginning. GM will close those nine plants in the U.S. in the coming year and many more in the years to come. This is the future—and some people are going to do very well." I looked around at the crowd that was giddy over the thought that *they* were the chosen ones to pack up the U.S.A. (or at least its most precious national resource—its jobs) and move it to sunny Mexico.

It was both nauseating and breathtaking, the scope of what I had witnessed over this weekend. A well-oiled machine was already revved up and in motion to snuff out the American middle class. And, I thought, *"Nobody knows this!"* Here I was, wining and dining among the plotters. In the ensuing years, I would witness the wholesale destruction of towns like Flint across the country, and I would think, *I was there! I saw the murder being planned! The plot to kill the American Dream was hatched and enacted right in front of my eyes.* A witness to an impending execution—and the executed had no idea yet that the gun had been fired and the bullet well on its way.

On the plane ride back, the seersucker suit neatly packed in the overhead, I thought long and hard about all of this and what I was planning to do.

Gratitude

I KNEW NOTHING about making a movie, and I wish I could tell you some cool story about how I started shooting films when I was six on my dad's 8mm Bell & Howell, or that I went to NYU film school with Spike Lee, and that Martin Scorsese was my teacher. All I knew, all I did, was go to the movies. And I mean *go*. In a good week I would try to see at least four or five films at the local multiplex (in other words, everything that opened that weekend). If I was lucky, I'd get to borrow the car and head down to Ann Arbor to one of the half-dozen film societies that showed a classic or foreign movie every night. A really special Friday night would mean a trip to the Detroit Film Theatre at the Detroit Institute of Arts. On the rare occasion, I went on a foreign journey to Chicago because I couldn't wait the month or two for the film to open in Michigan.

And then there was that insane, pure batshit-crazy, spur-of-the-moment "Get in the car! I *refuse* to see *Apocalypse Now* in Flint because it does *not* have the new surround sound stereo *and* the ending that Coppola *wanted!*" The studio would play *that* version only in New York, Los Angeles,

and Toronto. And so I drove the three hundred miles to Toronto so I could see the alternate ending.

I looooved the movies.

I always did. Like most kids of my era, my first films
were *Bambi* and *Old Yeller, Swiss Family Robinson* and *The
Alamo.* But the first movie I remember having a strong reaction to was *PT 109,* the story of John F. Kennedy in World
War II. It had everything an eight-year-old boy could want:
action, suspense—but in this case, the story of a hero who
initially screwed up and ran his boat into the path of a Japanese destroyer. Yet he didn't let his mistake defeat him. He
saved his crew and found a way to get them all back to safety.
He was a rich boy, and probably could have gotten out of
being on the front lines, but he wasn't that kind of American.
Even at eight, I got that.

I came of age as a teenager when the great films of the
late sixties and early seventies blasted their way onto the
screen. *Out* were the stiff, formulaic movies of the aging studio system, overblown fare such as *Hello, Dolly!* and *Doctor Dolittle. In* were *Easy Rider* and *The Graduate, Midnight
Cowboy* and *The Last Picture Show, Deliverance* and *Taxi
Driver, Nashville,* and *Harold and Maude.*

At seventeen, I saw Stanley Kubrick's *A Clockwork Orange,* and then I saw everything else by Kubrick, and after
that there was no looking back. I was hooked on the potential
and the power of cinema. I took two Introduction to Cinema
classes as a freshman in college, and the professor, Dr. Gene
Parola, had us watch all the greats, starting with *M* and *Metropolis* and landing on *Blow-Up* and *Who's Afraid of Virginia
Woolf?* My friend, Jeff Gibbs, took both classes with me, and
we would spend hours afterward dissecting every nuance of

these movies. Two years later I opened my own "art house" in Flint where, for just two nights a week, I would show everything by Truffaut, Bergman, Fassbinder, Kurosawa, Herzog, Scorsese, Woody Allen, Buñuel, Fellini, Kubrick, and all the masters of cinema. Each film would get four showings, and I would spend my Friday and Saturday evenings watching all four shows. On the first viewing I would sit close and enjoy the experience. On the following three screenings, I would sit in the back and study them, sometimes taking notes. This became my one-room, one-student film school.

I did not like documentaries, and so I rarely went to see them. Documentaries felt like medicine, like castor oil—something I was *supposed* to watch because they were good for me. But most were boring and predictable, even when I agreed with the politics. If I wanted to listen to a political speech, why would I go to a movie? I'd attend a rally or a candidates' debate. If I wanted to hear a sermon, I would go to church. When I went to the movies I wanted to be surprised, lifted, crushed; I wanted to laugh my ass off and I wanted a good cry; and when I left the theater afterward, I wanted to glide out onto the street as if I were walking on air. I wanted to feel exhilarated. I wanted all my assumptions challenged. I wanted to go somewhere I had never gone before, and I didn't want the movie to end because I didn't want to go back to where I was. I wanted sex without love and love without sex, and if I got the two together then I wanted to believe I would have that, too, and forever. I wanted to rock and be rocked and five days later I wanted that film ricocheting around in my head so madly that goddammit I had to go see it again, right now, tonight, clear the decks, nothing else matters.

And I felt *none* of that when I went to see a documentary. Of course, it was rare, rare, rare that a documentary would play in a movie theater in Flint, let alone any other place in the state. But when it did, and when it was constructed as a *movie* first and as a documentary *second,* then it would fuck me up in ways that no work of fiction could. I sat in the Flint Cinema on Dort Highway and saw the devastating Vietnam documentary *Hearts and Minds*—and to this day I have seen no finer nonfiction film. Another time I drove to Ann Arbor and saw something I didn't know was possible—a humorous film about a depressing subject, *The Atomic Café*. In Detroit, at the Art Institute, I saw the cinema verité classics by D. A. Pennebaker (*Don't Look Back),* and Richard Leacock and Robert Drew (*Primary*), and the radical work of Emile d'Antonio (*Point of Order*). Later, I would see the films of Errol Morris (*The Thin Blue Line*) and Ross McElwee (*Sherman's March*) and an outrageously experimental nonfiction film with Barbie dolls by a young Todd Haynes called *Superstar: The Karen Carpenter Story.* And one day, without the use of any substances, long after I had dropped out of college, while collecting $98 a week on unemployment after being fired during Labor Day week by a rich liberal, and having just spent the scariest weekend of my life in Acapulco—my mind brought all these films and filmmakers together and gave me an idea unlike anything that I had seen before, a film that began to unspool in my head and simply started to project itself onto my imaginary screen in my frontal lobe. I was broke, depressed, shunned, and three thousand miles from home. I was on Mount Parnassus in San Francisco living under a giant microwave telecommunications tower, and I wanted to leave and go back home *and make a movie!* It was nuts, I knew it, but the bus had already pulled out of the station and there was no turning it around, no going back. I did not have a day of film school in me, let alone much of any college schooling at all. I didn't care. I had my idea. And I had a new friend. His name was Kevin Rafferty.

Kevin was a documentary filmmaker. He made *The Atomic Café*, a smart, funny film, in the early 1980s. He and his brother Pierce, and friend Jayne Loader, put together ninety minutes of scenes and clips from the archives of the U.S. government, defense contractors, and the television networks of the Cold War era. With no narration, they strung the footage together in such a way that made the arms race and fear of the Red Menace look exactly like the madness that it was. Footage showing how you could survive an atomic attack in your basement or at school, by ducking and covering your head under your desk, said more about the stupidity of the two superpowers than any political speech or op-ed. The effect was both hilarious and debilitating—and when you came out of the theater you were certain of two things: (1) never, ever believe at face value anything a government or corporation tells you; and (2) these Rafferty brothers are not only great filmmakers, they proved to me that a documentary could be both funny *and* profound.

Ronald Reagan had been president for just a year when *The Atomic Café* came out. The American and Russian people were tired of spending billions on the Cold War, and this movie hit that raw nerve. It became a big hit on college campuses and among those who loved good movies. When the political history of an era is written, the honest recorders of that history will write about the impact that the *culture* had on the political changes that took place and how it shaped the times. (You can't tell the story of the Civil Rights and Vietnam eras without mentioning the impact of Bob Dylan, Joan Baez, or Harry Belafonte.) I would like to now say, for the record, that for every "Mr. Gorbachev, tear down this wall!" there was also a "Born in the U.S.A." and an *Atomic Café*. Art has a searing impact in a thousand simple, unnoticed ways. This work by Kevin and his brother and friends had that kind of impact on me.

Flint was the Forgotten City in the 1980s. Once a vibrant, thriving metropolitan area that was the birthplace of the world's largest, richest company — General Motors — it was now an evil science experiment for the rich. *Question: Can we increase our profits by eliminating the jobs of the people who not only build our cars but also buy them?* The answer was yes — *if* you kept the rest of the country working so they could buy your cars. What the mad scientists didn't count on was that those car workers would not only stop buying the cars once they were jobless, they would also stop buying televisions, dishwashers, clock radios, and shoes. This in turn would cause the businesses which made those items to either go under or make their products elsewhere. Eventually, those who had the remaining jobs would have to try to buy the cheapest stuff possible with their drastically reduced wages, and in order for manufacturers to keep that stuff cheap, it would have to be made by fifteen-year-olds in China.

Few foresaw how the taking of just one itsy-bitsy little thread and pulling it out of the middle-class fabric would soon unravel the entire tapestry, leaving everyone struggling in a dog-eat-dog existence, a weekly battle to keep one's head simply above water. On one level, it was pure political genius, because the electorate, so consumed with its own *personal* survival, would *never* be able to find the time or energy to politically organize the workplace, the neighborhood, or the town to revolt against the mad scientists and politicians who had engineered their demise.

In the 1980s, though, it was just that first tiny thread that was being removed—but it was coming out of the place where I lived: Flint, Michigan. The *official* unemployment rate hit 29 percent. This should have been the canary in the American coal mine. Instead, few noticed. Sure, there were those who cared about our plight and sought to tell its story. There was a solid BBC story about Flint being the jobless capital of America, and then there was the...ah...the...um... Well, OK, that was about it. The BBC. From five thousand miles away. Not many others came to Flint to tell our story. They were too busy talking about the Reagan Revolution and how great it was that some people were prospering with the trickle-down economy. And they were right. Those who did well in the '80s did *very well,* and, frankly, there weren't that many places that looked like Flint, Michigan. Other than the steel towns of the Ohio Valley that had their comeuppance a few years earlier, and the textile mills in the northeast a few years before that, the country was still doing pretty well, a middle class still existed, and nobody paid much attention to the grimy, gritty towns that built their cars. The Brits from the BBC knew what a town on its knees looked like, and their DNA allowed them to not mince many words as to the cause of what was going on when they did their piece on Flint. *But who saw that?* Oh well, tallyho! Out of sight, out of mind. If you lived in Tampa, in Denver, in Houston, in Seattle, in

Vegas, in Charlotte, in Orange County, in New York, Flint's fate would never be yours! You were doing great and you would continue to do great. Yes, of course, poor Flint. Poor, poor Flint. Pity. Pity. Tsk-tsk.

One day in 1984, I was sitting at my desk at the *Flint Voice* and there was a knock on the door. Two men who did not look like they were from these parts were standing on the porch, peering through my screen door to see if anyone was home.

"Hi there," I said. "Can I help you?"

"Sure," said the taller one with the accent. "Is this the *Flint Voice?*"

"Sure is," I said. "C'mon in."

The two of them walked in.

"My name is Ron Shelton," the American one said. "I'm a screenwriter. I wrote *Under Fire*. It came out last year."

We shook hands. "Um, yes, I, I loved the movie," I said, a bit startled and thinking, *Is this guy lost?*

"And I'm Roger Donaldson," the Aussie said.

I knew him, too. "Uh, you didn't make *Smash Palace?*" I asked.

"That didn't play here, did it?" he asked, perplexed that there would be someone in Flint who had seen his indie film from New Zealand.

"No, I drive to Ann Arbor a lot," I replied.

I was trying to collect myself. What were these guys[*]

---

[*] Ron Shelton would go on to write and direct *Bull Durham* and *White Men Can't Jump,* and Roger Donaldson would direct the remake of *Mutiny on the Bounty* (*"The Bounty"*) and the Kevin Costner thriller *No Way Out.*

doing in my office? In Flint, Michigan? Not exactly Holly-wood. I was in a bit of shock, but trying to stay cool.

"Well, you're probably wondering what we are doing at the *Flint Voice*," Donaldson said.

"Not really," I responded with a straight face. "Writ-ers and directors pass through here all the time. Last week Costa-Gavras stopped by with Klaus Kinski." He laughed. I offered them each a chair and they took a seat.

"I'm writing a screenplay," Shelton said, "a sort of a modern-day version of *The Grapes of Wrath*. We've heard about the hard times Flint has been having, about the many people who've lost their jobs and have had to pack up every-thing and leave the state. So, the story follows a family who loses everything here in Flint and throws together what's left into the truck and heads to Texas in search of work."

"And when they get to Texas," Donaldson added, "they are treated the way the Joads were treated when they got to California."

I sat and looked at them and, goddammit, if I just didn't want to get up and hug them right there. Somebody — from Hollywood, no less — wanted to tell our story! I thought we'd been ignored, forgotten. Not so.

"So the reason we stopped by to see you is that we're col-lecting information and stories and research, and someone mentioned you would be a good person to talk to. And that your paper was really the only paper in town covering this story from the side of the workers."

"Well, I don't know what to say," I remarked, trying to find the right words and *be cool* at the same time. "First off, thank you. I can't believe you are actually here and give a shit. That means a helluva lot."

"We do give a shit," Donaldson said. "We think there really is this shift taking place in America, where those with the money want to turn the clock back to a time when everybody else has to scrape and scrap and beg for the crumbs. And we think that this will make for a powerful movie."

They talked to me for an hour, asking me to tell them some stories about life in Flint and what would I do if I were them to keep the story "authentic." I spoke a mile a minute, sharing everything I could think of and giving them my advice as to what I thought would make for a good movie. They took notes and seemed very pleased.

"We'd like to get a bunch of back copies of your paper and take them with us," Shelton said as we were wrapping up. "And we'd also like to subscribe to it. Can I pay for a subscription?" (I made sure to frame this subscription slip and hang it on my wall.)

"We'll be in touch if there's anything else we need," Donaldson said. "We're going to do the drive from Flint to Texas, scouting along the way. Thanks for your time. We'll be in touch."

They left as they came in, and I got on the phone and called everyone I knew. "Hollywood was just here!" I shouted into the phone a dozen times that day. I just couldn't believe the randomness of this encounter—and the fact that Flint was going to star in a movie, *a real movie!*

Around that same time, Nina Rosenblum, the documentary filmmaker from New York City, was making a number of trips to Flint. She, too, decided that Flint was a worthy subject for a film—and in her case, a documentary. I and others spent a lot of time with her, and she seemed ready to put our story down on film. This was exhilarating; we were glad that we were no longer going to be ignored. The movie people had shown up!

For whatever reason, neither film got made and, as fate would have it, I would soon leave Flint myself. Within a month of having made my move to California for the dream job of a lifetime, I was sitting in San Francisco both without a dream or a job and collecting unemployment. Dejected, I returned home to Flint to think about what course my life should take. Should I try to restart the *Flint Voice?* Should I run for office, like maybe mayor of Flint? Maybe I could get a job…well, there was nowhere to get a job.

When I wanted to be alone in those jobless days in late 1986, I would head to downtown Flint, which was like a ghost town within a ghost town. I would take a newspaper or a book or my legal pad into Windmill Place, a failed urban renewal project designed by the people who built the South Street Seaport in New York City. They promised to do for Flint what they had done for the Lower East Side of New York. But, alas, the Flint River was not the East River, and a few other things were missing, too. Nonetheless, a half-dozen restaurants struggled to stay open inside the food court that was empty for most of the day. My next-door neighbor from childhood worked behind the counter of the bakery in Windmill Place. I would go in there and she would warm up a chocolate croissant for me. The Chinese take-out place a few counters down made a mean moo goo gai pan, and that was what I was enjoying a few minutes before noon on Thursday, November 6, 1986, when, on the overhead TV screen in this desolate food court, the regularly scheduled program was interrupted by a live feed from the world headquarters of the General Motors Corporation in Detroit. Roger B. Smith, the CEO of General Motors, was standing before a podium, and he had an important announcement to make:

"Today, we are announcing the closing of eleven of our older plants. We will eliminate nearly thirty thousand jobs, with the largest cuts happening at our Flint facilities, where nearly ten thousand of these thirty thousand jobs will be eliminated."

I looked at this man on the TV screen, and I thought, *You motherfucking cocksucking son of a bitch. You're a fucking terrorist. You're going to kill another ten thousand jobs here after you've already killed twenty thousand others in Flint? Really? REALLY?*

I had forgotten about my moo goo gai pan. I calmed down and thought: *I need to do something. Now.* What could I do? I had an unemployment check in my pocket. I had a high school degree. I had about a quarter tank of gas in the car.

And then the idea came to me.

I walked over to the one working pay phone and called my friend Ben Hamper. Ben was the autoworker/writer I had put on the cover of *Mother Jones* before they fired me.

"Did you just see Roger Smith on TV?" I asked.

"Yeah. More of the same," Ben replied.

"I can't take this anymore. I have to do something. I'm going to make a movie."

"A movie?" Ben asked, a bit surprised. "You mean like a home video or something like we did for your going-away party?"

"No. A real movie. A documentary. About how they've fucking destroyed Flint."

"Why not just write a story about it somewhere, like in a magazine or something? I dunno."

"I'm done with magazines and newspapers. I need a break. They don't want me anyway. A movie seems better."

"But how you gonna make a movie when you don't know how to make a movie?"

"I've seen a lot of movies."

"Yes, you've seen a lot of movies."

"I've seen everything."

"No one will dispute that. I don't know anyone who goes to as many movies as you. What'd you see last night?"

"*Jumpin' Jack Flash*. No, wait—that was the night before. It was *Soul Man*."

"Jesus, why do you waste your time on such crap?"

"You're missing the point. I think I've seen enough movies to figure out how to make one. And I can make this movie. And I know someone who can help me."

My next call was to Kevin Rafferty.

"I'd like to come to New York and talk to you about something."

"Can't you just tell me over the phone?"

"No, I want to do it in person. You around this week?"

"Sure."

"OK. I can be in the city by tomorrow night."

I borrowed my parents' car and drove the twelve hours to New York. I met Kevin in a bar in Greenwich Village.

"I want to make a movie," I said to him straight up. "I want to make a documentary on Flint and GM. But I don't know the first thing about how to do that. And I was wondering if you could help me."

Asking Kevin Rafferty for help was a crazy move; yes, he was an award-winning documentary filmmaker, but he was clearly broke. It was like me asking a homeless guy to dig a quarter out of his pocket cause I wanted a latte. I had no idea what Kevin's situation was financially, but suffice it to say that I looked like I was dressed by Saks Fifth Avenue compared to Kevin. With him it was always the same torn black T-shirt, the same plaid shirt over it, the same worn-out loafers. Making documentaries made no one any money, even if you made great ones like Kevin. His mop of red hair looked like he cut it himself. Understandable, considering his chosen low-paying profession. He was tall and lanky, the latter a condition I assumed to be the result of not having the money to eat three solids a day. I was glad to be taking him out for a meal, even if it was in a bar I couldn't afford. His one luxury seemed to be the constant stream of cigarettes he was smoking, the brand of which was unfamiliar to me.

"Well, that sounds like a great idea," he responded, making that the first time anyone had said they liked my outrageous plan. "What would you need me to do?"

Uh, everything?

"Well, for starters," I said timidly, "you could show me how the 16mm camera works."

"I could come to Flint and shoot some of it for you," Kevin said out of nowhere. I wanted him to repeat that, but I was afraid if he did, it might turn out that he had actually said, *I'll have another Heineken, please, from the tap.*

"Really?" I asked, fingers crossed.

"Sure. I could bring my equipment, and maybe some of my crew would come. I think even Anne Bohlen [his co-director on their American Nazi film, *Blood in the Face*] might come."

This was way beyond what I was expecting, and, if truth be told, I was really thinking a "good luck" and "see you next time" would be all I'd get.

"Wow," I said, my face feeling flush, "that would be so incredible. I mean, I wasn't expecting that, but..."

"No, it would be fun. And I can show you what you need to know. I could give you a week of my time."

A whole week? In Flint?

"Kevin, I'd be happy with whatever you could do. Do you think you can teach me this stuff in a week?"

"It doesn't take long to know how the equipment works. The most important part about making a movie is what's in your head, your ideas, and then the beats and rhythms it moves to. Knowing how to say more with less. Having a sharp eye. Listening for the stuff happening between the lines. Having some balls. I watched you when we came to Michigan. You'll do fine."

At some point it dawned on me that I would have to pay him for his time, plus his crew and equipment. I was on the public dole, so I was hoping for a little mercy.

"Of course, you know, I'll pay you for this," I said. "Maybe we can work out something?"

"Not necessary," he replied. "You did us a big favor with our film and *we* didn't pay *you*. So we'll return the favor. You don't have to pay us anything."

The table did not break when my jaw hit it.

"Um, wow—I don't know what to say. Thank you. Thank you so much. I've had nothing but one door after another shut in my face for the past two months. This is really beyond necessary. I can't thank you enough."

I wanted to break down right there, but I was in New York sitting at a table in the Village with a top filmmaker, and I wanted to act as cool as possible. So I smiled. A big smile.

Kevin took me over to his edit room which was in (and I will be polite here) some back-alley location you have to walk on 4 x 12s to get there. It was in a basement on MacDougal Street. The place looked like the kind of room where a cheap Chinese restaurant might store its garbage, or maybe a dead body. No, strike that—no one would do this to the deceased, not here, no matter how rotten they were or who they owed money to.

He saw the look on my face and said that the owner of the building did some deal with him that didn't cost him that much to put his Steenbeck editing machine down in the basement. In addition to the Steenbeck, there was what he called a "rewind table," a few "trim bins," and stacks and stacks of developed film. He turned the machine on and showed me some of the scenes from the Nazi film he was working on. It was cool to see the things he had shot in Michigan, and even weirder to hear my voice and see my mug on this little screen. Other than my parents' home movies, this was the first time I'd ever seen myself in a film. I hated it and I loved it.

"You made a lot of this possible," Kevin said. "All your best stuff will be in here."

I went back to Flint and started to think about what I would shoot. I had to get back to San Francisco where my wife was packing us up to move to Washington, D.C., where we both had found jobs. We arrived in D.C. in January 1987, and while I was happy to have the work and the income, my thoughts were on the movie I wanted to make.

I got word that the UAW in Flint was going to hold a rally on February 11 to mark the fiftieth anniversary of the Great Flint Sit-Down Strike. I thought this might be a good place to start shooting. I called Kevin to see what he thought about that.

"Good plan," he said. "I'll get everybody together, we'll bring all the equipment with us, and I'll go buy the film and put it on my credit card. You can pay me back when we get there."

I wanted to say, *You have a credit card?!* but I didn't want to offend him. I was just glad that he had one.

"Thanks," I said.

"It's about $200 for a ten-minute roll of Kodak. I'll bring about sixty rolls. That'll be about $12,000. Can you handle that?"

"Um, yeah," I said, lying.

"Good. You don't have to develop the film right away, but it's best if you do. That'll cost you about $12,000 more to do the developing and sound transfers."

Gulp.

I had some money saved from my four-month job in San Francisco, but that would not be enough. I would have to sell the building that was the office for the *Flint Voice*. It was a four-bedroom house with a yard in a nice part of town.

The depressed economy in Flint would get me a whopping $27,000 for it. I was all set.

Kevin, Anne, and the others arrived from New York the day before the first shoot was to begin. A friend offered his home as a place for them to stay. We met that night in his house and invited a few Flint people over to discuss ideas for the movie. Everybody had a good idea about what this movie should be. I was getting a little overwhelmed and Kevin motioned me to step outside so he could have a smoke — and a talk.

"Movies are definitely a collaborative process," he said to me outside in the cold. "But they are not a democracy. This is your movie. You don't hold meetings and have discussions. We shoot your ideas. We just need to get out there tomorrow and start shooting."

Kevin's philosophy was to just film whatever happens, cinema verité style.

"I do have an outline of the things I'd like to get," I said, pulling the list out of my pocket.

"I don't use shot lists," he said. "I just shoot. But this is your movie, so we'll do it your way." He did not like my idea of having a little bit of a plan, but he was willing to go along. "Let's just call this meeting to an end and get some sleep and get to work in the morning," he said as his cigarette concluded.

"Roger," I said — which reminded me of the title that I had come up with for the film. I decided to wait for another time to tell him. I figured he wouldn't think much of titling something before you knew what you had.

But I knew what I had. I'd been living it for thirty years, all the while taking notes in my head. I'd been writing about Flint and GM for over a decade. I was already operating at

24 frames per second, even though I had not yet encountered a woman who raised bunnies to sell for "pets or meat," or a deputy sheriff who evicted people from their homes on Christmas Eve, or a future Miss America parading down Flint's main street on top of a convertible and waving at the boarded-up stores, or the elite of Flint dressing up at a party like the Great Gatsby and missing the irony, or one tourism scheme after another to convince people to spend their vacations in Flint. And I was yet to meet a man named Roger Smith.

None of that was known to me as the very first roll of film made its way through the sprockets of Kevin's Aaton 16mm camera on that cold February day in 1987. We filmed the Sit-Down Strike remembrance, and we shot thirty other scenes in the next seven days. The plasma center where the unemployed sold their blood, the free cheese line, the GM flak who said GM was only in the business to make money and not to help out its hometown. We filmed from sunup to long after dusk.

I watched what Kevin and Anne did as they pointed out things to me about how it's sometimes the little moments that you grab with your camera or microphone that tell the bigger story. They talked about how, with only ten minutes of film in the camera (after which you would have to stop and reload, thus shutting the shoot down for a few minutes), you had to operate as a sort of on-the-set editor and do it all in your head. This discipline would not only save you from wasting film, it would force you to think about what exactly it was, this story you were trying to tell. They did not see the ten-minute restriction as an impediment; they saw it as a creative benefit.

"Imagine if we had an hour's worth of film in the camera and film was as cheap as paper," someone on the crew observed. "We'd just get lazy and shoot everything. Wouldn't have to think about it while shooting. Worry about it later!"

"I want to go down to GM headquarters and see if Roger Smith will speak to us," I told Kevin. "Are you up for that?"

"Are you kidding?" he said with his typical droll, sarcastic voice. "I was wondering when things were going to get interesting."

And so we drove down to Detroit and entered the lobby of General Motors. I went straight to the elevator and hit the button. The doors opened and we went inside. I pushed the button for the fourteenth floor, where Smith's office was. The button wouldn't light up. I kept pushing but nothing happened. The doors wouldn't shut. And that was when a security guard asked us to step outside. He was a polite, older man and he told us to hang on while he called someone. He came back and said that we needed an appointment, and to come back when we had one.

For the next two-plus years I tried to get that appointment. And when I couldn't, I made numerous trips to Detroit to just show up and see what would happen. The search for Roger, to get him to come to Flint so I could show him the damage his decisions had caused, became the thread of the movie. But the real mission of the film had nothing to do with Smith or GM or even Flint. I wanted to make an angry comedy about an economic system that I believed to be unfair and unjust. And not democratic. I hoped that would come through.

Our week with Kevin was up. I thanked him profusely for all that he and Anne and the others did to give me my start.

He said he would help in any way he could, just give him a call. I showed him an application I had received to apply for a grant from the Michigan Council for the Arts. I asked him if he could help me fill it out, as I assumed this was something he had to do all the time.

"What do I put in this box here," I asked him, pointing to the line that asked for my "occupation."

"Filmmaker," he said without missing a beat.

"I'm not a filmmaker," I responded. "I haven't made a film."

"I'm sorry," he replied curtly. "You write down that you're a *filmmaker*. You were a filmmaker the second that film started rolling through this camera."

And so I wrote "filmmaker." And for the next two and a half years, I made a film. There would be over a dozen more shoots. Kevin connected me to friends of his in the documentary community, most importantly to a couple from San Francisco, Chris Beaver and Judy Irving. They, too, came to Flint and shot for me for a week. The rest of the time it was just me, my wife, and a few friends (plus a cameraman or two from Detroit) bumbling around with the equipment, trying my best to make a movie. There were never more than four of us in the car as we drove from shoot to shoot. Left on our own, we would constantly screw up the camera and the sound recorder—so many times in fact that by the end of shooting in 1989, only about 10 percent of the footage we shot was usable.

I was having a hard time staying above water financially and so the film lab, DuArt in New York, said I could defer payment until I was done. It was run by an old lefty, and he liked seeing the footage as I shipped it in. I heard about an event in New York where distributors and funders came together to look at films in progress. If you paid them a fee, you could show them fifteen minutes of what you had. But none of my footage had been edited together because, well, I didn't know how to edit. Again, Kevin to the rescue.

"I'll put a reel together for you," he said. "When can you come to New York?"

"Whenever you say," I said.

Three weeks later I revisited his editing "suite" in the Village. I sat down and watched the fifteen minutes of my movie he had put together. I was blown away. It *looked* like a movie! He showed me how the Steenbeck worked. He showed me his editing system and how I could create my own. I spent hours watching him as he worked on his Nazi film, how he made decisions, how he knew just how long to hold a scene and when to get out. He did not believe in narration, or himself being on camera, or using music.

One day in the edit room, I asked him how he learned how to do all this.

"Well, I got a film degree."

"From what film school?"

"I didn't really go to film school," he said.

"So where did you go?"

He paused. "Harvard."

"*The* Harvard?" I asked, dumbfounded.

"Yes, that Harvard," he answered, not wanting to.

"Shit. I mean, wow. Cool."

How on earth did *this* guy get into *Harvard?* I didn't want to pry, especially into matters like how the hell could he afford it. After all, Harvard has scholarships, too. Not everyone who goes there is rich. Don't be a bigot! One thing was clear: the dude was smart, very smart, and so that was clearly his ticket.

I set up an edit room in Washington, D.C., and hired a close friend from Flint and a local woman from suburban Maryland to be my editors, even though neither of them had ever edited a movie. So the three of us taught ourselves, with Kevin's guidance, how to edit a movie. Our edit room was a cut above the ambience of Kevin's, yet we did have our own cockroach-and-rodent problem. We had a room on the ninth floor of a dilapidated building on the corner of Pennsylvania and Twenty-first Street, about four blocks from the White House. There was a Roy Rogers burger joint next door to us, and the exhaust from that spewed into our edit room on a daily basis (that alone should have made the three of us vegans on the spot, had such a thing existed in those days).

Bit by bit, we figured out how to put the movie together. My two friends became amazing editors. The film was funny and it was sad. We stopped making a "documentary" and decided to make a film we'd take a date to on a Friday night. It would have a point of view, but not the point of view of the rigid, unfunny Left. I felt no need to fake the sort of "objectivity" that other journalists deceitfully hid behind. And I could sit there in our cramped edit room and see an imaginary audience in a big dark theater howling, cheering, hissing, and leaving the movie house ready to rumble.

We were working 'round the clock in the edit room, trying to finish the film before the bill collectors shut me down. And then, on a cold morning in January 1989, a new presi-

dent was to be inaugurated at noon that day. His name was
George H. W. Bush, Ronald Reagan's vice president.

I couldn't think of a better way to spend the day, so I bundled up and headed over to the National Mall, where anyone from the public could watch the swearing-in of President
Bush and Vice President J. Danforth Quayle. It was not very
crowded, and I found a way to get closer to the Capitol steps
than I thought would be possible. Looking up at the stage, at
all the muckety-mucks sitting behind the new president, it
was there that I saw Kevin Rafferty.

"Jesus," I thought, somewhat in shock. "I think that's
Kevin up there!"

It did, in fact, *look* like him—but this guy was dressed
up in a suit and tie and a fancy winter overcoat. There was
no way this was him. Or if it *was* him, well, he's got a good
gig for the day, filming an inauguration! But I didn't see any
equipment.

A few days after the inauguration of the elder Bush as president of the United States, I tracked down Kevin at home. I
had to know if that was him.

"Kevin," I said into the phone, "I was at Bush's inauguration the other day and I could have sworn I saw you up by
the podium. Was that you?"

Silence.

"You were *there?*" I pressed.

More silence, then a drag off his cigarette, then the ex-
haling of the smoke. "Yes, I was there."

"On the stage?"

Another drag. "Yes."

"Jeez! How cool! What the hell were you doing up there? How'd ya get in?"

A sigh.

"My uncle is the president of the United States."

"Hahaha. That's a good one. My uncle's Dan Quayle!"

"No. I'm not kidding," he interrupted. "My uncle is George Bush, the president. My mom and Barbara Bush are sisters. His four sons and his daughter are my first cousins. I'm a member of the family. That's why I was there."

I've had many things told to me over the years: personal things, shocking things, the kinds of things everyone gets to hear at some point or another from someone— *"I'm gay." "I'm leaving you." "Only Austrians may depart this plane."*—but nothing in life had prepared me for this piece of news. What Kevin was saying to me was that he had been working with me for nearly three years, first with me helping him with his movie, then him shooting my movie, then editing the first part of my movie—but, more important, being my mentor, my one and only teacher, a one-poorly-dressed-man film school—and now he was telling me that his uncle was the President of the United Friggin' States of America???

My head was spinning.

"Look," he said, "I know you're probably pissed at me for not telling you. But try to look at it from my vantage point. Whenever someone finds out who I am, they immediately start acting different, treating me different, judging me, wanting something from me—you name it, it's a drag to have this around my neck. And frankly, I thought you knew. I thought I told you—or tried to tell you. But you wouldn't believe it. I thought Anne might have told you or someone had or you figured it out—but when it became clear to me that you didn't know, well, I liked it that way. Because right now, now that you know, you're sitting there thinking, *He's one of those fucking Bushes!*"

I jumped in. "No, no, none of that! I don't make those judgments. But Kevin—*shit, man!* You could have told me."

"Yeah, well, I thought I did."

"I mean, so during this whole time, your uncle was the vice president and now he's the president? What were you thinking whenever I said something negative about him or Reagan?"

"Nothing. I agreed with you. I don't share his politics. And to be honest, the family stuff is complicated. Personal. And I don't want to talk about it."*

"Sure, I get it. This is still fucking me up a bit. I'm just being honest. *A member of the Bush family has been a significant part of not only making this movie but also teaching me how to be a filmmaker.* Whew. Fuck. I mean, really, fuck!"

"Well, there you have it. Do with it as you will."

"This changes nothing, Kevin. Don't worry. And I'm glad you finally told me."

---

* When the movie was released, the White House called the production office and asked if a print of the film could be sent up to Camp David for the weekend, as the president wanted to have a screening for the family of the movie Kev worked on. I tried to get invited to this, but that was not going to happen. I later asked Kevin if he'd heard anything. "I think they admired my camera work," he said in typical fashion. "Otherwise I guess it was pretty silent." I told him that someone from the studio heard that there was one family member who really loved it and was howling hysterically throughout. "Apparently it was one of Bush's sons," he said. And apparently the laughter may have had some pharmaceutical assistance (yes, his name was George, too). I told the studio rep, "It must be sad to be the son of the president and then end up never amounting to much?"

Seven months later I finished the film. I had shown a cut of it to three film festival selection committees—Telluride, Toronto, and New York. They all liked it and accepted it to be shown at each of their festivals in September 1989. I had also shown an early rough cut of the movie to my two sisters. They sat with me in our parents' home and watched it. They said nice things to me and encouraged me to keep working on it. What they didn't tell me (until years later) was that they were mortified about how poorly put together they thought the film was. They spoke quietly to one another—"What should we say to him? How can we let him down easy?"—but they couldn't find a way. They didn't want to burst my bubble as I seemed so excited about what the final film would look like. So they said nothing. But they did make a pact with each other to be there at the first film festival screening so that I wouldn't be alone in my moment of public humiliation.

The first festival turned out to be in Telluride, Colorado, over Labor Day weekend. The festival paid my way (as I was truly broke by then). Some of my crew got out there and back on the money they'd raise by hawking handmade silk-screened T-shirts and buttons of the movie's logo on the streets of Telluride.

The week before the festival I went into a panic that I had picked the wrong title for the film. I called up the festival organizer, Bill Pence, and told him that I was changing the name of the film to *Bad Day in Buick City*.

"No, you are not," he said quite forcefully into the phone. "The name of this film is the one you gave it—*Roger & Me*—and that's the perfect name. You're not changing it.

Besides, we already sent the program guide to the printer."
I was bummed out but afraid to say anything else. I hung up
the phone.

When I arrived in Telluride and was handed the program
guide, I noticed something awful: the festival had decided to
schedule my opening at the same time as their big opening
night gala film, *The Cook, the Thief, His Wife and Her Lover*
by the British director Peter Greenaway. The opening gala
film would be held in the town's historic Opera House. My
film would have its "world premiere" in Masons Hall down at
the other end of town. Masons Hall! Was I supposed to feel
good about this? Like, be thankful it's not the Kiwanis? Or,
God forbid, the Elks Lodge? I tried to see all the positives in
that. Well, I mean, after all, who was I? No one here knew
me, I had never made a movie, and, let's be honest: it *was* a
documentary! So I guess I understood why its opening was
being buried. Oh well.

Before the Telluride Opening Night Gala, the town
blocks off the main street and throws an opening night party
for all the filmmakers and passholders to the festival. My sisters and their husbands and kids had driven all the way from
San Diego—they were following through on their promise
to each other to be there in Telluride to catch me when I
fell. My crew and I showed up to the party early and availed
ourselves of the free food (while selling more buttons and
T-shirts). It was then that I spotted the film critic, Roger
Ebert, who, along with his TV co-host Gene Siskel, were
the most well-known film critics in the country. I decided
to approach him and invite him to my movie.

"Hi," I said. "My name is Michael Moore. I'm from Flint,

Michigan, and I have a film here in the festival. It's called *Roger & Me*. And I'd really love for you to see it!"

"I *am* going to see it—tomorrow at noon at the Nugget Theater," Ebert responded, as he reached for another hors d'oeuvre. I was impressed that he already knew about me!

"Well, it's going to have its world premiere tonight, in about an hour, at Masons Hall. I'd love for you to be there."

"Thank you, but I have tickets for the opening night gala at the Opera House."

"That's what I figured, but I think you should be at the *very first* screening of my movie. I think you'll really like it. And you can say you saw it here first!"

"Like I said, I have tickets to the opening. I've already spent something like eight hundred dollars for them."

"But Roger," I pleaded, using his first name as if we knew each other, something that he clearly didn't like. "I just know you will want to be at the premiere of this. You haven't seen anything like it. It's about the Midwest where we're both from. It—"

He cut me off.

"Listen," he said pointedly, "I *said* I would see it tomorrow and I will, and that is that. And now if you'll excuse me." And with that, he walked away from me, perturbed, annoyed, maybe even pissed: *Who was this jerkoff from Flint bugging the shit out of me?*

I felt like an idiot. Now, I'd be lucky if he even came tomorrow, let alone end up liking the movie. Why did I have to slide into that stalker voice? Oh, the desperation that was painted like a billboard across my face!

One of my buddies who worked on the film, Rod Birleson,

tried to console me. "Don't worry, Mike. He said he'd come tomorrow and he will. He probably appreciated your enthusiasm."

"Yeah," I said. "The enthusiasm of a serial killer."

The street party was drawing to a close, and the well-heeled were heading into the Opera House for the gala. The rest of us wandered down to the end of Main Street, to where the Order of Masons meet, to unspool our masterpiece.

Remarkably, when we got to the "theater," even though we were put up against the opening night film, the place was packed.

About five minutes before showtime, I looked out the window of the hall and saw a lone figure, a stout man, waddling down the street toward Masons Hall. It was none other than Roger Ebert. He walked in the door and saw his stalker standing there.

"Don't say a word," he ordered, putting his hand up and averting his eyes from mine. "I'm here. That's all that needs to be said."

"But—" I said, disobeying him—and being cut off by him in the same instant.

"I'm only here because there was this strange look in your eyes, a look that told me maybe I better be there. So here I am." He went into the theater and took the last available seat, three rows from the back. No pressure now.

I went in and took my seat in the last row. My sisters had positioned themselves on each side of my seat so they could both sit directly next to me, to comfort me in their role as the good sisters that they were (and are), to be there for me in my moment of impending embarrassment and failure. The lights in Masons Hall began to dim, and as the theater went dark, Anne and Veronica each grabbed a hand of mine and held it tightly. All would be well, no matter what.

At that moment, the music began and the title of the film appeared on the screen....